W9-CCE-343

THE ART OF

Wiccan
Healing

Hay House Titles of Related Interest

Books

*AFTER LIFE: *Answers from the Other Side*, by John Edward

BORN TO BE TOGETHER: *Love, Relationships, Astrology, and the Soul*, by Terry Lamb

CHAKRA CLEARING: *Awakening Your Spiritual Power to Know and Heal*, by Doreen Virtue, Ph.D.

CONTACTING YOUR SPIRIT GUIDE (book-with-CD), by Sylvia Browne

DIARY OF A PSYCHIC: *Shattering the Myths*, by Sonia Choquette

POWER ANIMALS: *How to Connect with Your Animal Spirit Guide*, by Steven D. Farmer, Ph.D.

PSYCHIC NAVIGATOR (book-with-CD): *Harnessing Your Inner Guidance*, by John Holland

SPELLBINDING: *Spells and Rituals That Will Empower Your Life*, by Claudia Blaxell

SPIRIT MEDICINE: *A Guide to Healing in the Sacred Garden*, by Hank Wesselman, Ph.D., and Jill Kuykendall, RPT

SPIRIT MESSENGER: *The Remarkable Story of a Seventh Son of a Seventh Son*, by Gordon Smith

A STREAM OF DREAMS: *The Ultimate Dream Decoder for the 21st Century*, by Leon Nacson

THE WAY OF WYRD: *Tales of an Anglo-Saxon Sorcerer*, by Brian Bates

*Published by Princess Books; distributed by Hay House

Card Decks

ARCHETYPE CARDS, by Caroline Myss

GODDESS GUIDANCE ORACLE CARDS, by Doreen Virtue, Ph.D.

MAGICAL SPELL CARDS, by Lucy Cavendish

TRUST YOUR VIBES ORACLE CARDS, by Sonia Choquette

***

All of the above are available at your local bookstore, or may be ordered by visiting:

Hay House USA: www.hayhouse.com
Hay House Australia: www.hayhouse.com.au
Hay House UK: www.hayhouse.co.uk
Hay House South Africa: orders@psdprom.co.za

THE ART OF

Wiccan Healing

A PRACTICAL GUIDE

SALLY MORNINGSTAR

HAY HOUSE, INC.
Carlsbad, California
London • Sydney • Johannesburg
Vancouver • Hong Kong

Copyright © 2005 by Sally Morningstar

Published and distributed in the United States by: Hay House, Inc., P.O. Box 5100, Carlsbad, CA 92018-5100 • *Phone:* (760) 431-7695 or (800) 654-5126 • *Fax:* (760) 431-6948 or (800) 650-5115 • www.hayhouse.com • **Published and distributed in Australia by:** Hay House Australia Pty. Ltd., 18/36 Ralph St., Alexandria NSW 2015 • *Phone:* 612-9669-4299 • *Fax:* 612-9669-4144 • www.hayhouse.com.au • **Published and distributed in the United Kingdom by:** Hay House UK, Ltd. • Unit 62, Canalot Studios • 222 Kensal Rd., London W10 5BN • *Phone:* 44-20-8962-1230 • *Fax:* 44-20-8962-1239 • www.hayhouse.co.uk • **Published and distributed in the Republic of South Africa by:** Hay House SA (Pty), Ltd., P.O. Box 990, Witkoppen 2068 • *Phone/Fax:* 27-11-706-6612 • orders@psdprom.co.za • **Distributed in Canada by:** Raincoast • 9050 Shaughnessy St., Vancouver, B.C. V6P 6E5 • *Phone:* (604) 323-7100 • *Fax:* (604) 323-2600

Design: Leanne Siu and Scribe Design Ltd

All rights reserved. No part of this book may be reproduced by any mechanical, photographic, or electronic process, or in the form of a phonographic recording; nor may it be stored in a retrieval system, transmitted, or otherwise be copied for public or private use—other than for "fair use" as brief quotations embodied in articles and reviews without prior written permission of the publisher.

The author of this book does not dispense medical advice or prescribe the use of any technique as a form of treatment for physical or medical problems without the advice of a physician, either directly or indirectly. The intent of the author is only to offer information of a general nature to help you in your quest for emotional and spiritual well-being. In the event you use any of the information in this book for yourself, which is your constitutional right, the author and the publisher assume no responsibility for your actions.

Library of Congress Control Number: 2004115024

ISBN 13: 978-1-4019-0609-2
ISBN 10: 1-4019-0609-5

08   07   06   05   4   3   2   1
1st printing, June 2005

Printed in the United States of America

For my partner Bill, a rare and special man it is my
joy and delight to know, love and celebrate.

From the Editor: To our American readers, please note that we have maintained the British spelling, grammar, punctuation, and syntax of the original text in order to preserve the editorial intent of the author (who hails from the United Kingdom).

Contents

Acknowledgements

Peter Mills was a generous contributor to this project. I would like particularly to acknowledge his valuable contributions to Wiccan origins and history and Chapter Three, and his artwork throughout, as well as thank him for sharing his knowledge of coven activities as a Wiccan High Priest, especially in Chapters one, two, five, eight and eleven. I would also like to thank my dear friend and agent Cheryl van Blerk; Angie Francesco, a truly remarkable friend and healer; and my beloved son LJ, a very special young man. My thanks too to everyone at Hay House, and to all who have helped me along the way with my own healing journey – thank you for being by my side! Ultimately, I would like to acknowledge the Earth herself, without whose gifts we could not be.

Introduction

The definition of a witch: a man or woman who venerates the Goddess and Horned God and follows the ways and ethics of the (pre-Christian) Old Religion.

Witchcraft – a Healing Tradition

It may be surprising to read that witchcraft has largely been a healing tradition since its inception thousands of years ago, but back in the ancient past it was the people who would later be termed 'witches' who were the herbalists, midwives, counsellors, protectors, healers and guides for their community, of which they were a vibrant and respected part. In those days there were no doctors' surgeries, hospitals or pharmacies at the end of the high street. People relied heavily upon the witches' knowledge of healing, which would have been passed down to them by a relative or wise one, a practice that is still alive today within the hereditary arm of witchcraft.

Unlike practitioners of the majority of other religions, witches do not separate the spirit from the flesh, nor deny their humanity; they work to bring spirituality into their daily lives. Because of this there is no inherited sin in Wicca. Wiccans have ethics about what is right and wrong, but the concepts of 'original sin', 'hellfire and damnation' and 'the wickedness of the flesh' are entirely alien to Wiccan beliefs. Wiccans see themselves as children of the Earth, children of the Goddess and the great Horned God. They honour the seasons with their festivals, celebrate the diversity of nature, are respectful of life and work for the highest good. What this means is that witches attempt not to harm any other life form.

Over the years witchcraft has both provided a profound spiritual creed for its practitioners and answered a need within community life – the need to keep that community healthy, happy and secure. In fact, the term 'blessing witch' was often given to the wise people and cunning folk of older times.

The Peasants' Doctor

The term *Wicca* originates from the Anglo-Saxon language (c.-600-1066 CE), and it is within this period that the word became a recognizable expression. *Wicca* was the term used for a male witch, and *wicce* was used for a female one.

Up to the end of the Middle Ages, medicine was a blend of the beliefs of the Christian religion and the existing pagan folk medicine (which includes Wicca and other non-Church-based traditions), both of which were practised side by side by the common people. The divide between those who practised medicine and those who practised healing was therefore often blurred, but herbs played a prominent part in treatments and cures. The common folk would not have been able to read or write, so although they had a vast working knowledge of medicinal treatments, it was the literate monks who recorded the ancient medical practices.

One such document still in existence is a herbal manuscript from Anglo-Saxon times called *The Leech Book of Bald* ('leech' comes from *læce*, Old English for 'healer'), which was compiled between 924 and 946 CE by a monk named Bald. Although a monk, Bald would have obtained much of his information from treatments used by the common folk. *The Leech Book of Bald* contains many herbal recipes and remedies which use plants like vervain, mugwort, plantain, violet and yarrow – names still recognized today.

The Anglo-Saxon approach to medicine was to treat both the physical and the spiritual, and in those days there was little separation between magical and herbal cures. Belief in malevolent possession by faeries and maladies caused by 'elf-arrows' (flint arrowheads, believed at that time to be supernatural) was common, and Bald dedicates a chapter of the book to the treatment of elf-shot, which was believed to cause great harm to both man and beast! Here is the treatment for a horse:

> 1. If a horse be elf-shot, then take the knife of which the haft is the horn of a fallow ox and on which are three brass nails, then write upon the horse's forehead Christ's mark and on each of the limbs which thou mayest feel at: then take the left ear, prick a hole in it in silence, then strike the horse on the back, then it will be healed. And write upon the handle of the knife these words – *Benedicite omnia opera Domini dominum.* Be the elf what it may, this is mighty for him to amend.

Because of their belief in magical influences, the Anglo-Saxons used amulets and charms as well as herbs, chanting and prayers to heal the sick. Open sores, cuts and wounds would often be sung into with special incantations to speed the healing process, because it was not until medicine became a science that there was any separation between the spiritual/magical causes of disease (spirits and daemons) and the ills of the physical body.

Between the fifteenth and seventeenth centuries, medicine began to be classified as a science, and alchemists and apothecaries made treatments available to the wealthy. The poorer classes could not afford these treatments, so they continued to turn to the shaman or 'wys' man or woman for their cures. Such people, although providing Wiccan-type services, would not have considered themselves witches as such, because they were nothing more than local people working with what they knew best for the benefit of the community. Even in those days, wealth commonly bred arrogant selfishness, which cared little for the hardships of poverty. The goodness of the heart of the healer, whether witch or otherwise, had to go underground in order to survive.

The Christian Church actively discouraged such practices. It had imposed the worship of a single god, Yahweh (also referred to as Jehovah), a vengeful god whose religion was strongly male-oriented and reduced women to the status of second-class citizens. Society was expected to commune with this god through layers of male-only ministers. The term *witch* was a derogatory one adopted by the Church in its attempt to annihilate pagan practices. It became a title that was often hysterically used to describe literally anyone, with or without any healing knowledge, just because they were pagan. By this time the policy of eliminating witches, subjugating women and banishing magical healing practices was very firmly in place.

The Roots of Modern Medicine

Our modern-day medicine was influenced by an ancient Greek physician called Hippocrates, who is considered the founding father of modern medicine. He introduced the Hippocratic oath for the medical practitioners of his day (around 400 BCE), which begins with the statement:

> I SWEAR by Apollo the physician, and Asclepius, and by Hygea and Panacea, and all the gods and goddesses, that, according to my ability and their witness, I will keep this Oath.

This oath formed the basis for allopathic (modern scientific) medicine's code of ethics and is still referred to today during medical training. Although no longer sworn, it reveals that the moral values of modern medicine grew from a very pagan past where health and healing were considered to be under the mystical governance of the gods.

Further proof that in our ancient past deities were considered important in daily life includes an ancient invocation to the Earth Goddess, translated from manuscripts said to date back to 400 CE. It is one of the earliest surviving texts of Goddess worship and records the belief that it was the Goddess who granted health, wealth and blessings for all the children of the Earth. It is a field blessing ritual that calls upon the Goddess to make the land fertile for the crops and to keep them safe:

Eastward we stand, asking for the blessing of life!
We beseech the illustrious Lord of all things,
We beseech the mighty Lord,
We ask the guardians of holy heaven.
Earth we ask, and the realm of spirit,
And heaven's mighty and high halls,
That we may, with this prayer,
By the gift of the Gods,
Fill the Earth with strength through our firm faith,
And beautify her green meadows,
That all may be wholesome in Earth's realm.

Erce, Erce, Erce, Earthen Mother,
Give forth life that is waxing and thriving,
Increasing and full of strength:
Trees and plants, beasts and birds,
And all beings of earth and sea.
Grant, ye Holy Ones of heaven and earth,
That Earth's life be warded against all foes,
And defended against every ill
that is sown by the wicked throughout the land.

Be thou healthy, Earth, Mother of all!
Be thou growing in God's embrace,
Filled with food for the use of all,
Full acres of food for every living thing.
Brightly blooming, be thou blessed!

Translated from the Anglo-Saxon by Peter Mills

We can surmise from this that, in the past, gods and goddesses formed a major part of daily life and so it is not unusual for Wiccans to be continuing this tradition by honouring the Goddess and her consort, the Horned God, in the present day.

Witches As Healers

Throughout ancient history, healing and health were largely the domains of the female (wise woman), as the ways of the spirit were largely the province of the male (shaman). Exceptions to this can always be found, but generally speaking it was the women who carried herb lore and folk medicine through the ages. It is interesting to note that running alongside the Church's subjugation of women was their institutionalized exclusion from the study and practice of medicine from 1858 until the National Health Act of 1948, almost 100 years later. At that time, all medical establishments in England were required by law to open their doors completely to women once more. Today in Western-oriented countries, women can study all aspects of medicine without restriction.

In the present day, witchcraft maintains its ancient connections with healing, and so, as in the past, every coven meeting or ritual event carries the option for healing, whether this is a Sabbat or esbat. A Sabbat is a sacred festival that honours certain dates during the year. An esbat is less formal, usually held at the full moon, and includes teaching modules, discussion and honouring the moon as a symbol of the heavenly presence of the Goddess.

All Wiccan activities have at their foundation the guiding 'rede' to work for the highest good of all:

> *By the Wiccan law ye must*
> *In perfect love and perfect trust*
> *Eight words the Wiccan rede fulfil*
> *An it harm none do what ye will.*
> *Follow this with mind and heart*
> *Merry meet and merry part.*

This means that although healing is offered, the witch will always honour free will and personal choice and will work at whatever level is acceptable and honourable, even if this means acknowledging an individual's decision to take no action at all.

The Myth of Witchcraft As Evil

Within the witch's code is the ethic to 'harm none', though it would be true to say that perhaps not all people calling themselves witches have adhered to this over the years. But cursing, hexing and manipulating free will for any kind of personal gain are not part of modern-day Wicca.

Within all traditions, however, one can find dubious practitioners. It has been the same with witchcraft. Sadly it is almost entirely the sensational that has been reported, which has produced a rather warped view of witchcraft and its true essence.

I recently came across a website from someone calling themselves a witch. The site invited individuals to join. Looking down the list, one of the groups you could participate in was labelled 'Satanic'. It is very important to state right from the start of this book that there is no Satanism within Wicca and there never has been. This is a Christian phenomenon. Wicca has no devil and no hell, and no concept of one vengeful god. Instead it honours life, celebrates individuality, works for peace and goodwill, lives in harmony with nature and sees all deities and archetypes as aspects of the human spirit we can aspire to.

Witches have been persecuted unjustly for centuries, blamed for all sorts of society's ills and made the scapegoat for a great deal of human aggression and intolerance. This book will give you the opportunity to explore the true context of our healing practices and to understand a little more about this ancient Craft of the Wise.

Wiccan Healing

This is both an explanatory and a practical book, taking you from the origins of witchcraft to what it is today and explaining how witches heal. I shall be guiding you through ways to perform healing rituals, sharing some traditional treatments and helping you to find magical alternatives to those everyday problems that bring stress or 'dis-ease' into your life. I will explain how to make charms and reveal ways in which you can work more closely with nature through herbs, flowers and trees and the seasons, moon and stars. You will also be able to make up your own healing rituals and will be given all the guidance that you will need to perform them with confidence. You can learn how to create a *doppelgänger* – an astral helper – and to raise a cone of power for healing others, as well as learning how to use the runes in simple healing charms. You will also be able to explore working with Elemental spirits from the natural world, such as the Dryads, Gnomes, Salamanders and Sylphs.

The book also contains some of the more traditional witchcraft 'cures' such as knotting spells, charming, cord magic and candle magic – all of which can work to focus the mind – a vital ingredient in any magical or healing practice, because the psychological aspects of disease are well documented. Research has revealed quite clearly that the mental belief in a 'cure' can be as important as the cure itself.

The powers of the mind, along with a developed character and deep knowledge of the self, feature strongly in all Wiccan philosophy, and so part of this book is dedicated to developing focus, concentration and willpower in order to build up an awareness of how powerful a thought, especially when it is backed up by emotion, can really be. I am sure that all of us have experienced how unpleasant it is when negative thoughts are directed at us; in a similar way, positive thoughts produce a pleasant reaction. When we send the energy of love, healing or encouragement to someone else, they will feel that too.

Our inherent powers include our thoughts, feelings and energy. In developing recognition and understanding of their colours and flavours on levels both seen and unseen (the physical and the energetic), witches, and all spiritual seekers, can evolve and empower themselves and thus their magic. To know oneself really is the key to a magical life.

Witches do not concentrate just upon human beings – they are also concerned with animals, minerals, plants and the ecosystem. Therefore, this book also takes us through nature lore, animal healing and the performance of Earth blessings, as well as self-development exercises aimed at loosening conceptual thinking and social conditioning. The Wiccan belief system is based upon the knowledge that all the answers to our questions lie within our own being.

Medicine and the Law

The Wiccan healer can legally respond to heal the spirit (sometimes referred to as 'faith healing'), work on a magical level with the energetic elements of a disease, help calm emotional stresses and strains and acknowledge that illness is a journey that often craves a companion and friend. It is well known that a contented patient recovers far more quickly than a depressed one, and so the Wiccan healer can be of benefit by supporting, caring for and understanding a person's needs.

There are, however, several conditions known as 'notifiable diseases' which no one except a properly qualified medical practitioner is allowed to treat. These include cancer, TB and other infectious conditions. By law the medical authorities must be notified if one of these diseases is suspected. At no time must anyone, Wiccan or otherwise, attempt to treat or effect a cure for these, nor state that they can cure or have cured them. This does not preclude a Wiccan healer from stating facts, as long as they do not claim that a cure has occurred due to their acts and therefore imply that it is possible to achieve again. There is still no place for the magical or the miraculous within medical science and only those witches who are recognizably qualified to diagnose ailments and internally administer such things as herbs, tinctures and medicines can practise these arts in modern society.

The ways of the Wiccan healer always include the caveat that one must remain within the confines of the law. Also obvious, but nonetheless extremely vital to remember, are personal limitations. You should not attempt to treat anything on any level that you feel is beyond your capabilities. Never be afraid to refer your client to someone better qualified than you are. In the simplest terms, you can offer spiritual healing, emotional support, practical help and magical stimulus, as long as you don't mislead or misguide your client in any way.

The Domain of the Wiccan Healer

We no longer see the travelling 'doctor' with his unguents, salves, tonics and cure-alls, nor visit the leech, witch or cunning person for herbal potions, charms and protection, but instead visit our GP when we feel unwell. Because of the displace-ment of the services traditionally provided by a community wise-person, there is now increasing pressure upon doctors to treat such things as malaise, stress and lifestyle problems. Perhaps the re-establishment of the witch, the cunning folk or the wise ones could go some way to alleviating some of the pressures falling upon the medical profession, for all those things that they have little time to treat fall very easily into the Wiccan domain and, in fact, often do!

To give you some examples: Martin was 40. He had been suffering from debilitating depression for several years and had received medical treatment from psychiatrists, including electric shock therapy. His most recent prescriptions were for powerful mind-numbing drugs that had several side-effects. He had attempted suicide twice by the time he came to see me. We talked for about four hours, during which he revealed his hopes, his fears and his dreams. He began to feel calmer and I offered a hot drink. Then he informed me that he would like four sugars in his tea. Sugar can play havoc with the immune system, the nervous system and blood sugar levels. We talked some more about his eating and drinking habits, and it emerged that his diet was jammed with sugary-sweet foods and drinks and very little else. Throughout the next four weeks, we worked together to cut his sugar intake down (and eventually out of) his eating plan and to replace it with wholesome, natural, nourishing foods. Within one month a no-longer suicidal, nor desperate individual was returning to his GP to seek less powerful medicines, was seeing a future for himself and was holding a far more balanced and happy perspective. To this day Martin must beware of sugar in his diet, because of his depressive reaction to it, but he now knows what triggers his psychological problems and so has the power to avoid them.

In another instance, Charys, a 54-year-old who was on her feet almost all day, had suffered from a swollen knee for over two years. Throughout that time she had repeatedly experienced pain but was not fond of taking painkillers or seeking treatment. I happened to be talking to her about her limp and offered healing to her should she so wish. She readily agreed. That night I performed what is called an absent healing ritual, which is a healing ritual done on someone's behalf without them being present, using some traditional Wiccan methods, and then promptly forgot about it. Two days later, I called in to see Charys, who was buoyant and ebullient. 'Whatever you did,' she said, 'it has completely cleared it. I have absolutely no pain or swelling whatsoever.' To this day, two years later, there has been no recurrence of her condition.

So, was it magic, was it a 'sugar pill'? Were the gods nearby and listening? Or was it coincidence – or fate? I leave that decision up to you!

We Are a Circle

The circle of life gives each of us, if we are so destined, approximately 70 years to walk this Earth and fulfil our highest human potential. Some of us are lucky enough to live a life of relative freedom. For others this is still not a reality. At the moment our planet, its people and its kingdoms are in dire need of healing, due to our increasing abuse of her gifts and, indeed, of each other. All over the world, people are becoming increasingly aware of the importance of healing, and especially of the need for more positive religious and cultural attitudes, but often feel powerless. Apathy could be classified as the greatest 'dis-ease' of the twenty-first century. But the Earth's ecosystem, her people and her creations are all under threat and we really must do far more to preserve this planet.

This book will enable you to understand the ways in which you can make a difference by exploring witchcraft. It will show you how you can work for positive change within your own life and then touch the lives of others with love and respect. First, heal yourself, then be of service to the healing of your community and from there you can move out into the world and colour it with love and healing if you choose to do so.

Your life matters – it is important and it does carry meaning. To turn away from our potential is to deny our purpose. To ignore our blessings and to refuse our joy is to deny our true spirit. And to ignore the causes of starvation, greed, domination, torture, war and want is to deny the true human heart. It hurts to feel it, to see it, to comprehend its existence and to actively seek to heal it – but I believe this is what we must all do if we are to lift humanity back into its rightful place in Creation.

This book explores the art of Wiccan healing, encircled by the Wiccan tenets of veneration of Earth and Sky, of Creation and her Creatures, of self-development, wisdom, love and truth. I hope that your journey with me touches your heart, your soul and your knowing, and that you remember who you truly are: a child of the Earth – an Earthchild.

You are invited to join the Circle, to offer your life to the highest good and to explore at a magical level who you are and why you are here. Step into *The Art of Wiccan Healing* and prepare to be spellbound by what you find!

Chapter One
Where Does Wicca Come From?

In order to understand the nature of Wiccan healing, it is helpful to know something about the tradition and the principles and ethics involved. A definitive chronological description of witchcraft is no longer possible, because several periods of its history and practices are lost to us today; however, I have attempted to provide as holistic a picture as possible of its age-old connections to the healing and magical arts.

The Nature Goddess

Way back in our distant past the tribal healer, wise person, shaman or herbalist would not necessarily have been known as a witch. Local dialect names would have been applied to them, such as the 'cunning man' or the *wys wyf* of Old England, the *strega* of Italy or the *incantatrix* of ancient Rome. Further back in time, wise folk would have been known by many other names. It is within these hazy mists of antiquity that we must search for the origins of witchcraft.

Fertility was vital to our ancestors. If the crops failed, if livestock numbers fell or if no babies were born, the tribe would die out. Fertility was life itself; its absence was total extinction. Therefore, the concept of fertility and motherhood was embodied in the form of a great Earth Mother. Stone Age people carved beautifully crafted images of this fertility and nature Goddess, who is still worshipped today by Wiccans. These figurines, called 'Venuses', indicate that witchcraft, as a spiritual belief, is at least 25,000 years old – and perhaps older.

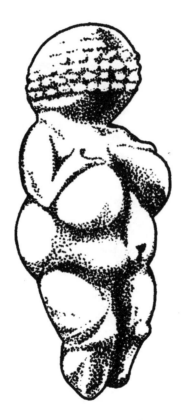

The 'Venus' of Willendorf from Europe, about 25,000 years old

Images of a male consort or 'husband' to the Goddess have been found dating back a similar age, complete with horns or antlers on his head as a sign that he represents not only human beings but also the entire natural and animal world. There is an example of this on a wall of *Les Treize Frères* cavern in France. This cave painting, thought to be about 13,000 years old, has been nicknamed

'The Sorcerer', a cave painting dating back approximately 13,000 years

'The Sorcerer' and shows an upright human figure with a horse-like tail, a beard and large antlers on his head.

When farming arrived, these ancient gods became deities of the crops and harvest, the rain and sun, the flocks and pastures, the fruits of the Earth and the seasons.

The Warrior Aristocracy

It was the discovery of metalworking at the dawn of the Bronze Age that tilted the spiritual balance in a new direction. Those who possessed sharp bronze weapons came to dominate the population. Chieftains and kings gathered armies to extend their power even further and so gave rise to a new type of social order: the warrior aristocracy. The temple friezes and stelae of Egypt, the clay tablets of Nineveh and Babylon, the *Vedas* and *Upanishads* of India and the Hebrew scrolls of the Talmud, which became the basis of the Old Testament of the Bible record a succession of battles, wars of conquest, territorial disputes and invasions, all beginning at this time.

During this period of violent and bloodthirsty cultural upheaval, the god known as Yahweh was venerated. The warrior kings of the Metal Age required a strong male god, because in their world the male was the lord of creation.

It was thought that only sons, not daughters, could carry the inheritance of a bloodline to the next generation; and in order to ensure that every son was recognized as the child of his father, with no possible doubts about lineage, the warrior society controlled sexual union by enslaving women. In all the realms over which the single male god hovered, women were made the subject of stringent laws to ensure that no impregnation could occur other than by their 'legal owner'. Penalties were severe. The Bible relates how a woman caught in adultery would be stoned to death. To this day under Islamic law an adulteress still faces the death penalty.

So the religious beliefs of the warrior caste dictated that women became the property of men. The ancient and more compassionate belief, however, the Old Religion of humankind, in which the Ultimate Creator was female and women were the leaders, never entirely vanished from the face of the Earth: it became known as witchcraft.

The First Healers

From the remotest eras of human history, every tribe, village and community had its wise person, its 'witch-doctor', its medicine man or woman, its driver away of demons and ghosts and curer of ills and ailments. Many of these people were grouped together under the epithet 'witch', and their various skills have been called 'witchcraft' for many centuries.

Knowledge of all natural things – plants, berries, roots, fruits, leaves and herbs – was the lore of the witch, as was the ability to make magic and cast out evil spirits. Healing on all levels, whether mental or physical, was the witch's most important skill within the community and, since it involved exclusively natural ingredients, it was considered that the witch was held in high esteem by the Goddess and Horned God of nature, so they were held in great honour.

Thus healing and witchcraft have travelled hand in hand down the long centuries from the early Palaeolithic to the present day.

The Historical Evidence

After the First World War, a distinguished archaeologist and anthropologist, Dr Margaret Alice Murray (1863–1963), was drawn to investigate witchcraft after returning from excavations in Egypt. She approached it from the point of view of an historical and anthropological research project. In 1921 she published *The Witch Cult in Western Europe* and followed this up some years later with *The God of the Witches*. These books helped to bring witchcraft to the attention of the modern world and began to generate an enormous popular interest in its beliefs and customs.

Dr Murray advanced for the first time as a scientific theory the idea that what was popularly referred to as witchcraft was actually the survival of a pre-Christian fertility and nature religion, which had been widespread before being driven underground by the hostility of Christianity and which was still surviving within our folklore and old traditions. For example, the custom of dancing round the maypole is the enactment of an ancient pagan fertility rite.

Proof that the Old Religion continued to be important to ordinary people through Saxon, Norman and mediaeval times can be found in churches in the small ornamental carvings of a stylized woman, 6 inches to 2 feet (15-cm to 0.5-m) in height, in a sexually overt pose, representing the prehistoric pagan fertility Goddess worshipped by witches. These figures are known to archaeologists as 'sheelas', from their Celtic name *Sheela-na-gig*. There are over 70 in Ireland and 23 in mainland Britain, most in Christian churches. In at least one surviving example, at the eleventh-century church of Whittlesford in Cambridgeshire, there is also a depiction of a male partner, a naked man with an animal's head, possibly representing the Horned God.

In his book *The Lost Gods of England* (1957), Brian Branston remarks, 'There can be little doubt that we have in the sheela the actual representation of the Great Goddess Earth Mother on English soil... What may be surprising is that the "idol" should so clearly retain characteristics which go back to the figurines of the Stone Age.' He also gives the significant statement: 'That the cult of the Great Goddess did not end with the Middle Ages but still flourishes today is indicated by the resurgence of "white" witchcraft, "wicca", in Great Britain ...

there are certain modern Wiccan rites which are traditional with roots going back to the Middle East of at least 2500 years ago...'

The Persecution of the Old Religion

The earliest-known written reference to witchcraft is nearly as old as writing itself, appearing on a clay tablet from the reign of King Hamurabi of Nineveh around 1700 BCE. It was not until well into the Christian era, however, that the authorities began to recognize witchcraft as a belief that was opposite to that of the established Church.

At first Christianity, like all imported ideas, took root most readily in the great ports and trading centres such as Londinium Augusta, today's London, while in the rural areas, the Old Religion continued to survive. This division between town and country was even more pronounced in older times and the Latin word for country dwellers was *pagani*, from which the word *pagan* originated.

After the Roman withdrawal in the fifth century, Britain entered a new age in which so few records were made that it became known as the Dark Ages. During this time Christianity became extinct in Britain, and any herbal and medical lore was retained largely in the folk medicine of the local cunning man or woman. Eventually the Church of Rome sent a new wave of missionaries to convert the pagans of the British Isles and to re-establish its presence.

During the early years of the Christian revival in Britain, Christianity and paganism co-existed with little conflict. Then, slowly at first, the native pagan religion was ostracized and then outlawed altogether. Thus, under Church and state persecution, followers of the Old Religion formed an underground movement. The old ways began to be observed in secret.

The Anglo-Saxons, whose language was a form of German rather than what we would now recognize as English, had a name for the followers of the Old Religion: *wicca*, pronounced today as 'wikka' but in Anglo-Saxon correctly pronounced as 'witcha'. From this word came a more modern version: 'witch'.

In the middle of the tenth century King Edgar ordered every priest in the land to promote Christianity with the utmost zeal. A little later, the witan (council) of King Ethelred directed that wherever witches, magicians and certain other offenders were found, they should be 'diligently driven out of this country...'

Anglo-Saxon England was defeated by the Norman invasion of 1066 and the new ruler, William the Conqueror, publicly stated his own disbelief in witchcraft. Nevertheless, four years later, when Hereward the Wake and his guerrilla army were successfully defying the Normans in the marshes of Cambridgeshire, William was persuaded, rather against his better judgement, to engage the services of a local witch as a means of dislodging the rebels. This plan collapsed together with the high wooden tower built for the witch to stand on to aim curses at the Saxons: the witch was plunged headlong into a swamp.

In the early 1400s, as the Dark Ages faded into the Renaissance, society began once more to expand its knowledge and understanding. Medical treatment increasingly became the province of alchemists, who performed many experiments in their quest to find new chemical cures, sometimes using mental patients and prisoners as their subjects. These experiments involved the treatment of syphilis with mercury (quicksilver), a highly dangerous poison, but the results were adequate enough to merit continued experiments by these 'quacksilvers', as they were known. It is from here that we get our word *quack* to describe anyone who works with as yet unproven medical hypotheses.

By the sixteenth century the rising influence of the alchemists had led to so much confusion about the law concerning the divide between them and the more traditional botanical therapists that King Henry VIII passed an edict which stated:

> ...it shall be lawful to every person being the King's subject, having knowledge and experience of Herbs, Roots and Waters or of the operation of same, by speculation of practice within any part of the king's Dominions, to practice, use and minister in and to any outward sore, uncome, wound, apostumations, outward swelling or disease, according to their *cunning*, experience and knowledge in any of the diseases, sores and maladies before-said and all other like to the same, or drinks for the Stone and Strangury, or Agues without suit, vexation, trouble, penalty or loss of their goods...

This confirms that herbalism and healing by cunning folk was still acceptable during his sovereignty, although he also introduced the first Witchcraft Act (1542). This first Act imposed the death penalty for invoking or conjuring evil spirits.

In those days witchcraft was not classified as it is today. The term *witch* was intended to be derogatory and literally anyone could be branded a witch just because a neighbour didn't like them, or because they had a physical affliction, or perhaps because the local cattle had just been struck down with a disease. The increasing suspicion of anyone who was in any way different from the norm led in part to the atrocities committed later during the witch-mania.

It was not really until the reign of Elizabeth I, however, that serious witch-hunting began in England. The sudden dramatic increase in witchcraft phobia was brought about by the return to England of the 'Marian exiles'. These were large numbers of extremist Protestants who had been forced to flee England when the Roman Catholic Mary Tudor, Elizabeth's predecessor, came to the throne. These religious fanatics had sought refuge in the Calvinistic towns of Europe such as Geneva and Zurich, where fierce witch persecutions and burnings were already raging. When Protestant Elizabeth was crowned, it became safe for the exiles to return home again, but they brought with them extremist continental notions about the nature of witchcraft and the way in which it should be eliminated.

In Europe and Scotland, witchcraft was defined as a heresy, a crime against the Church, and the punishment for such a crime was to be burned at the stake. In England, though, it was defined as a crime against the state, and the punishment was hanging. English Christians who found themselves on the wrong side in the Protestant/Catholic schism, such as Archbishop Cranmer, were burned; English witches were hanged. Some say millions, others say thousands were affected, but whatever the number, no one was safe from the witch-mania.

The Witchcraft Act of 1563 was replaced in 1604 by another even more severe Act which remained in force until 1736, when it was replaced by a new law that actually forbade the prosecution of anyone performing witchcraft, stating that there was no such thing. Instead the new law made it an offence for someone to *pretend* or *claim* that they were a witch. This enlightenment was a result of the flowering of the Age of Reason, in which learned people became more interested in the developing world of science.

The last English execution for alleged witchcraft was that of Alice Molland, who was hanged at Exeter in 1684, and the last witch to be condemned to death, although the sentence was never carried out, was Jane Wenham of Walkern in Hertfordshire, who was tried in 1712. Under the existing law the judge, one John Powell, had no alternative but to condemn her to death, since statutes had to be obeyed, but he managed to delay the execution until he was able to secure a royal pardon for her.

The propaganda campaign of the Christian Church against witchcraft was so successful, so merciless and applied for so many centuries, however, that it forms a distinct undercurrent in society to this day. It is this legacy that forms the root of so many of the current misconceptions of witchcraft – for example, that witches are Satanists, that witches worship the Devil, that witches perform human or animal sacrifices, that witchcraft is evil and that witchcraft is a blasphemous parody of Christianity. None of these things are true, although the accusations have remained firmly planted in the depths of public consciousness, fertilized by the Church and the media, and from time to time this old hysteria bubbles to the surface again.

The Emergence of Wicca

While the law of 1736 reduced the 'crime' of witchcraft to one of fraud, no parliamentary law could eliminate the negative beliefs about its practices that had been drummed into the average person for so many centuries by the Christian Church. Sporadic incidents of 'witches' being hounded and sometimes killed continued to occur for a long time. Secrecy still had to shroud the practice of witchcraft.

Herbalists and other healers remained popular, however – so much so that in 1847 the American Medical Association was established, which effectively eliminated any 'non-regular' practitioner from performing any form of medicine. In this way alternative medicine virtually disappeared from the United States for the next 60 years, the knowledge held only by the Native Americans and other folk traditions.

In the United Kingdom the picture was largely the same. In 1854 the Medical Reform Bill put before Parliament was intended to ban the use of herbal medicine unless practitioners were registered with the British Medical Association. There was a united uprising against the Bill, however, and it was dropped, thus allowing the continuance of the practice of herbal medicine up to the present day.

The Wiccan Revivalists

The modern emergence of witchcraft was driven essentially by two people: Dr Margaret Murray, whose popular books we have already mentioned, and Gerald Gardner. Many others made significant contributions to the spread of knowledge and interest in the subject, but these two individuals remain paramount.

Gerald Brosseau Gardner (1884–1964) had a deep interest in the religious customs of the tribes he had encountered in the Orient. It is believed that he was a member of a witchcraft coven based in the area of the New Forest in Hampshire. This would have been a 'Traditional' Wiccan coven, one of those groups following the Old Religion that had survived down the centuries. It is thought that Gardner was initiated into witchcraft in 1939 by a woman named Dorothy Clutterbuck.

During the 1940s Gardner published a book about witchcraft called *High Magic's Aid*, but because claiming to be a witch was still a criminal offence, this highly accurate book was written in the form of a novel. However, after the Second World War, in order to comply with the newly formed United Nations Organization and its Universal Charter of Human Rights, Britain was obliged to repeal the Witchcraft Act of 1736. This disposed of the legal restriction on witches themselves openly publishing books on witchcraft.

In 1954 Gerald Gardner published what was to become his most influential book, *Witchcraft Today*, in which he affirmed that, despite centuries of persecution, groups of witches were still thriving throughout the country. He immediately received floods of letters from interested people, and many were initiated into witchcraft by Gardner and his High Priestess, the late Doreen Valiente, and later went on to start up covens of their own. Within a few years there were groups of witches all around the country.

Gardner, however, did not teach the kind of witchcraft that was being observed until his time. One theory holds that his parent coven in the New Forest had told him he must keep some of their rites and customs secret. This cannot be proved. However, Gardner fashioned for himself and his followers a new variety of witchcraft, drawing from old pagan sources, including many aspects of Traditional witchcraft, for which he made use of the ancient Anglo-Saxon word *wicca*. It is perfectly possible that Traditional covens prior to Gardner called what they were doing Wicca, but I believe it was Gardner's followers who made the term widely known and who became the greatest influence on the spread of witchcraft and the term Wicca during the 1950s and 1960s.

Gardner's work led to an explosive flowering of Wicca during the 1960s, when people were searching for new values and beliefs after the imposed austerity of the post-war era. The type of witchcraft that Gerald Gardner promulgated soon came to be called Gardnerian Wicca, and today this is probably the most popular variety.

Other varieties of Wicca were soon branching off the main stem established by Gardner. During the 1960s Alex Sanders with his wife Maxine founded what was to be named Alexandrian Witchcraft after him. Sanders incorporated into his system many elements drawn from branches of the occult, such as the Qabbalah (an ancient Jewish occult system) and the inclusion of Judeo-Christian 'words of power' written around the edge of the working Circle.

There are also Dianic Wiccans, taking their name from Diana, one of the many ancient names for the witch's Goddess, who form female-oriented covens in which few or no men are admitted.

There are, however, no vast divisions within witchcraft, or Wicca, as there are for example between Catholics and Protestants in Christianity. All witches regard their individual varieties of the Craft as being branches and twigs upon the main family tree of witchcraft, whose trunk rises throughout recorded history and whose roots lie buried deep within the earth of our prehistoric past. It is from the bond of this common heritage and widespread living Craft that Wiccan healing derives.

We can now see that Wicca was born from a very turbulent background, involving war, subjugation, abuse and derision, even though for thousands of years prior to 'Churchianity', witches, pagans, shamans and healers were all keenly sought and their skills greatly respected. The existence of such people right up to the present day is living proof that pure science cannot supply all the needs of human society and that magic has its place within healing.

Chapter Two

What Is Wiccan Healing?

Part of Wiccan philosophy is to work for the highest good. In practice, this means that genuine Wiccans will, as far as possible, make themselves available in service to all life, and this would include healing. All spiritual traditions have their particular healing beliefs and practices, which are reflected in the various types of healing offered. In Wicca there is always magic, nature and spirituality involved at some level.

Wicca has no centralized doctrine or scriptures and celebrates personal freedom. The drawback to this for someone who writes about Wicca is that there are as many different opinions about it as there are Wiccans; however, there are certain things that apply more or less universally.

Types of Wiccan

There are basically only two kinds of Wiccan: those who prefer to work as part of a coven (group) and those who prefer to work alone, normally referred to as 'solitary witches'. There are many different varieties of witchcraft today, but this coven/solitary option runs through all of them. In general, anything a coven does, a solitary witch can also do, and vice versa. (Some may argue that a coven is able to raise more energy, but this is only a difference in energy levels, not in techniques.) A witch is a witch, regardless of how they practise, and so there is nothing that precludes a solitary witch from working in a coven now and then, nor a coven-based witch choosing to also work alone.

Somewhere in between these two basic preferences is the hereditary witch, who may be either solitary or a member of a coven. This is someone who is a witch because it 'runs in the family' and the knowledge has been passed down from generation to generation.

There is also the hedgewitch, who is normally expert in the healing properties of herbs, plants and natural remedies and is also closely aligned to the spirit world, someone akin to the village shaman.

The Wiccan Tools

The whole ideology of Wicca is based on simplicity. This does not mean that ritual equipment is not used, but that witches are able to work by just using the powers of the Craft within their own being. An evolved witch should be able to work magic anywhere, at any time, without any elaborate preparations or equipment. However, we could say that the same applies to a medical doctor. If someone has a heart attack in the street, a doctor will know exactly what to do to help them, but at the same time he or she would prefer to get them as quickly as possible to a hospital, where all the equipment is waiting. In a similar way, if there is no urgency, witches will generally prefer to work magic with the assistance of their magical equipment and in a properly cast Circle. (Because it is a sacred place to Wiccans, the word *Circle*, when used to denote a witches' meeting-place, is conventionally spelled with a capital letter.)

A typical coven will usually set aside a period of time at its meetings for healing. First, the meeting-place is prepared and the altar made ready; it is upon this that the Wiccan tools are placed and made ready for use. These tools are often referred to as the 'Wiccan Elemental working tools'.

The Elemental Working Tools

One of the basic factors of Wicca, and most other magical traditions, is the use of the four Elements of Earth, Air, Fire and Water. In the next chapter we will go into the Elements and their applications in magic more thoroughly; here we are concerned with their relevance to the witches' working tools.

The belief in four Elements goes back a great many centuries and was first defined by the ancient Greeks, although a fourfold division of the universal energy is a common theme in many religions and can be dated back even further than that. For example, at the root of Judaism, God's name was formed out of four Hebrew letters, YHWH (הוהי), which it was forbidden to speak out loud. In occult belief, each of these four letters represents a primordial cosmic vibration that became one of the four Elements. In Christianity there are the four gospels, in nature four seasons, and so on. In the magical tradition, all of the possibilities for change and evolution are governed by one of the four Elements. (As a convention, in magic the word *Element* is often spelt with a capital 'E' in order to distinguish it from the many chemical elements.)

In magical practice, the four Elements are associated with the four points of the compass. For example, when Wiccans open their working Circle, they place Earth in the North, Air in the East, Fire in the South and Water in the West, creating four quarters within their sacred space that represent the four Elemental qualities. These correspondences date back to an age before the world had been explored and when it was still thought to be flat. The reasoning was that the further North you travelled, the colder, damper and darker the world became, and what is Earth but cold, dark and damp? The further South you went, the hotter the sun grew, so South was obviously the domain of Fire. To the East, before Marco Polo travelled to India and China and taught Europeans of these countries, the endless Russian steppes reached up to the edge of the world under a huge sky where the winds constantly blew – a suitable abode for the spirits of the Air. And before Columbus it was thought that the ocean went West until a ship would plunge over a huge waterfall at the rim into the home of the Water gods.

In order to work magic with the energies of the four Elements, witches make use of four Elemental tools:

> The pentacle – Earth
>
> The athame (sometimes the sword) – Air
>
> The wand – Fire
>
> The cup or chalice – Water

There are different opinions regarding the exact nature and applicability of these tools, depending upon the particular tradition being followed and upon the preferences of the individual coven. The Earth pentacle and Water chalice are just about universal, but the Fire wand and Air dagger/sword are subject to the interpretations of various schools of thought. Some feel that because a wand grows on a tree waving in the breeze, it is more suitable to represent the Element of Air rather than Fire, and because a dagger or sword is forged in a furnace, these are more suitable to be Fire tools. Some witches use them in this way and others in the more traditional way. It is actually not important; what *is* important is that whichever interpretation you decide to use feels comfortable and logical to *you*, regardless of what others may say. In this book, we will use the more traditional associations, but this does not mean that I am saying this is the only way.

Another difference of opinion relates to the use of the sword by witches. It must be remembered that witchcraft is an incredibly ancient belief and has come through some violent and oppressive times. In certain parts of the mediae-val period it was forbidden for anyone not of the nobility to own a sword, and as most witches were peasants, they did not have the money to purchase one anyway. Swords were frequently used by ritual magicians and sorcerers, who were mostly members of the upper classes, and because of this ancient memory, some covens regard the sword as a symbol of those who oppressed the Craft and consider that it should not form a part of coven equipment. Other witches have freely adopted the use of the sword, and there is some evidence that the wealthier witches of the past also made use of it, even though there was risk attached.

Let's look at the individual tools in more detail.

The Pentacle

The pentacle that represents the Earth Element is simply a plate or platter, very often decorated with various magical designs and emblems, specifically the five-pointed star. It can be made from wood or copper, because copper is a metal associated with Elemental Earth. Some magical practitioners say that copper is also associated with the planet Venus. It is, but in times past the goddess Venus was an Earth goddess, and copper, because it turns green and can conduct electrical currents, is also associated with planet Earth. The easiest and most cost-effective material to use for a pentacle, however, is wood, a material also associated with the Earth. A round wooden breadboard can be painted to make a very effective pentacle.

The pentacle is considered an 'earthing' tool. It is used for protection, for grounding unwanted magical energy (just as a lightning conductor earths electrical currents) and for any magical working that comes under the influence of the Earth Element.

The Athame

As a general rule, a witch uses a special black-handled knife or dagger, known as an athame, as a 'pointer', a means of focusing their energy in any direction. Although this can be used in all works of magic, it is particularly associated with the Air Element.

The sword, if used at all, is used for more powerful acts of focusing, such as casting the Circle *(see Chapter Seven)*. It is also generally associated with Air, but can be viewed as being powerful enough to represent a kind of 'united Elemental force', especially when used for Circle casting.

The coven sword can also be a symbol of the authority of the High Priestess within the Circle, where in Wiccan belief she becomes the embodiment of the Goddess.

The Wand

The wand is the tool of the Fire Element and is the most famous and clichéd of all the magical tools. The stage magician's 'magic wand' with its black shaft and white tip is actually a debased memory of an ancient design in which the wand had a 'positive' and a 'negative' end.

In Wicca, the emphasis is on simplicity and also, very importantly, on nature and natural forms. The typical Wiccan wand therefore more usually consists of a live-picked piece of wood about 9-inches (23 cm) long that has been ceremoniously cut from the tree. It can be left exactly as it is, or trimmed, stripped of bark and wax polished, depending upon individual taste. Traditionally, it can also have magical symbols engraved upon it, or else a suitable inscription in a magical alphabet, perhaps Runic or Theban. The Runes are the ancient northern European alphabet and are relatively well known *(see Chart 14 on page 168)*. Theban is sometimes called 'the Witch's Alphabet' and is very suitable for magical inscriptions. *(This alphabet can be found on page 174.)*

There is a lot of tradition associated with the making of a wand, such as the belief that it must be made of ash wood that is cut at the stroke of midnight at a full moon using only the single stroke of a knife. If this kind of complicated symbolism works for you, then by all means use it. However, any wood is appropriate, cut at any tree-friendly time and in any respectful manner. Another salient point is that some people may prefer to use fallen wood and may come across just the right piece lying upon the ground. There are no hard and fast rules – simply follow your own heart as to what feels right. One thing that is important, however, if you do decide to take live wood, is to remember to respect the tree by asking if you may cut a branch from it and being appreciative afterwards.

The Chalice

The cup or chalice is the tool of the Water Element. Most covens will consecrate their water during the ritual of opening the Circle by sprinkling a pinch of salt into it and imparting energy to it through lowering the point of an athame into it while a blessing is spoken.

The cup is used as a working tool during rituals involving Water magic. Once consecrated, the water in the cup can also be used to sanctify the Circle as it is cast.

Other Wiccan Tools

Apart from the four Elemental tools, there are various other items that can fall into the category of 'witchcraft tools'. Not every witch or coven will have all of these things, and there is no need to feel in any way inadequate if you do not have them; their presence is – as in the case of so many Wiccan items – purely a matter of personal taste, feeling and availability.

The Cauldron

The cauldron is an item used by many witches, not for bubbling up 'magic potions' but as a symbol of the pagan fertility Goddess. The round hollow basin of the cauldron symbolizes the cosmic womb of the Great Mother and the Earth. Its size is not important. It is frequently just a small token cauldron little larger than a cup.

Cords

Cord magic is an important part of Wiccan practice *(see page 162)*. Witches use cords during rituals; knots tied in the cord are used to 'bind' a spell. To release a spell after it has fulfilled its function, the knot is ceremonially untied.

Cords are normally consecrated and when not in use can be placed as symbolic ornaments on the altar.

Many covens also use coloured cords worn round the waist to indicate the particular Wiccan degree of individual witches. There are three degrees in conventional witchcraft: white cord for a prentice (first degree), blue cord for a High Priest or Priestess (second degree) and red cord for a female and black cord for a male third-degree witch.

Candles

Candles are used by Wiccans universally as illuminators within the Circle, where electric light is generally not used at all. Coloured candles are chosen for the particular qualities of those colours, such as red for energy, in order to bring appropriate correspondences *(see Chapter Five)* to the working Circle.

Wiccans also light different-coloured candles depending upon what day of the week it is or what festival they are celebrating. Monday is white or silver, Tuesday is red, Wednesday is yellow, Thursday is turquoise, blue or purple, Friday is green, Saturday is indigo or black and Sunday is orange or gold. *(For candle magic, see Chapter Ten.)*

Coloured candles are also displayed and lit during traditional Wiccan festivals. At Imbolc (2 February) they are white, at Beltaine (30 April) gold or green, at Lughnasadh (31 July) orange and at Samhain (31 October) black, orange and white. We shall be studying the traditional Wiccan festivals and their meanings in the next chapter. What is important to state here is that when choosing candles, personal connection is of more significance than adherence to hard and fast rules.

It is interesting, however, how the traditional colours came to be used, because it is through a very pagan association. Unlike the Latin-based names for the days of the week used in European languages, which are named after the Roman gods, the English names are based on the Viking gods, because huge areas of England were once a Danish kingdom (the Danelaw) in which there were at least as many Danish-speaking people as there were Anglo-Saxons who spoke English. Only one Roman god survives in the English week: Saturn, who of course gives us Saturn's Day or Saturday. Sun-Day and Moon-Day are fairly obvious and very pagan, and Tuesday is Tiew's Day (also Tiwaz' Day), Wednesday is Woden's Day, Thursday is Thor's Day and Friday, Freya's Day. The traditional Wiccan candle colours for each day derive from the colours associated with these god forms. Freya, for example, was the Scandinavian equivalent of the Roman goddess Venus, whose colour is green.

Figurines

Many Wiccans will have statues or busts on the altar representing the Earth Mother Goddess and Her consort the Great Horned God. These are not 'idols', for an idol is a carving that is itself worshipped and believed to *be* a deity. The Wiccan figurines are more akin to being 'reminders' of what we worship.

Wiccan statuettes of the Goddess and God can take many forms. In some covens they are Egyptian, in others they are Celtic, in others mediaeval, and so on. The artistic and cultural style will depend upon the preferences of the individual Wiccans using them.

The Scourge

The scourge plays a small symbolic part during modern Gardnerian initiations and can also be used during part of the ritual casting of the Wiccan Circle. It has been associated with witchcraft for untold centuries and there are grounds for believing that it is the surviving relic of the ancient Egyptian crop-flail, which can be seen in statues and paintings of pharaohs, where it is held on the breast crossed with the shepherd's crook.

The Bell

The bell is a tool of the Air Element (the Element of communication amongst other things) and throughout time has been used as a tool by heralds and summoners. Most covens have a bell of some kind on the altar, which the High Priestess (or someone she may nominate) uses to announce the start and finish of ceremonies and other parts of a coven meeting, such as the 'Cakes and Ale', the traditional feast that follows a Sabbat. It is also used to signal the start and finish of periods of meditation and so on. Bells are used by solitaries and hedge-witches in the same way.

Incense Burner

Incense forms an important part of Wiccan ritual, the precise scent being chosen to correspond to the nature of the meeting, the season or the type of ritual to be undertaken. Although the simplest variety is the incense stick, it is considered more effective and more personal to use loose incense grains, which are placed on ignited charcoal. There are many beautiful brass incense thuribles available. Using loose incense gives the opportunity of mixing your own blend for special occasions.

The Book of Shadows

Most covens have their own book of Wiccan lore containing rituals, ceremonies, recipes for incenses, information about herbs and some form of almanac that gives details and dates of the Sabbats. Frequently included are diary notes about the progress of the coven, or the individual if they are a solitary practitioner. Very often, this 'Book of Shadows' is propped up on the altar open at a relevant page.

It is not really correct to consider this to be a form of 'Wiccan bible', for the Bible itself is a static book, whereas a Book of Shadows grows as the years pass, like a living thing. There are as many different Books of Shadows as there are Wiccans who keep one, even if they were originally copied from the same source. By tradition, a newly initiated witch is lent a Book of Shadows by someone in the coven and is required to copy it out 'in their own hand of write', as an old Wiccan ruling puts it. However, after this is done, they will then keep on adding their own knowledge, wisdom and experience in further pages, according to their own degree of development within the Craft.

A solitary Wiccan, such as a hedgewitch for instance, can quite legitimately compile their own Book of Shadows according to their own ideas, without the necessity of having to copy it from another.

The Loving Cup or Wine Cup

The main altar cup or chalice, as described in the Elemental working tools above, contains consecrated water with salt added and is unsuitable for drinking out of. Indeed, as it is a consecrated magical tool, it would be an insult to attempt to drink from it. Many Wiccans, therefore, also include a drinking cup or loving cup on their altar to contain wine or some other traditional drink such as mead. If wine is used, then according to tradition it should be red wine.

This loving cup is placed on the altar at the outset, when the altar is 'dressed' in preparation for use, and the wine or mead then becomes consecrated during the ritual of opening the Circle. Before the Circle is closed at the end of the proceedings, the wine is blessed in the names of the Goddess and Horned God by the High Priestess, who will pour a libation to deity into a small bowl before taking a sip and then passing it round for everyone to share a sip at a time. Traditionally, it is handed from female to male (if the numbers are equal) with a kiss and the loving greeting 'Blessed be!' A solitary Wiccan may simply make a suitable toast of thanksgiving to the Goddess and God before drinking any themselves.

Robes

There are many different schools of thought regarding Wiccan robes. Some covens, particularly Traditional Wiccan ones, wear uniform robes all of the same colour and style, usually in natural tones such as green, brown, black or white. Other Wiccans wear their own individual robes, each different from one another and in colours chosen by the people themselves. Other covens, such as Gardnerian Wiccan covens, work 'skyclad' in the Circle. *Skyclad* is a poetic term meaning 'naked', and there is ample evidence that this is how witches worked rituals in ancient times. Even robed covens generally conduct initiations skyclad, and the convention is that robes or loose-fitting gowns are worn until just before the commencement of casting the Circle. Other Wiccans just wear ordinary casual clothes such as jeans and T-shirts, although this can certainly detract from the important magical 'feel' of the occasion.

Whatever kind of robe or clothing, or absence of it, is decided upon by the solitary Wiccan practitioner, it should be something that they themselves feel adequately expresses their magical persona and that they do not connect with their ordinary lives and activities. The purpose of special robes or of going skyclad is to make the Circle feel extremely *different* from normal life and activities, and to ensure that witches can fully escape, within the Circle, from the regimentation and oppression of social dictates.

Jewellery

This, too, can be considered a 'Wiccan tool', because if it is worn in ceremony or ritual it will have been consecrated and activated to carry magical energy. Many witches wear silver jewellery such as a pentagram or Goddess pendant, rings or even, in the case of a High Priestess or High Priest, a special witchcraft crown. It is the usual practice for a witch to purify their jewellery, perhaps at their initiation ceremony, thereby cleansing and consecrating the items.

As a general rule all trinkets, bodily adornments, watches and non-spiritual jewellery are removed prior to working in the Circle. Hair is undone and knots in belts or ritual clothing are unfastened prior to undertaking any knotting or cord magic to ensure a clean slate from which to create the knots for the new spell.

Having now established what constitutes part of the Wiccan working Circle and the individual choices that can be made with regards to Wiccan tools and equipment, you can set up your Wiccan altar knowing what each tool represents and how each is used in a working Circle.

The Wiccan Altar

The Wiccan altar is a designated surface upon which Wiccan tools are laid out for ritual, and it is a traditional part of any activity where there is the casting of a Wiccan Circle. The altar is the physical centre of spiritual energy, as is the case with all religions that make use of one, and is prepared before the ritual and cleared away upon completion of the ritual.

The Wiccan altar is normally laid out so that each working tool can be easily reached, with the most regularly used items being placed in the most easily accessible positions. As a guideline, your loving cup can be filled with mead or red wine (or spring water or apple juice if you do not take alcohol) and can stand on, or in front of, the pentagram in the centre of the altar. Place a small bowl of salt to the right of the pentagram and your chalice of water to the left. The Goddess statuette can be placed to the left of the pentagram and the God to the right. The candlesticks are best placed towards the back of the altar at the left- and right-hand outer edges. The flail is placed atop the wand in a crossed

('X') position with the athame, and the bell placed within easy reach. The incense holder, charcoal and herbs are placed where space allows. If a sword is used to cast the Circle, it is laid respectfully upon a cloth at the base of the altar or at the front of the altar itself. The Book of Shadows is placed either by the side of the altar or between the candlesticks.

Once set up, the Wiccan altar becomes a place of sanctity and is considered very sacred.

The Healing Altar

Whereas the Wiccan altar is a ceremonial place for ritual tools to be placed during full Wiccan healing rituals, you can also set up a simpler altar to someone who is unwell to act as a focal point for your healing energies. This type of healing altar comprises anything that you choose to lay out upon it and does not have to include the more formal placements of the Wiccan tools and equipment. It can include, for example, items like photographs, possessions of the person needing healing, healing crystals, items of personal meaning that can link you to them, flowers, power objects, and so on. It can be indoors or outdoors, whichever feels more appropriate.

There are several ways a healing altar can be put together, depending upon the healing focus required. For example, if someone you know is going in for surgery, your central point of focus would be the magical correspondences for surgery. Correspondences are things that blend together well and, through co-operation, help to enhance or increase the potency of any magical workings. For surgery the correspondences are the planet Mercury, Wednesday, the colour yellow, an agate crystal, caraway seeds, lavender incense and the god Thoth, to name but a few *(see Chart 1 overleaf)*. From these you can choose items for a healing altar dedicated to successful surgery and display them any way you choose. You could, for example, just have yellow candles and a photograph of the individual concerned and burn lavender incense. Alternatively, you may decide to have one of the patient's personal items, such as a piece of jewellery, surrounded by agate crystals and caraway seeds. You may decide to use all the correspondences; the choice really is up to you.

Chart 1: Correspondences for a Healing Altar

Day of week	Planet	Governs	Candle colour	Gem	Planetary sigil	Herbs	Fragrance	Deity
Monday	Moon	Healing/Family life/Emotions	Pale blue	Clear quartz		Camphor	Jasmine	Isis Hecate
Tuesday	Mars	Conflict/Strength/ Power	Red	Ruby		Coriander	Pine	Woden Thor Brigid
Wednesday	Mercury	Health/Medicine/ Surgery/The mind	Yellow	Agate		Caraway	Lavender	Thoth Hermes
Thursday	Jupiter	Luck/Fortune/ The law	Purple	Amethyst		Nutmeg Oak	Honeysuckle	Hera, Zeus, Jupiter
Friday	Venus	Relationships/ Love	Green	Emerald Rose Quartz		Myrtle Violet Vervain	Rose	Branwen Aphrodite
Saturday	Saturn	Karma/Restriction/ Obstacles	Indigo	Obsidian		Ever-greens	Cypress	Cronos Nemesis
Sunday	Sun	General health and well-being	Orange	Amber		Marigold Bay Laurel	Frankincense	Lugh Sekhmet

A healing altar can remain in place for as long as necessary and can be freshened up every 24 hours or so, with replacement flowers, candles or other items to keep the energy fresh and bright.

Ideally, it is best to understand what type of healing is required before you lay out an altar and then to work with the appropriate correspondences. When you are seeking protection during an illness, for example, or wish to call for a change in your 'fate', you can work with Jupiter and set up your altar on a Thursday with purple candles, amethyst crystals, honeysuckle incense, oak leaves, and so on. If someone is suffering setbacks in their personal life and health due to difficult relationships, you could choose to work with either Venus (personal) or the Moon (family), in which case you would choose herbs, colours, deities and crystals that were appropriate to them. If, on the other hand, the individual needing healing felt weak and unable to face up to whatever was causing their ill health, you might decide to work with Saturn or the Sun. The Saturnian powers would be invoked to bring assistance in finding the reason behind any medical/psycho-spiritual condition; the Sun could be invoked to bring the strength needed to rise above the conflicts of poor health and thus help to speed the healing process. For stress-related difficulties you could choose to work with Mercury (mental stress) or the Moon (emotional stress).

When working with correspondences to set up a healing altar, the possibilities are endless and can therefore be a little confusing at first. I would advise you to refer to correspondence charts, start at a basic level, keep it simple and remember that your intent, your love and your goodwill are the real potentizers of any healing altar that you create and that what feels right for you is the most important quality to respond to.

Activating a Healing Altar

To activate your healing altar all you need to do is to light your candles, focus your thoughts upon the individual concerned and send them healing through your hands by sitting with the palms of your hands facing upwards whilst they are resting in your lap.

Open your healing with words appropriate to the healing required (as an example I have used surgery):

An it be for highest good and harming none, I call you, Mighty Thoth [you would state your chosen deity's name here]. It is I, [state your name], come to you to appeal for your protection and healing during the surgery for [state patient's full name]. May you bring confidence and surety to the surgeon. May all be made well under the guidance of your wise counsel. So mote it be!

If working with another deity, simply change the wording a little to accommodate the change of focus. With a relationship issue, for example, you could say:

An it be for highest good and harming none, I call upon you, Gracious Lady Branwen. It is I, [state your name], come to you to appeal for your loving wisdom and guidance to touch the hearts of [state the names, as required]. May you bring warmth and reason to their relationship. May they be guided by love and your wise counsel. So mote it be!

The Working Circle

Witches do a lot of their magical work inside a Circle that is traditionally 9 feet (2.7-m) across, although it can be any size that is required. It does not necessarily have to be a visible Circle, although it can be outlined with cord, string or chalk. The most important point is to visualize it clearly, whether or not it is a physical Circle. Most covens do not visibly mark out their Circle but visualize it all together.

Once the room and altar are ready, the Circle is cast. The Circle is actually a sphere, like a huge bubble, with the Circle resting where this invisible bubble intersects the floor or ground. Within this magic Circle, the laws of the mundane world do not apply, for the Wiccan Circle is held to be beyond space and time and is considered part of a magical dimension. Witches work within this sphere to help to retain the energy of the magical field and to define a clear boundary between the magical and the mundane world. Most religions have a special place for meetings, such as a church, mosque, temple or synagogue; the Circle is the Wiccan equivalent, being what is called a *psychic construction* rather than a physical one.

During the ceremony, the coven members are welcomed into the Circle that has been prepared by the High Priestess and High Priest, with the exact timing depending upon the particular variety of Wicca. The High Priestess may then ask whether any coven member knows of anybody who requires healing. This question can come at different stages of the proceedings depending again upon the type of Wicca and upon the customs of the particular coven. In Traditional Wicca, healing is generally the very first item on the agenda.

The High Priestess, aided and counselled by her High Priest, must form a judgement about the morality of any request. For example, a particular coven member might be approached by one of their friends, who knows of their link to witchcraft, to ask if anything can be done to help a sick relative. This is not always a straightforward matter. For example, the applicant may believe in witchcraft, but his ill brother might be from another religion and unaware of the request being made on his behalf. The High Priestess may decide that it would be morally wrong to conduct a healing in this case, since it is highly probable that if he knew about it, the brother might not agree to any help from witches. This would be a fairly clear-cut example, but other cases may be far more difficult to come to a decision about.

Before leaving this chapter on the background to Wiccan healing, we can summarize that it is based upon faith in the goodness of the Goddess and the God, on utilizing the gifts from nature's garden, on working with the Elements and their tools, honouring all life as sacred and adopting moral values when performing any healing work. What is also important is the emphasis upon being part of Creation, the cosmos and the stars.

Chapter Three
Earth, Sun, Moon and Stars

The Zodiac has played a major part in magic since astrology was first established, at least as long ago as the ancient Babylonians and Egyptians, who both had well-developed Zodiac charts and images. There are very few magical systems in the world that do not incorporate some aspect of astrology within their tradition, and healing is no exception.

Unlike astronomy, which is the pure science of the Universe, astrology deals with the energies believed to link events on Earth with the phenomena observable in the night sky. The argument about whether astrology works or whether it is baseless superstition has simmered for centuries. In the past, even the dates of coronations were arranged according to whether the stars were 'favourable' – for example that of Queen Elizabeth I, whose coronation date was decided upon by her court astrologer Dr John Dee. Whether we believe in it or not, though, there is no doubt at all that astrology has been a major part of the human belief system for thousands of years.

The First Astrologers

Detailed study of the stars and planets originated at the end of the last Ice Age, when farming developed. The first shepherds in the Middle East, where farming first started, had to remain on guard against wolves and other predators throughout the night. In order to pass away the time, they would gaze at the stars and see patterns in their arrangements, imagining suggestive outlines of mythological creatures, great warriors and heroes, as well as some of the animals they were familiar with.

Today there are still many clues pointing to the strong influence of Middle Eastern cultures in our astronomy and astrology. A great many of the stars have Arabic names, such as Rigel, Mizar, Altair, Sirius, Mira, Vega, Betelgeuse and Antares. In the constellation of Taurus the Bull the star *Alpha Tauri*, one of the brightest stars in the sky, is called Aldebaran (Old Arabic: *Al de-beran*, 'the eye of the bull').

The early observers also noticed two other facts over a period of time and devised their own ideas to explain them. They noticed that the sun always rose in a certain group of stars at the same time every year and that there seemed to be 12 such groups. The fact that these 'sunrise stars' seemed to be grouped into 12 distinct constellations is pure chance; there might have been fewer or more, but to the first shepherds there seemed to be 12. This is why from that time onwards we have 12 months in our year rather than, say, 10 or 15. To the minds of the first observers, these particular 12 constellations were favoured by the sun and so were more important than the other star groups that the sun never visited. These 12 special constellations formed a band or belt around the sky that became known as the Zodiac, and the figures formed by the special stars became the signs of the Zodiac.

The second fact noticed by early observers was that there were two different kinds of stars in the sky. The majority of them never changed their position and were called the 'fixed' stars. (Actually, they do change their position, but so slowly that it takes many lifetimes before it becomes noticeable.) However, there were a few stars that did change their position very rapidly, being in a different place every night. Five of these moving stars were visible altogether and they were called 'wandering' stars. The Greek word for 'wanderer' was *planetes*, and these wandering stars therefore came to be called 'planets'.

The five *planetoi*, it was noticed, only travelled *within* the band of the Zodiac, never above or below it. This is a simple result of the solar system being formed in the shape of a flattened disk so that most objects orbit the sun in one plane called the *plane of the ecliptic*. (It is as though the sun were an orange lying on a table and the planets were grapes and peas rolling around on the same tabletop, never spinning below or above the table, except for Pluto, which takes a different orbit, but was not known in those days.) This means that each sign of the Zodiac is visited by different planets on various occasions. The planets were believed to be the chariots of the gods, and therefore the gods spent time visiting the various constellations. Obviously (to pre-scientific thought), if a particular god was in a Zodiac constellation, it would produce a particular kind of influence on Earth and anyone who was born at that time would partake of this influence. This is the root of the concept now known as astrology.

Two other objects in the sky also possessed the ability to move amongst the background stars: the sun and moon, and these were also considered to be 'wanderers', or planets. Therefore, in the ancient world, before new planets were discovered after the invention of the telescope, there were seven planets altogether, each of which was the chariot of a god and was accorded its own particular day of worship. This is why, since that remote time, our week has consisted of seven days.

The mysterious celestial influence of the Zodiac upon the human world became the object of great study and speculation over the years. It forged the belief that each individual part of the human body was linked by some kind of invisible 'energy thread' or etheric vibration to a certain Zodiac sign and its influence and characteristics, modified by the presence of any visiting planet. If a good planet was in the sign that related to a particular bodily ailment, then the ailment was considered likely to start healing. If a bad planet were visiting the sign, however, the condition would grow worse. In the Middle Ages it was a common figure of speech when someone had a bad ache or sickness to say that they were suffering 'an attack of planet'.

There are two ways of regarding this entire subject, especially in relation to healing. Some people might wish to adopt an entirely 'scientific' attitude and dismiss the whole thing as groundless superstition. Others may realize that the human mind works in mysterious ways and that the unconscious mind has psychic abilities that can be controlled and released by the processes we call magic. The influences of the Zodiac signs on the human body may well be the result of the working of the unconscious mind, into which the ideas have been placed in a form of auto-suggestion, and not the result of any 'invisible link' with the stars themselves. The point is, it doesn't really matter, as long as a result is achieved. Whether the result is brought about by mystical energy networks linked to the patterns of the stars or by the powers of suggestion within the deeper layers of the mind, it is really only the result and the apparent cause and effect we should be interested in.

From the point of view of Wiccan healing, there is a fairly simple method of utilizing the influences of the Zodiac to aid the healing process. This method can be used on its own or as a background to any of the other healing techniques described in this book.

The essence of this particular method is that it provides two things: first, an appropriate day of the week to work any ritual or other healing; and second, a Zodiacal correspondence with any afflicted part of the body that can be utilized within a magical activity.

A Zodiac Healing

The first step is to establish what part of the body requires healing and then to refer to Chart 2 to find which sign of the Zodiac corresponds most closely to that part of the body. For example, if I have a bad knee, by referring to the chart, I can see that my knees are governed by Capricorn. I then refer to Chart 3 to find which element, day of the week, symbol and planet relate to Capricorn, and thus build the structure of a healing ritual, charm or talisman with these components. In the case of my bad knee, I would perform the ritual on a Saturday, with herbs or correspondences of the Earth element, utilizing the symbols for the planet itself and the Zodiac sign of Capricorn.

Chart 2: The Zodiac and Parts of the Body

Aries	Head, brain, face
Taurus	Throat, neck, diet
Gemini	Shoulders, arms, hands, lungs, nerves
Cancer	Chest, stomach, digestion
Leo	Heart, spine, back, eyes
Virgo	Abdomen, intestines
Libra	Kidneys, skin, lumbar region
Scorpio	Genitals
Sagittarius	Hips, thighs, arteries, liver
Capricorn	Knees, bones
Aquarius	Legs, ankles, circulation
Pisces	Feet, toes, lymphatic system

Chart 3: Zodiac correspondences

Day of week	Planetary symbol	Planet	Zodiac sign	Zodiac symbol	Element
Monday	☽	Moon	Cancer	♋	Water
Tuesday	♂	Mars	Aries	♈	Fire
			Scorpio	♏	Water
Wednesday	☿	Mercury	Gemini	♊	Air
			Virgo	♍	Earth
Thursday	♃	Jupiter	Sagittarius	♐	Fire
			Pisces	♓	Water
Friday	♀	Venus	Libra	♎	Air
			Taurus	♉	Earth
Saturday	♄	Saturn	Capricorn	♑	Earth
			Aquarius	♒	Air
Sunday	☉	Sun	Leo	♌	Fire

When performing a Zodiac ritual that is to treat/heal a body part, you can also plan your healing to coincide with the Moon passing through the Zodiac's governing sign during its 28-day cycle (in astrological terms, the Sun and Moon are conventionally spelled with capital letters). To work with the Moon in this way, you will need a lunar calendar. Conversely, surgery or any other invasive treatment should *not* be undertaken when the Moon is in the same sign as the relevant body part.

The Clockwork of the Earth

Even before the first systematic observations of the night sky came humankind's intimate knowledge of the seasons of the Earth herself. These, too, were seen as having connections with the sky, for it was obvious that the midday sun changed its position from a high place in summer to a lower point in the sky in winter, and that its rising and setting moved along the horizon in yearly cycles.

We can be confident that our ancient ancestors made these observations because of the stone circles they built. At Stonehenge, for example, the great stones are aligned with the midsummer and midwinter sunrise. However, far fewer people have heard of the Aubrey Holes, named after the antiquarian John Aubrey, famous for his book *Brief Lives*, who discovered them in the seventeenth century. The Aubrey Holes are a circle of 56 holes, now filled in by thousands of years of silt, surrounding the visible edifice of Stonehenge. In his book *Stonehenge Decoded*, Gerald S. Hawkins reported the results of his investigation into the alignments of Stonehenge carried out with the aid of an early computer at the Smithsonian Astrophysical Observatory, at Harvard College Observatory, at Boston University and at Stonehenge itself. He showed that if it were assumed that early humans placed several coloured posts or small marker stones in certain of these holes and moved their positions around the circle by so many places each year, so that some markers went round in a few years while others took many decades to complete a circuit, the whole complex became a highly accurate astronomical computer, like a gigantic clock, which accurately predicted solar and lunar eclipses, the 18-year solar cycle and the 56-year lunar cycle.

The origins of witchcraft lie in the same remote epoch, if not far earlier, and it is a central part of Wiccan belief that time is not linear, stretching out in a long line of dates from past to future, but cyclical, turning through each year and each sequence of seasons like a majestic clock, like the observations maintained at Stonehenge 3,500 years ago, or like a great wheel.

The Wheel of the Year

The Wheel of the Year is a term used by witches for the yearly cycle. It takes us through the seasons of nature and honours her changing faces with festivals that acknowledge the importance of each part of that cycle. In the olden days people literally survived or died according to the weather and the health of their crops and livestock. The Old Religion, as a nature/fertility religion, is still based upon the same festivals that our ancestors celebrated and ritualized in order to do all that they could to safeguard their survival. For example, as the winter begins to lose her grip, we have the festival of Imbolc (pronounced 'Imolk'), the return of the virgin bride, who brings the promise of the rising light of a new spring. At this festival, Wiccans celebrate the fact that winter is fading, spring flowers are emerging and life is once more waking up from its long winter sleep.

Then at the eve of May we celebrate Beltaine, the festival of blessing the seeds, the fields, the stirrings of growth in plants and crops and the warming of the earth. At this festival, more familiarly known to non-pagans as May Day, the maypole, a phallic symbol, has become a familiar sight. Its Wiccan significance lies in the fact that the phallus carries the seeds, germinates life and symbolizes fertility and virility. Without the seed, there would be no life, so at Beltaine Wiccans celebrate fertility, growth, the return of spring and all its vigour. At this festival, rituals centre around uniting masculine and feminine forces and binding them joyously with love and good fortune. It is the traditional time for handfastings (the Wiccan equivalent of a wedding), for blessing livestock and affirming friendships. It is also the time for partings.

At August eve we celebrate Lughnasadh ('Lou-na-sah'), the festival of Lugh, a Celtic Sun god. By this time of year the harvest is nearly ripe and ready for picking. Lughnasadh rituals focus upon appeals to the Sun god to shine upon the fields until the harvest is brought in. During the same season (13 August) we have a day dedicated to the goddess Hecate, when appeals are made to her to keep storms away until the crops are safely home. At Lughnasadh there is thanksgiving for grains and bread. Some traditional pagan practices involved scattering the first loaf made from the new crops onto the fields as an offering to the gods or making a corn dolly from the last sheaf of grain to be cut in the harvest and ritually scattering its ashes onto the fields the following year to symbolically maintain continuity.

On the last evening of October we have Samhain ('Sow-en'), commonly referred to by non-pagans as Halloween. Its spooky connections are rooted in a more reverential pagan past where it was — as it still is — the festival of the ancestors. Samhain is the time of year when honour and respect are given to the ancestors as they are remembered through activities like a Dumb Supper, where two extra places are laid, one for spirit and one for the ancestors. The meal is eaten in total silence, for to speak would be disrespectful to those unable to do so. This is the traditional time to acknowledge the past, to practise all sorts of divination, especially for the year ahead or for a future partner, and to reflect upon the passing year as a new one rises. In the Celtic calendar, Samhain marks New Year's Eve.

These four festivals are known as agricultural festivals and are referred to as Major Sabbats in the Wiccan calendar. In summing up, we could define them as:

Imbolc: The blessing of the fields and wells

Beltaine: The blessing of the seeds

Lughnasadh: Thanksgiving for a safe and fruitful harvest

Samhain: Remembrance of the ancestors, the land and our spirituality

Crossing these on the four quarters of the wheel are the Winter Solstice (around 21 December), the Spring Equinox (around 21 March), the Summer Solstice (around 21 June) and the Autumn Equinox (around 21 September). These solar-based festivals were a later introduction to the Wiccan calendar and are referred to as the Lesser Sabbats.

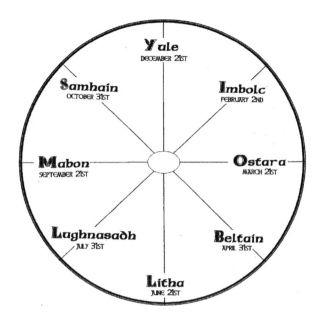

The Wheel of the Year, the cyclical non-Christian calendar favoured by Wiccans and other pagans, reflects the concept that time is not a straight line from past to future but an ever-repeating mystical and magical cycle of seasons.

So we have eight Sabbats on our Wiccan wheel. Between these festivals are the full Moon celebrations, important to Wiccans because of their close connection to the Goddess (personified in Moon, stars and Earth). At these esbats, as they are called, there is the opportunity to honour the Moon at her fullest power, to study and learn, to share and celebrate and, as at the Sabbats, to perform any requested healings. There are 13 Moons within a solar year, and with the combination of the Sabbats and esbats, Wiccans build up very strong bonds with the natural world as well as with natural forces.

Earth, Sun, Moon and stars all play their part in the broader Wiccan healing picture, because we are not separate from the Universe but part of its Creation. By developing a deeper sensitivity to the rhythms and cycles of life, we can also find a deeper connection to our own particular rhythms and to the circles and spirals that make up our world.

Chapter Four
The Elements and Elemental Spirits

The natural world, and in fact our whole Universe, is comprised of the four Elements of Earth, Air, Fire and Water manifested in space (or Ether or Spirit, as it is also called). This chapter explains the healing qualities associated with each Element and includes simple guidelines on Elemental healing rituals that you can perform for yourself or for others. We will also explore ways in which we can link into the natural world and communicate with her Elemental spirits in order to develop our spiritual nature.

The Four Elements

When working magical rituals, it is important to know which Element corresponds with the magic you intend to perform. If you have an inbuilt understanding of each Elemental signature, it becomes far easier to put a ritual or healing event together. An effective place to start is with each Element's physical characteristics:

The **Earth Element** is solid and tangible. It supports us, feeds us and holds us within our physical existence, providing everything that we need in order to survive.

The **Air Element** is moving and changing, bringing gentle breezes as well as storms. It provides the air we breathe and the weathered winds, yet is invisible to the naked eye.

The **Fire Element** is hot and transformative. It always requires combustible materials for its existence. Fire provides warmth and light upon our Earth.

The **Water Element** is cool and moist. It can be calm and deep, or violent and destructive, as can all the Elements.

All four Elements are contained within a fifth Element known as Ether or Spirit.

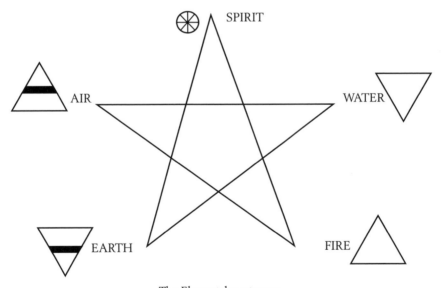

The Elemental pentagram

Elemental Connections

When we build up an understanding of the Elements and how they operate in nature, we also come to understand how they manifest and move through us.

All of the Elements are wild and unpredictable and can be both destructive and creative in nature, very much like the human character – so already we can see similarities between the human being and the natural world.

The magical Elements of Earth, Air, Fire and Water are held to be slightly different from the pure chemical elements of science, because each is believed to exist on the spiritual plane as well as in the physical world. For example, Elemental Fire will embody the spiritual essence of fire and not the physical burning flames of a real fire. The spiritual essence of Fire consists of the energy, transformative qualities and fuel used by the human spirit when aspiring to actions requiring courage and strength. With Earth the spiritual essence is protection and defence and safe discharge of energy; with Air it is constructive thought, mental processes and intellect; and with Water it is the emotions, perceptions and feelings. It is this fact that, according to Wiccan belief, allows the spiritual essence of an Element to connect with the physical realm, linking its spiritual aspects with its material qualities and thereby bringing spirit into matter, or the spiritual into the physical world – a vital ingredient in Wiccan practice and healing.

Let us say, for example, that someone you know is feeling tired and drained and doesn't really know why. She has come to you and asked for help. (Always be aware that any significant changes in health should be monitored by a GP or health professional.) With this in mind, how could you best work with the Elements to bring about healing for your friend?

For me, as I listen to her, I am made aware by some of her comments that people are taking advantage of her good nature, even going so far as using her. Therefore this is where I would start my magical work, because her confusion and exhaustion will automatically disappear once she has found the ability to say 'no'. If we look at Chart 4, we can see that any of the Elements could be used to help her – Earth to support her physical body, Air to help her with more effective communication, Fire to build the courage and vitality to speak her truth and Water to help her develop right relationship to others.

So which one would *you* choose and why? Again, you should move into your own spirit and contemplate which feels most right for her. Let us say that your friend is a Water sign and so you could decide to work with the Water Element

Chart 4: The Basic Elemental Correspondences				
Element	Direction	Season	Sense	Colour
Earth	North	Winter	Touch	Black/White/Olive green/Ochre
Air	East	Spring	Smell	Yellow
Fire	South	Summer	Sight	Red
Water	West	Autumn	Taste	Blue
Ether/Spirit			Hearing	Black

with her. Looking at Chart 6 on Elemental correspondences *(on page 56)*, you will see that if you utilize the Water Element, you could work with Isis, mirrors, the colour blue and perhaps otters. Isis is a healing deity, amongst her other qualities, who can be called upon to assist in building a right relationship to others. You could utilize a mirror to symbolically reflect exploitative energies away from your friend. You could call upon the playful and joyful energies of the otter to show her how to play with life, how to say 'no' without fear of offending anyone. And you could contain all of this within the colour blue to soothe stretched and strained emotions, so that she feels calmer and more at ease.

This is just one way of utilizing the information in the Elemental chart. Let your imagination and wisdom find ways to bind the information together into your own magical ritual. How to put a ritual together is explained in Chapter Thirteen. In this chapter we are exploring what to put with what and how we come to certain conclusions, so that when it comes to understanding the spirit of nature and her magical abilities, you are fully aware of the principles and practices of working in harmony with nature and all of her gifts.

Elemental Spirits

Each Element has what is called an Elemental spirit associated with it. This spirit is the essence of the Element which has been magically 'personified' into:

> Gnomes: Earth
> Sylphs: Air
> Salamanders: Fire
> Undines: Water

You can work with the Elemental spirits when you wish to receive teachings about a chosen Element or when seeking assistance with a healing. This is extremely simple and just requires you to find a place in the natural world where you feel comfortable, such as a woodland clearing or the bank of a lake, and calling for the spirits to hear your appeal. There is no set way to communicate with them, except with respect and honour. Speak from your heart, from your feelings, and be open and honest. Begin by outlining your need and end with your thanks.

When working with Elementals, it is important to remember to give them appropriate gifts as a way of thanks for their assistance, otherwise we are taking without giving. Refer to the sections that follow for gift suggestions. You may also like to leave little organic offerings for them on a more regular basis – just as a gift, without seeking a return.

With all the Elemental spirits, you can work with them on the issues that they govern, utilizing your imaginative and visualization skills. Whether you perceive their presence or not, they will be there.

Sylphs

Sylphs, the Elemental spirits of the Air, are lovers of movement and change. They are associated with the mind, with thought and with creative energy. It is said that each of us has a Sylph assigned to us throughout our lives. Our personal Sylph will be able to help us release addictive patterns of behaviour or unhelpful habits, will help us to express our creativity and will assist at those times when we are fearful of change. Sylphs are most closely related to faeries and angels, and some people may choose to refer to their personal Sylph as their guardian angel. Sylphs are intensely curious by nature and are responsible for helping us to build strong mental capacities and clear thinking. Their Elemental responsibility is for the air that we breathe and for fragrance and scent, creativity and evolution.

To connect with your Sylph, sit quietly outside on a day with a gentle breeze and clear your mind of all thoughts except those of meeting your personal Sylph. Remain quiet and contemplative. Call for a visit from your Sylph and wait patiently. Remember that Elemental spirits are not physical, so you will not necessarily 'see' a Sylph so much as sense it with your perceptions or psychic vision. Have no expectations and see what happens.

A suitable gift for these airy spirits would be burning an incense stick or offering a small bunch of fragrant flowers or perhaps even a single scented rose.

Salamanders

Salamanders are the Elemental spirits of the Fire Element. They are associated with all fire-based phenomena such as volcanoes, flames, heat and light, as well as with the more spiritual aspects of Fire, such as courage. The Fire Element is sacrificial in nature, which means that in order for transformation to take place, something has to be sacrificed. With an open fire, for example, it is wood or coal. In a candle it is the waxen body that burns. In its higher aspect, the Fire of courage normally involves some kind of personal sacrifice such as the willingness to face danger.

When working with Salamanders, approach them with caution and a clear definition of your needs, as they are capable of great enthusiasm and fervent activity. Their Elemental responsibility is for heat and light, spiritual ideals, vitality, energy and transformation from a lower state to a higher one, so you would choose to work with them when seeking these attributes in your own life or calling for them in healing someone else.

When invoking Salamanders, always have a flame burning. Meditate upon the flame and visualize a Salamander rising up in the heat and manifesting before you. Communicate your need very clearly and carefully.

Salamanders draw energy from fire, so a burning candle or carefully controlled bonfire would be a suitable gift for them – the equivalent of providing them with a tasty snack!

Undines

Undines are the Elemental spirits of Water. They will be found wherever there is water, including its more spiritual aspect, the emotions, which means that they live within us, as do all the Elementals.

The Water Element requires boundaries in order to maintain its form. For instance, without banks, a river would not have a shape, because water flows until it reaches resistance or a boundary. Likewise, emotions without boundaries are a weakness, but with boundaries, they are a strength. This is why people with a lot of Water in their character can feel uncomfortable around change, because it brings up a level of insecurity until a new form has been created.

Undines are responsible for our feeling nature and our emotions, also for healing, conception and birth, fertility and imagination, our relationships and dreams. You can call on them when you are working with these aspects in yourself or others, especially when wishing to ease any troubled feelings.

Undines often come to us in our dreams. You can also connect with them at all watercourses, wells and springs, or simply through a bowl of spring water in your home. Leave a shell or crystal offering in the water before sitting quietly and calmly, and meditating upon Undines coming to help you. Again, all that is required is an open heart, honesty and respect. Trust that your heart will say what you need.

Gnomes

Gnomes are the spirits of the Earth Element. They are responsible for all aspects of our natural world such as the trees, herbs, flowers, colours and minerals. Their primary focus is on protecting the Earth with buried treasure, both inner (hidden talents and abilities) and outer (physical finds), although they can also help with money issues, material matters and grounding. Gnomes can reach a great age and can often look like gnarled tree roots. They have a great sense of humour and may well be responsible for moving things, practical jokes and the disappearance of pennies! Having said that, they are extremely wise and can be approached whenever wisdom is being sought.

In my experience Gnomes can be elusive and suspicious of human motives because humans tend not to respect the Earth, which is their domain. To connect with Gnomes, take yourself off to a natural environment and then bury a silver coin as a gift before sitting nearby and asking for the Gnomes' assistance. If you live in an urban environment you can create an earthy haven for them to inhabit by filling a small baking dish with mosses, lichens, stones, leaves, berries and twigs. Then you can sit by this 'Gnome garden' to meditate.

Working with Elemental Spirits

The following chart outlines which Elemental spirit you could choose to work with in your healing rituals. You will see that each one has a personal requirement. What this means is that if you choose to work with a particular Elemental, you should be aware of what you will need to focus on in order to be able to

Chart 5: Nature's Elementals Healing Chart

Elemental	Air: Sylph	Fire: Salamander	Water: Undine	Earth: Gnome
Condition	Eases apathy	Eases depression	Eases rigidity	Eases mental stress
	Eases fear of change	Assists transformation	Releases trapped emotions	Protects against psychic attack
	For inspiration and creativity	For passion	Eases insomnia	For all practical concerns
	For clear thinking	For altruistic ideals	For perception/ clarity	For grounding and manifestation
	For exams and tests	For vitality, strength and bravery	For conception and birth	For material needs and luck
Personal requirement	Mental calm	Composure and definition	Boundaries and trust	Practicality and dedication
Spiritual quality	Clarity	Courage	Compassion	Realism
Gift	Flowers	Flame	Rock crystal/Shell	Shiny coins

correctly hold the Element you are working with. Uncontained Fire, for example, can burn you out, too much Air can lead to mental confusion, and so on. So when calling upon an Elemental spirit, make sure that you have the associated personal requirement in place too.

Elemental Herbs

Herbs also have their place within the table of Elemental correspondences, with each having specific attributes, healing qualities and connections. When working with the Elements with regard to healing, you can refer to the following pages and pick a suitable herbal offering, either to utilize in a charm or spell, or to display, wear or burn, depending upon your preference. As with all correspondences, pick the one that seems most closely to resonate with the condition you are healing.

Internal uses of these herbs have not been specified here, so please do not assume they can be made into herbal concoctions and make certain that the dosage, quality and herb are non-toxic and safe for you to drink. *Please do not work with herbs and oils if you are pregnant, unless under medical supervision, or if you are on medication.*

Herbs of Air

When working with Sylphs, the Air Elementals, you can use any of the following herbs to decorate your altar, to hold or wear upon your person, to burn or sprinkle, or to use as an ingredient in a herbal healing charm.

Anise

Part used: *Seeds*

Anise has associations with the planet Mercury, so is excellent for use in all bronchial and speech complaints, breathing and communication problems. It is a protective herb, expansive by nature, and it assists divination, clairvoyance and psychic development. It is a specific against nightmares.

Lavender

Part used: *Oil or leaves and flowers*

Associated with the elven kingdom, lavender is calming and sleep-inducing, and so an appropriate herb to include in calming charms and anti-stress and peace-of-mind rituals. It has strong associations with mental capacities and can also be used in the relief of tension headaches.

Mugwort

Part used: *Leaves*

Also known as artemisia, mugwort is one of the herbs of Artemis and is associated with mental healing, psychic powers and woodland Elementals. Work with mugwort to improve your second sight and psychic skills, and to increase stamina and wakefulness at those times when you feel fatigued, worn out or in need of a tonic. *Do not touch if pregnant, please.*

Rose

Part used: *Flowers*

Rose is associated with the Air Element primarily because of its beautiful scent. As a flower of love and harmony, it can be used during all rituals involving the healing of relationships or problems associated with the love of self or others, especially where mental thoughts, attitudes or beliefs are clouding reality.

Thyme

Part used: *Leaves*

Because of its links with other planes, thyme can be utilized when emotions are raw or when we must accept someone's physical departure or death and the feelings of loss that this incurs. It can be worn at funerals as a protective and supportive herb and is a helpful pain reliever, both of the emotions and of the physical body.

Vervain

Part used: *Leaves*

Vervain, also known as the enchanter's plant, is a truly magical herb. It protects, enhances, improves and inspires wherever it is present. It aids peaceful sleep, free from anxious dreams, and helps to calm the nerves. It can improve creativity as well, so is an appropriate herb in cases where anxiety should not be allowed to cloud decisions or where clear and inspired thinking is necessary in order to find a practical solution.

Herbs of Fire

When working with Fire Elementals, the following herbs can be used. Choose the one that seems most closely to fit your ritual or magical purpose.

Basil

Part used: *Leaves*

Basil can be used in a cleansing and purifying bath prior to fire-based healing rituals. It is transformative and promotes brightness of disposition, happiness and strength. Use basil when either courage or fortitude is required or a more positive outlook sought. It is a good heart tonic.

Bay

Part used: *Leaves*

Bay is another herb of transformation, as are all of the Fire Element herbs, for Fire is purgative and purifying by nature. Utilize bay leaves for protection during change, to help to overcome obstacles and to provide a shield against negativity.

Copal

Part used: *Resin*

Originating from South America, copal is also known as Mexican frankincense. It is a potent tree resin used in a similar way to frankincense, although it is more closely associated with spell-breaking, exorcisms and powerful protection.

Copal, therefore, is a suitable herb to work with when there is severe mental or physical breakdown, delusions, illusions or fantasies that are causing self-destructive behaviour or threatening the safety of the self or others.

Frankincense
Part used: *Resin*

Used for thousands of years to cleanse, bless and sanctify sacred spaces, frankincense is a well-known herb of grace. Burn it whenever you wish to cleanse or prepare a space for ritual working or to sanctify working tools and equipment. As a solar herb, frankincense is appropriate to offer to the Fire Elementals. In fact, it is a good all-round herb to use for any magical workings associated with solar energies.

Ginger
Part used: *Root*

Ginger is a spice that has spicy connotations and as such can be utilized as an offering to the Fire spirits when sexuality, fertility and conception issues are highlighted. It has aphrodisiac properties and is a general pick-me-up and energy booster, so it can also be used during rituals whose focus is upon energy and the need for it. Ginger cleanses the blood, but like many solar spices it can also burn sensitive areas of skin.

Rose Geranium
Part used: *Leaves or essential oil*

Rose geranium encourages self-assurance and self-belief at times when perhaps other people are holding more negative attitudes about us, to the point where they may be spreading rumours or causing mischief. Work with rose geranium when the healing ritual involves protection from the attitudes or behaviour of others and when confidence is low and a determined resolve required.

Herbs of Water

Herbs associated with the Water Element are often found growing by rivers or streams or in boggy areas, or are sweetly scented night-blooming flowers such as jasmine. They are always cool and soothing by nature. They also hold the signature of Water, which is cleansing and free-flowing. The Water Element can also become stagnant and inert, however, and so these herbs can often treat stagnant conditions in the body, such as catarrh.

Camphor

Part used: *Resin*

Camphor is a specific against bronchial complaints and breathing difficulties and can be inhaled with steam to help clear the symptoms of a cold. It has the ability to dull the senses and so can be worked with when the body is trying to throw off colds or fevers or hot-headed behaviour. It calms everything down and allows rest to occur. Most camphor is synthetically produced today, so try to find a pure source of the actual resin if you can. *Never take camphor internally.*

Jasmine

Part used: *Flowers*

This sweetly scented and most delicate flower is associated with the Moon, who herself governs the Water Element. Because of this, it is an appropriate herb to work with when emotions are involved or when family or home issues are highlighted. Jasmine helps to improve our spiritual outlook and give us a wider perspective on why something is pushing our emotional buttons.

Lily

Part used: *Flowers and leaves as a votive offering in water*

Lily, especially the water lily, because of its watery location, is another Water-based plant. It is specifically for calling in new beginnings, helping us to release what is standing in our way and bringing a new state into our lives. It brightens our disposition so that we can remember our own beauty and live by it.

Lotus

Part used: *Powder, root or joss stick*

The lotus flower has long been associated with spiritual liberation and peace. It can most often be found in the Western world in the form of incense and so can be easily utilized in that way. Burn a lotus joss stick whenever you wish to raise spiritual vibrations, to increase a sense of ease and to bring peace and security to a sick room or environment.

Myrtle

Part used: *Leaves*

Myrtle is a herb that has associations with the love and relationship aspect of the Water Element. Utilize the power of myrtle whenever personal relationships are problematic or causing health problems such as stress or depression. Myrtle will help to open the heart and release the difficulty by encouraging a more positive state of being.

Herbs of Earth

Herbs of the Earth Element have earthy qualities and associations with earthly matters such as security, practicality, material concerns and grounding. The Earth Element is also responsible for psychic protection, as it has the ability to earth excess energy and thus balance any extraneous astral forces that may be causing anxiety or stress.

Cypress

Part used: *Leaves or oil*

An evergreen tree, the cypress is also known as the Tree of Death because of its connections to death, dying and completion. It is excellent in any magical work involving grief, terminal illness or any issue related to death and dying, due to its ability to cleanse and clear away energies that it is no longer appropriate to hold on to. Cypress can also help us to release the past and thus come to a point of completion. A sprig of cypress cast into the grave of a loved one is said to help them on their soul's journey in the afterlife.

Ground Ivy

Part used: *Leaves*

This is a very common and overlooked little plant that is considered a creeping menace in gardens across the world because its growth pattern means that it can take over any hedgerow or wasteland and push out other plant life in its way. It is these very qualities, however, that you can call upon when seeking to clear obstacles around you, or when you are trying to find your roots of identity after disturbing times or changes in personal circumstances. Ground ivy helps us to connect to the animal kingdom, to honesty, protection and regeneration.

High John the Conqueror Root

Part used: *Root*

This magical herb is often employed in charms involving a change of fortune, where dynamic and vibrant energy may be required in order to bring about an improvement in circumstances. It potentizes any spell, giving purpose and strength, and can help at those times when confidence, clarity and direction must be managed and maintained.

Rue

Part used: *Leaves*

Rue leaves were the inspiration behind the suit of clubs in playing cards and in the Middle Ages rue was a favoured strewing herb, being one of the four anti-plague herbs of the time. It is said to improve vision both on the inner and outer planes and so is an excellent choice when you are trying to see your way through material difficulty, obstacles or limitations. Known also as the Herb of Grace, it improves levels of compassion, understanding and wisdom, whilst at the same time offering its protection.

Sage

Part used: *Leaves*

Sage is easily obtainable today as loose leaves or in bundles and provides a quick and easy way to cleanse both yourself and an environment. It has been venerated throughout history as a plant with health-giving qualities. Regular intake of sage is not recommended, however; it is best burned or crushed and included in charms. It offers good protection, cleansing and purification wherever it is burned.

Yarrow

Part used: *Flowers and leaves*

Yarrow is one of the most significant herbs to use against psychic attack, which is why it is placed here amongst herbs of Earth (the Element to use for ground-

Chart 6: Elemental Correspondences					
Element	Deities	Governs	Colour/s	Magical tools	Associations
Earth	Cronos Cerridwen Demeter Gaia	Practical and material matters Personal identity	Olive green Black	Pentacle Salt Gems Rocks Soil	Bull Stag Badger Cow Gnomes Scarabs Cornucopia The World
Air	Thoth Mercury Hermes	Communication Travel Change Study, tests Mental health	Yellow	Bell Athame Incense The Breeze Breath	Birds Butterflies Sylphs Mercury
Fire	Brigit Lugh Sekhmet Apollo	Transformation Vitality and health Energy Willpower	Red Gold	Wand Candle	Dragons Lions Dragonflies The Ram Salamanders The Sun
Water	Isis Aphrodite Hecate	Healing Relationships Emotions	Blue Silver	Chalice Cauldron Mirrors Rain	Fish Frogs Otters Sea mammals Undines The Moon

ing excess psychic energy). It is also a specific against fear. Utilize the powers of yarrow whenever personal fears and/or phobias are affecting your health or well-being. Yarrow helps to change perspectives, whilst at the same time providing protection on all levels. Drinking yarrow tea can increase perception, but as with all herbs taken internally, please ensure that it is appropriate for your disposition.

It should now have become obvious that the four Elements and their magical correspondences play a vital role in all Wiccan activities, because at both a spiritual and physical level, we are Elemental beings ourselves, made up of Earth, Air, Fire, Water and Spirit. To learn about the Elements, therefore, is highly recommended, especially if you are wishing to deepen your connection to Wicca, to life, the Universe and beyond!

Chapter Five
Magical Correspondences

Everything that exists has its own unique signature, and these have been mapped and charted over the centuries to produce what are known as *magical correspondences*, things that blend together well and, through co-operation, enhance or increase the potency of any magical workings. For example, when working with Mercury, we can also consider the Air Element (Mercury as the winged messenger is linked to communication, which is associated with the Air Element) and so, especially when working with the communication aspects of Mercury such as ailments of the respiratory tract, we can also consider including any Air Element correspondences. Lists of correspondences have been compiled over a very long time span and they have been proven to work very effectively.

How Do Correspondences Work?

Correspondences can form a part of all ritualized magical working, acting like agents or foci for the magical practitioner to help to align inner and outer powers, thus ensuring the most appropriate actions and results. They are a way to create specific circuits within the unconscious mind where the root of magic is located. They have been described as signposts, but a better way to think of them is as points on a railway network: change just one set of points and the train goes somewhere else, change many sets and the train travels along a particular route, change them all again and the route is entirely different. In magic, correspondences can include scents, colours, images, symbols, actions, words, deities, tools, Elements, compass points and many other things. Think of correspondences as being the points on a railway journey that can be arranged according to the destination (result) required.

The use of a particular set of correspondences in magic – a certain incense, a particular colour, a magical tool and a ritual gesture – will form links deep within the unconscious mind that focus the psychic powers of the person onto a particular result.

The fact that various items placed together in association can guide the mind to form a specific thought can easily be proved with non-magical correspondences. Consider the following items: lawn, mower, greenhouse, plants, path and flowerbeds. The mind automatically sees a garden, even though the actual word *garden* has not been written. Likewise, spark-plugs, exhaust, wheels, travel, controls, seats and steering-wheel will bring to mind the image of a car. But change just some of the correspondences – spark-plugs, exhaust, wheels, travel, controls, seats, *joystick, wings, undercarriage* – and the image becomes a plane and not a car. This is how correspondences work – they are subtle messages to our psyche that, when combined in different variations, guide the unconscious mind to different destinations.

Correspondences are also known by another name, the Doctrine of Signatures. This relates to the defining and categorizing of organic ingredients such as herbs, minerals and spices, as well as other aspects of Creation such as archetypes, planetary forces, seasonal variations and Elemental influences. These form a range of similarities or complementary powers that work together rather than in opposition to each other.

To give you an example: if we take the scenario that someone has asked for spiritual healing for a sick dog, we could begin by considering the deities that are specifically associated with dogs, such as Diana, Selene, Hecate and Pan (Lord of all animals). Perhaps we might decide to work with Diana, because the dog in question is a hunting breed (Diana is associated with hunting). From this initial decision we can begin to build up associations with Diana, with dogs and with animal healing in order to form our ritual or healing event. Diana is a lunar goddess and the Moon is associated with healing, so we can call upon lunar healing herbs to make our own incense for the dog's healing ritual, too. When we know the actual condition the animal is suffering from, we can add other specifics such as minerals, herbs, colours and fragrances that support the healing process that is required.

Making the connections as to why a plant, deity or colour has its particular associations is part of the Wiccan journey of discovery, as well as that of the other pagan traditions that work with correspondences, such as the druids and occult magicians.

Corresponding with Your Inner Spirit

Although initially it can seem complicated, mastery of correspondences is possible. Perhaps the most appropriate place to start is with your potential gifts and skills. If you feel uplifted by trees, for example, then spend a good amount of time in their company, in meditation and communion with them, and look at their leaf shape, fruit, berries, trunk, growth patterns, place in the environment, flowering time, and so on. Trees do communicate. They 'speak' to the spirit, move the spirit and relate to the spirit of our humanity, as we can do with them, once we open to trusting our intuition and feelings. How do we do that? We do that by first testing and then trusting what comes, and by acting in accordance with our inner promptings. It is this that strengthens the growth of the heart and the spirit – learning to recognize, discriminate, trust and act upon what we feel or sense.

Alternatively, if being with animals strengthens you, spend time in their company exploring the richness of the experience together. All animals communicate through the psychic realms, and so visual rather than verbal images and impressions may rise in the mind. These are perfectly easy to understand, because we all have psychic faculties. In order to communicate with any other life form we choose, it really is a question of expanding our perceptions and embracing our place as part of the natural world, using the language beyond words, the language of the heart – true feelings and perceptions.

Perhaps gardens or wild places are what stirs your spirit, in which case travel through some chosen habitats at different times of the year and see how the seasons change the landscape, what they bring, what they affect and why. Experience each item and each season within your being. Make notes as to which plants and herbs appear or flower at which times, because this will be part of their potent time. Just as the stag grows antlers for its power time in the autumn, so a plant produces flowers, bulbs, blossoms or leaves for the right time of its year.

A very clear example of this can be seen in the properties of spring flowers. Spring is the traditional time of year when we humans spring-clean, go on detox diets and clear out the old. Looking at most of the plants that grow in the spring, we can see that they are primarily for cleansing and detoxing, or for changing our outlook. Springtime itself provides us with all that we need in order to meet a new year.

There is a rather amusing tale about communing with nature: in East Anglia, farmers in the old days would test when to plant their fields by seeing whether they could sit comfortably on the ground without their trousers on. For if the ground was warm enough for them, then it was warm enough to germinate their crops. Perfectly sensible!

There are charts of correspondences throughout this book for you to refer to. These will be a helpful reference when you are working out your own rituals, charms and magical spells.

Timing Healing Events

To everything there is a season, a time of rightness. In line with this, Wiccans work to the best of their ability to time a particular healing event to occur at its most opportune moment, referring to the planets, day of the week and phase of the moon.

Chart 7 *(on page 64)* outlines a way in which you could begin working with correspondences by choosing the most appropriate day of the week for your healing ritual, using the appropriate colour correspondences for candles, cloths and flowers, displaying or burning the suggested herb for that day of the week, and saying your healing wish to the deity listed for that day. The ritual does not have to be performed during daylight hours – you may like to work in the evenings or even through midnight. It is up to you what time you prefer.

To give an example, perhaps someone you know has a health problem because of legal pressures or employment issues. In this case you could work with Thursday and its associations and entreat your chosen deity's assistance with a request to them, such as:

> Mighty Thor, god of storm and thunder, hear this plea I make on behalf of [state the recipient's name]. May you bring strength and justice. May all be made right according to the ancient Law. If it be for the highest good and harming none, may there be positive resolution of [state situation]. So mote it be.

Ultimately, we come to understand that time, space and energy can be related to and aligned in any moment without constraint or direction. This may, however, take a long time to develop. This is why so many tools, techniques and rituals exist, in order to provide the framework for such a development in understanding to occur.

Corresponding Days of the Week

Each day of the week has been named and associated with certain energies, deities and qualities: Monday with the moon, Tuesday with Mercury, Wednesday with Mars, Thursday with Jupiter, Friday with Venus, Saturday with Saturn and Sunday with the sun. If you refer to Chart 7 *(overleaf)* you will see that it is quite easy to put a simple healing ritual together once you know what kind of healing is required. Where there is perhaps more than one option that seems appropriate, choose whichever day of the week that you feel most comfortable with or that you feel most drawn to work with. Alternatively, you may prefer just to work with the two main healing celestial bodies: the Moon (in one of her aspects) or Mercury. For the maintenance of health or build up of stamina, however, it would be the Sun that would be the most appropriate planet.

Chart 7: Healing Correspondences of the Days of the Week

Day of the week	Planet	Healing ability	Colour	Herb/Incense	Deity
Monday	Moon	Emotions Home, family and children Healing generally	White: new Silver: full Light blue: waning	Lotus Sandalwood Cypress	New: Artemis Full: Isis Waning: Hecate
Tuesday	Mercury	Positive change Improved health and vigour	Yellow	Lavender	Brigid Thoth
Wednesday	Mars	Courage Strength	Red	Rose geranium	Tyr
Thursday	Jupiter	Justice Change of fortune Protection	Purple	Honeysuckle	Thor
Friday	Venus	Relationships Fertility Motherhood	Green	Rose	Demeter
Saturday	Saturn	Understanding the limitations of an illness Karma Release Endurance	Indigo blue	Cypress	Cronos
Sunday	Sun	Health, vitality Success Male issues	Orange Gold	Frankincense Marigold	Lugh

Phases of the Moon

As she passes through the heavens, the Moon has what are called different phases. These correspond to the three stages of woman – the maiden, mother and crone being the new, full and waning/dark phases. Each of these phases has a particular energy or quality attached to it. With the new moon (maiden), the Moon is increasing in strength. This is the time in her cycle where increasing rituals or rituals of attraction can be performed, for example rituals to improve health, to strengthen resolve or to draw new circumstances in. This definition remains in place right up until the moon becomes full. An appropriate deity for new moon healing rituals would be Artemis.

The full moon (mother) is the Moon at her most potent. All healing rituals can be performed at this time, whether for the attraction of good health or the removal of symptoms and release from a condition. The most appropriate use of the full moon, though, involves the powers of 'manifestation' – in other words, calling for an actuality such as healing, or the manifestation of whatever is needed in order to bring that about. A healing deity associated with the full moon is Isis.

The waning moon (crone) represents release, letting go and the removal of ailments or conditions, and so this is the time in the moon's cycle when one can ask for the relief of symptoms or the removal of illness, stress or any other condition. In this case you would work on a Monday and refer to Chart 7 for some simple correspondences. Your appeal would not be to Thor, but to Hecate, a goddess of endings.

The dark moon (the one night when there is no moon visible in the sky) is not a time for performing any rituals, due to the fact that the moon is neither waning nor quite new. It is the time in the moon's cycle which is best honoured as a night of rest, reflection and preparation for a new cycle.

Colour

Colour is also part of the correspondences continuum. Each day of the week has a particular colour associated with it, as you have seen from the healing correspondences chart. The vibrations of colour run through all things within the visible light spectrum. Perhaps interesting to note is that when we see a red tomato, for example, the tomato itself is everything *but* the colour red. It absorbs all colours except red, which it reflects. The same is true of all coloured objects. When we see that a leaf is green, to take another example, in fact it is every colour except the colour green. So, in this world of ours, even colour is not what it seems on the surface.

It is common knowledge that colours can also be used to describe emotional states, such as 'green with envy', 'seeing red' and 'feeling blue'. These descriptions point to the qualities of each colour. Seeing red, for example, refers to the fact that red is a hot colour, a dynamic colour, an active colour, a powerful colour. To see red, therefore, means to increase one's energy. Feeling blue reflects the opposite. Blue is cool on the colour scale. Its associations with the Water Element mean that by its nature it is cold and wet, unless it is tempered with some Fire Element, which will warm it up. Making these types of connections can help to build an understanding of correspondences and how they work.

Flashing Colours

Each and every colour has a complementary opposite that is called its 'flashing colour'. This can be demonstrated if you stare at a chosen colour and then turn your gaze to a plain wall, where you will see another colour – the flashing colour of the first one.

Taking the tones of a black-and-white photograph as an example, whatever is black becomes white, and vice versa. Developing a photograph shows this process in the production of a negative – a reversed tonal image of the original. Printing the negative onto a second paper that reverses the situation and restores the final picture to its original tones creates a copy of the original image.

This process can also be seen with colour photographs. Each colour on the original shows up as its flashing colour on the negative until it is passed through the negative onto its final print.

Magicians and occultists throughout time have been aware of these flashing colours and used them accordingly. In magical practice the flashing colour is a wavelength or vibration of the electromagnetic spectrum which, when used in conjunction with its complementary colour, enables it to draw on the Akashic current or spiritual energy flow, partly from the outside Universe (macrocosm) and partly from the magician's own inner self (microcosm), so that a spiritual energy vortex is formed that is as complete as possible.

Flashing colours should ideally be used in equal measure to produce a harmonious and symmetrical result. For example, when using candles in a ritual centred on colour, you could decide to use a blue candle for healing and an orange candle as its flashing complement, thus creating colour balance in your ritual.

You can either refer to the chart below to find each colour's complement, or you can look at an object and then gaze upon a plain wall to see which colour appears. You might also like to try the following exercise on colour awareness.

Chart 8: Table of Flashing Colours	
White	Black
Red	Green
Blue	Orange
Yellow	Violet
Olive	Darker violet
Blue-green	Red-orange
Violet	Citrine (lemon)
Reddish orange	Green-blue
Deep amber	Indigo
Deep lemon yellow	Red-violet
Yellow-green	Crimson

Colour Awareness

Visualize something of uniform colour that you are very familiar with, such as a field of grass. Visualize your field as strongly as possible in its usual colour. When the image is strongly in your mind, replace your colour with its flashing colour. The green field, for example, now becomes a red field. Experience what it feels like to view something as its flashing image.

When you have become familiar with using a flashing colour for a single colour, take something that has more than one colour associated with it, such as a tree, and change the brown trunk into a deep dark blue-purple and the green leaves into their complement, red.

This exercise helps us to loosen our habitual thinking about what reality is and also helps us to look at life through different, less blinkered eyes.

Chart 9: The Basic Occult Elemental Colours

Element	Main colour	Flashing colour
Earth	Black	White
Air	Yellow	Violet
Fire	Red	Emerald green
Water	Blue	Orange

Working with flashing colours builds up a relationship to the Elements, their astral counterparts and complements, and with correct application can provide keys to opening the occult or spiritual levels of each Element. This has been demonstrated in the Hindu tattwa system, which differs slightly from the occult system, but follows the same principles.

The Tattwas

The tattwas are an Oriental expression of the four Elements and the fifth Element of Spirit and have been used in Indian mysticism for many centuries. In this Eastern method, the same four Elements are used as in the Western system of magic, but they have been given their own specific symbolic shapes, known as the tattwas. These basic shapes can be used to help develop psychic and astral awareness.

By creating a set of these shapes and meditating upon them regularly, you can build up your concentration as well as your understanding of the interrelationships between the Elemental forces, because each Element can contain parts of every other to form, for example, Earth of Air or Spirit of Water or Fire of Earth or Water of Air, each one subtly different from the others. A full set would comprise 25 cards. Those interested in the tattwas could benefit greatly from creating their own personal set of cards and meditating with them.

The tattwas

This chapter has outlined the importance of learning about correspondences, from appropriate colours to days of the week, from phases of the moon to corresponding with your inner spirit. These are part of the correspondences picture and will combine well in any ritual, charm or magical design you may wish to use in healing.

Chapter Six
Healing Deities and Archetypes

Throughout the ages, deities and archetypes have been part of our lives, and some of the oldest known deities are associated with health and healing, such as Hygaea, Panacea and Asclepius, or Demeter, Isis and Brigid.

The Family of the Gods

It is an extraordinary thing, perhaps, but in cultures all over the world the same family of gods and goddesses with the same qualities and spheres of application are found, with only the names and costumes being different. For example, Zeus from ancient Greece becomes the Jupiter of the Romans, who in turn is known as Thor in the Norse tradition and the Dagda of the Irish Tuatha de Danaan. The same is true for female deities such as Aphrodite/Venus/Freya. Ultimately, however, in Wiccan belief, there is only one Goddess and God, and all deities are aspects of one of them. So although we have several healing deities available to call upon, we are effectively summoning the aid of an aspect of the one omniscient Goddess or God.

The reason why these different gods and goddesses have been created is simple. If I had a broken bone, for example, I would definitely want to go to a bonesetter. I would not in this instance want to make an appointment with the director of the Medical Association, or with an administrator or a chemist. I would want to be referred to the right person for the job. It is the same with deities. Ultimately, at the top of the tree, are the one Goddess and God. Beneath them are representations of different aspects of their energy, such as healing, birth, protection or success. If I can find the most appropriate personification of the Goddess or God for what I have need of, I am then referring to the right 'department' for that need. These aspects of deity act as a clearer focal point, brought as close as possible to physical reality by identification with an aspect of deity closer to the human realms, rather than the slightly more abstract and nebulous attempts we could make to connect to the Goddess in Her totality, or conversely the God. It all becomes much more personal when a specific aspect of these two archetypes is worked with.

Having said that, I often go into the wilds to talk to my spiritual mother (Goddess) and father (God). I speak directly to them and seek their advice and guidance. They have never let me down, and why should I expect them to, for I am one of the Earth's children and as such will always be heard by them. I love and respect them and serve them as best I can. They return my love for them with spiritual guidance and opportunity by subtly guiding me towards what I need – maybe with the sudden appearance of someone who can help or a particular book falling open at a page which explains something to me, and so on. I am very real with them, and take my 'warts and all' to their embrace, for they already know who I am, so there is no reason to hide any of myself from them. Try it yourself the next time you feel in need of some support. They will come and be with you somehow or other.

One way to begin working with deities is to see which best suits the healing required. If a loved one is in hospital, for example, about to have surgery, then Anubis would be an excellent choice to work with.

In all cases you can refer to the deity's details as given on the next page to see what votive offerings can be made and so make up an altar to your chosen deity whilst your loved one is in need. This serves not only to support them but also provides you with the opportunity to feel you are doing something for them. You will see that if you choose to work in another instance with Apollo, for example, you have all the references you need to set up a ritual to him, perhaps using orange candles, with gold-coloured items on the altar and the option to wear a laurel crown or make an offering of a bunch of laurel leaves you have gathered yourself. You can also see you would perform a ritual to Apollo on a Sunday.

When deciding which deity to work with, remember to check what phase the moon will be in for your planned healing event. If it is waxing, you can work with your chosen deity to draw something new to you or the invalid with regards to health. If it is a waning moon, it is best to work with your chosen deity in order to 'release' a condition, ailment or situation. If the moon is full, then either of these two options will be possible. If the moon is dark, wait for the new moon.

Hospitals and Surgery

Anubis

Colour: Terracotta

Offering: Silver objects

Mineral: Jet/obsidian

Day of the week: Tuesday

Anubis is an ancient Egyptian deity depicted with the head of a jackal or wild dog. He is a protective archetype, able to navigate the soul through vulnerable times. He has associations with hospitals and surgery and so is an appropriate deity to work with under these circumstances.

There is no fixed way to set up rituals to particular deities these days, and so references and correspondences can be interpreted in whatever way you feel appropriate. With Anubis, for example, you may decide to use terracotta clay pots for candle-holders. You may decide to display silver objects or say an invocation to Anubis whilst holding an obsidian crystal. You could use silver candles or cloths, or you could just display a piece of jet or obsidian. It is a good idea to obtain an image of your chosen deity. The internet can prove invaluable for this.

Convalescence and Recovery

Hecate, Demeter and Persephone

Colour: Red

Offering: Poppies, garlic, fish, grains

Mineral: Haematite, lodestone, sapphire

Day of the week: Saturday

Demeter is mother to Persephone, and the two are most often invoked together, though traditionally it was Demeter, Persephone and Hecate who were invoked as a triad, Hecate as the maiden, Persephone as the mother and Demeter as the crone, for Hecate, as a shape-shifter, can be maiden, mother or hag. Indeed, she was once known as a maiden goddess, and it was the edict of invading religions that relegated her to her dark goddess status with capacities for evil. Hecate is not evil, she is powerful, and it was precisely this power that 'Churchianity' needed to subdue by instilling fear of her worship.

This triad of goddesses can provide a multi-layered curative of past, present and future and thus align the soul with its potential for health and well-being. Between them they preside over Earth, Moon and the underworld, or the three aspects of our soul (higher self, physical self and subconscious self).

An altar to this triad could include red candles, poppies (or a small bowl of poppy seeds) or cloves of garlic, and a mineral placed perhaps over a photograph or possession of the individual concerned. Use your imagination and perception when building your altar, remembering that there is no set way it should be done.

Kali

Colour: Red

Offering: Spices and sweet delicacies

Mineral: Heliotrope

Day of the week: Saturday

Kali is a Hindu deity who walks side by side with other powerful female archetypes, and who has her place within the Wiccan tradition, albeit not at the forefront, due to her primary links with Hinduism. However, she is a patroness of witches and as such can be invoked when undertaking Wiccan practices.

Kali is a no-nonsense deity who will not tolerate abuse on any level of women or children. She has immense regenerative powers, being a deity of both life and death, and as such can help during recovery from illness when good strong energy is required.

Shock or Trauma

Ishtar

Colour: The seven colours of the rainbow

Offering: Sacred spring water, clear quartz

Mineral: Lapis lazuli

Day of the week: Friday

Ishtar is a Mesopotamian mother goddess also referred to as Astarte of Phoenicia and Inanna of Babylon. She is associated with the planet Venus, the planet of love and harmony, and is therefore an appropriate deity to call upon when someone you know has experienced a shock or trauma from which they need time to recover, or need healing in order to regain their balance and composure.

Natural and Herbal Medicines

Artemis

> *Colour:* Silver
>
> *Offering:* Juniper, acorns, willow branches, mugwort (do not handle if pregnant)
>
> *Mineral:* Moss agate
>
> *Day of the week:* Mental healing: Wednesday; Medicinal herbs: Saturday

Artemis is an ancient Greek goddess of wild places. Also known as 'the Many Breasted', she has strong nurturing powers and dominion over natural medicines such as herbs. Her specific ability rests with mental healing, and she can be called upon whenever stress-related problems are affecting the mind. Work with Artemis at those times when you or the patient are trying to find the right natural medicine or herb to treat a complaint, asking for her guidance to lead you to an appropriate practitioner or a revelation of the correct treatment. Please do remember, however, not to treat maladies in yourself or others that are beyond the everyday.

The ideal time to work with Artemis is from the sixth day of any new moon up until the moon is full.

Pain Relief

Juno

> *Colour:* Violet
>
> *Offering:* Vervain (Juno's tears), peacock feathers, pomegranates
>
> *Mineral:* Malachite
>
> *Day of the week:* Thursday

Juno has been a goddess of women of all ages throughout time. She is sister and wife to the god Jupiter and is a goddess of the Earth. She has strong associations with pain relief, so is an appropriate deity to choose where health issues are causing pain. I have worked with Juno on numerous occasions and found her to be an excellent choice in the relief of painful conditions.

Harmonizing Forces

Baldur

Colour: Gold

Offering: Frankincense, mistletoe (poisonous berries)

Mineral: Amber

Day of the week: Sunday

Baldur, known as the most beautiful of gods, is the son of the great Norse god Odin. He was thrust into the underworld on a spear of mistletoe, and although he died, he is to be resurrected at Ragnarok, the Nordic name for the end of the world, when he will bring beauty back to this Earth once more. His major attributes in relation to healing are the powers of harmony and reconciliation. Although it was mistletoe that killed Baldur, mistletoe is also the source of his resurrection, hence its relevance as an offering to him.

What is it that we must sacrifice within ourselves in order for harmony and reconciliation to once more prevail in our world? By offering mistletoe to Baldur, we can find what it is that is 'killing' harmony in our lives and be shown what is inside us festering in the dark and waiting for liberation.

For Men and Masculine Health Issues

Apollo

Colour: Gold

Offering: Laurel leaves, peonies

Mineral: Gold

Day of the week: Sunday

Apollo is an ancient Greek solar archetype who is brother to Artemis. He is associated with medicine and with miraculous healings. As a solar deity he is very appropriate for all masculine-based health issues, or when wishing to invoke courage and strength as well as fortitude. Work with Apollo when strength is required for recovery, or when asking for a positive outcome from illness for both men and women.

For Women, Children and All Feminine Issues

Isis

> *Colour:* Indigo
> *Offering:* Lotus, rose, the ankh, figs
> *Mineral:* Turquoise, bloodstone, carnelian
> *Day of the week:* Monday

Isis is an Egyptian deity, wife of Osiris and mother to Horus. She is a mother goddess, and as such understands all the problems one can encounter in relationships. She has also suffered the murder of her husband, so has a profound understanding of grief.

Isis is often depicted with outstretched wings, and in fact the throne upon which ancient Egyptian pharaohs sat had these wings of her protection carved into its design. As a mistress of magic and enchantment, she is also a fitting goddess to work with when weaving magical charms or rituals.

Diagnosis, Learning and Understanding

Thoth

> *Colour:* Yellow
> *Offering:* Figs, reeds
> *Mineral:* Amethyst
> *Day of the week:* Monday

Thoth is an ancient Egyptian deity of wisdom, medicine and magic. As scribe to the gods, one of his gifts is the ability to speak the words of Creation. He is a lunar deity and in the magical traditions he has a palace on the dark side of the moon, a place of wisdom and teaching for the soul.

Thoth is an excellent deity to work with when wisdom or understanding are sought as to why an illness is present in our lives, and what its teachings might be, as well as for all issues requiring some level of understanding, integration or acceptance.

Making a Fresh Start, Post-Recovery

Brigid

> *Colour:* White
>
> *Offering:* Rowan, snowdrops, flame
>
> *Mineral:* Shells
>
> *Day of the week:* Tuesday

A Celtic triple goddess, Brigid was so important to the ancient people that she was also absorbed into the Christian religion and sanctified as Saint Bridget. Her priestesses were always 19 in number to represent the 19-year cycle of the Celtic calendar. She is a goddess of hearth, healing and poetry, and her most sacred festival is Imbolc on 2 February. She represents the virgin returning to the Earth with the sacred flame that symbolizes the rising light of spring. As a fire goddess, she has transformative powers that can be called upon whenever there is a need to start again, and she can be called upon to help with conception, birth and all female-related issues.

Death and Dying

Hera

> *Colour:* Red
>
> *Offering:* Marjoram, apple, white lily
>
> *Mineral:* Gypsum
>
> *Day of the week:* Monday

Hera is an ancient Greek deity associated with death, dying and purification. She provides the stability needed when we must face the impending or actual loss of a loved one, as well as guiding and protecting souls in the afterlife.

Hera is an appropriate deity to work with during any dying process, such as major life-changing events that mean letting go of certain lifestyle patterns, the ending of relationships, and death itself. Call upon Hera when travelling through any grieving process and she will protect you.

Nut

Colour: Midnight blue

Offering: Milk, star icons

Mineral: Lapis lazuli, silver

Day of the week: Monday

Nut, an ancient Egyptian sky goddess with dominion over the heavens and the stars, receives the souls of the dead and acts as their protector as they find their way through the astral planes. In cases where someone you love is dying or dead, you may perhaps like to call upon Nut to offer her protection and guidance to them.

A Healing Appeal to a Deity

Once you have chosen the deity you wish to work with, you can set up an altar with their iconography, offerings, minerals and coloured candles and perform a ritual appeal to them on the recommended day of the week.

I have already stated that it is not the ritual itself but the alignment of intent and the level of focus and concentration that are the most important factors. Therefore, as long as you are holding these with respect and integrity, whatever you say or do will be acknowledged favourably. Try to 'feel' the meaning and emotion behind your words.

To give you a working guideline, you could perhaps consider a healing appeal as follows (details on how to prepare for a ritual and how to open and close a sacred Circle are described in the following chapter).

Prepare the room and altar.

When you are ready, open your Circle, light your votive candle and say:

Here do I offer light and love to [state deity's name]. May you find favour with this appeal to your compassion and hear the words I speak. Across the winds of time I come, to seek [state deity's name], Great God/dess of [state their healing ability here]. I beseech thee if it be for the highest good and harming none, may thy grace and healing be bestowed upon [state the patient's name here]. May all be made right according to destiny and divine will. So mote it be!

After sitting in quiet communion with the deity of your choice for about 10 minutes, give your thanks, bid them farewell, close your Circle and snuff out your candles.

Shrines

My youngest brother died whilst I was writing this book, and because he left so unexpectedly, his departure shocked not only the family but also many of his young friends. A few days before his funeral, many of these friends came to the house with no specific place to put their grief and shock. We made a shrine by gathering things like a photograph of my brother, candles, flowers and memories, and all of us could then go to the shrine and send him love, talk to him and shed a few tears there, too. Once the shrine was in place, the charged atmosphere of the whole house calmed. The shrine was beautiful, and many of the items placed so lovingly there were put into my brother's coffin, giving a sense of connected-ness to his memory and to his place in our hearts.

I offer the building of a shrine to you, should you lose a loved one, because it can provide a focus for the feelings and be a hallowed place to share your love with the soul just departed.

We have now met the family of the gods, learned how to make appeals to them and how to make decisions about working with different deities for different types of healing, from making a fresh start to death and dying. In the next chapter we will look at how to cast a Wiccan healing Circle.

Chapter Seven
The Circle of Healing

The objective of casting a Circle for healing, or any other magical activity, is to provide a framework or container for the energy that you will be raising. This chapter includes details on how to cast a healing Circle either as a solitary practitioner or with a group.

There are two variations on a healing ritual: a simple one and one that casts a full Wiccan circle. The first ritual can be undertaken alone or with others present and is quick and easy to perform. It accommodates the solitary practitioner and those who are just starting out on their healing path and perhaps do not feel particularly confident. Although simple, it is a powerful piece of magic and can be performed at any time when healing is called for.

The second ritual is not really for the solitary practitioner. It can only be performed when there is a partner to work with you or a group of people wanting to contribute to the healing event.

Both rituals, however, can be adapted once you feel you understand the principles behind their structure.

Self-Preparation

Self-preparation is an important part of any ritual or magical activity. It helps to focus the mind upon the task ahead.

Self-preparation always involves bathing and cleansing. This is because it is a magical belief that a clean space prevents certain negative energies attaching themselves to any form of dirt. Water alone is perfectly adequate for this, although some practitioners may add a teaspoon of rock salt to a bath, which acts as a sanitizer. If you wish, you can elaborate upon your bathing ritual by adding cleansing herbs or purifying essential oils to your water.

Once cleansed by the water, you can, if you like, anoint your body with a suitable essential oil mixture or with rosewater, which is obtainable from pharmacies. Some ideas for cleansing and anointing mixes are given below.

Caution

Essential oils are highly concentrated. Do not use them undiluted on the skin. Please test a small area of skin with any essential oils and herbs in the recipes that you decide to use to ensure you have no adverse reaction to them, and do not use herbs or oils if you are pregnant.

A Cleansing Bath Mix

> 7" (17.5 cm) square of cotton muslin
> a handful of medium oatmeal
> a tsp of rock salt
> 3 drops of rose geranium essential oil
> 2 drops of lavender essential oil
> 1 drop of cypress essential oil
> cotton thread

Place all of your dried ingredients into the centre of the muslin. Add your drops of oil and blend the mix together with your fingers. Gather the four corners of the cloth together, tie them with thread and place the muslin bag beneath the flowing hot tap of the bath, or hang it from the showerhead so that the water runs through it.

Body Anointing Oil

Any vegetable oil can be used for making up anointing oils, as well as sweet almond, grapeseed and wheatgerm oils, although sesame oil is the least greasy of them all and so the least likely to stain furniture or materials.

> 7 fl. oz (200 ml) of sesame carrier oil
>
> 3 drops of pine essential oil
>
> 2 drops of palmarosa essential oil
>
> I drop of patchouli essential oil

Add your oils in the above order to the carrier oil. Mix, cover and leave to stand. Allow the oils to blend together for a few hours before anointing yourself or others with the mixture.

Area Preparation

Due to seasonal variations, many Wiccan rituals are performed indoors, although the same principles apply in preparing any area where magical working is to take place, whether indoors or out. Some might say that area preparation is unnecessary because the Circle acts as a protector, but Wiccans are aware that energy is as real and potent as matter, and so they attach importance to right and proper preparation at every level, both spiritual and physical.

Magic deals with psychic energies released from the depths of the subconscious mind in a deliberate pattern. If other kinds of psychic energy have recently been stirred up in the same general area, it can interfere with the magical results, perhaps even cancelling them out. These other kinds of psychic energy need not necessarily be connected to magic: an argument, for example, can produce waves of negative psychic energy. Emotions and stress can also do it, as can mental illness. These negative vibrations can interfere with magical work in a very similar way to a motor interfering with a TV set.

The answer is to cleanse the area in which you are to work of any potentially negative psychic vibrations that may interfere with your magic. Magicians have done this as an integral part of magical practice for a great many centuries, and because witches also make use of magic, they, too, frequently adopt this practice. In magic, such a cleansing is called a *banishing*, and there are a number of banishing rituals used by a variety of schools of magic. The most widely known and used of all is the Lesser Banishing Ritual of the Pentagram.

The Lesser Banishing Ritual of the Pentagram

The Lesser Banishing Ritual of the Pentagram can be traced back through many respected occult orders. It is used by high magicians in their magical rituals, and although it would not generally be considered part of traditional Wiccan practice, the ritual itself is highly effective. However, here is a variation of the banishing ritual that has been adapted to fit with Wiccan archetypes and ideals, focusing upon the Goddess rather than the Judaeo-Christian male godform imagery used by ritual magicians and occultists. Wiccans believe that the Goddess is the Supreme Creator of the Universe, and therefore a banishing ritual in which Her names or titles are invoked will be more powerful than any other kind.

The Goddess has had many different names in different lands and times, including (as a Wiccan chant states) Isis, Astarte, Diana, Hecate, Demeter, Kali and Innana. She is also often called Gaia, the Greek name for the Earth as Mother. However, the Goddess is also identified with the Moon as well as the Earth, the three stages of the lunar cycle (new, full and waning) being associated, as we have seen, with the three stages of womanhood: maiden, mother and crone. The names and images used in the following ritual have been drawn from these ancient traditions. It has been created around the Triple Goddess and her three representations of maiden, mother and crone, specifically as the three Fates or Sisters of Wyrd, who as creator, preserver and slayer are believed to weave the destinies of both gods and men. The three Fates are sometimes multiplied into nine – the nine Muses, or the nine Morgans of Celtic myth and legend, for example.

Ritual Gestures

The idea behind a ritual gesture is to set up resonances within the subconscious mind. A right-handed person uses their right hand for this. Likewise a left-handed person uses their left hand. However, the starting-point of any diagram remains unaffected.

The Banishing Ritual

Face the North and visualize a beam of silvery-white light shining down upon you from the stars, a light from the highest source you can imagine. Touch your forehead with both hands and say: 'She who has always been...'

Touch your heart in the same way and continue: 'Is and always shall be...'

Touch your abdomen with both hands, continuing: 'Blessed Mother of Earth...'

Spread your arms, palms facing towards the sky at your hips either side of you, continuing with: 'Queen of Moon and stars and Mistress of magic and mystery...'

Raise your arms towards the skies: 'Now call upon the Goddess to stand strong at the mighty gateways to...'

Lower your left arm (if you are right-handed) to your side and point the index finger of your right hand in front of you.

Still facing North, draw in the air the symbol of the Triple Goddess as in the illustration overleaf. This should be drawn starting at the arrow on the diagram in one continuous motion without pause until the same left-hand point of the symbol is reached again. The size should be about as wide as your arm will stretch.

'Touch' the centre point of the symbol with your index and middle fingers held together, and as you do so, say in a commanding voice: 'Earth!'

The symbol of the triple Goddess – maid, mother and crone

Now turn to face East. Drawing the identical symbol, 'touch' its centre with the name 'Air!'

Turn to face South, repeat the same symbol, 'touching' it with: 'Fire!'

Turning to face West, the same symbol is drawn for the fourth time and is 'touched' with: 'And Water!'

Lower your arm. Continue to walk clockwise until you are facing North again. Raise your left index and middle fingers again and point northwards, saying the words: 'Before me Morgana ...'

Lift your arm over your shoulder to point behind you without changing position and say: 'Behind me Diana ...'

Point your right hand to the right and say: 'To my right side Artemis ...'

Bring your hand back in front of your body and point and in the same manner, say: 'To my left side Erynis ...'

The invocation is concluded by saying: 'Around me stands the Goddess. Above me and within me her loving presence shines.'

Once you have cleansed your working area, you can then move on to setting up an altar for either the simple or full healing ritual outlined in the following pages.

A Simple Wiccan Healing Ritual

This ritual can be performed at any time of day or night. However, a Monday evening during a waning moon would be considered the most appropriate timing, as the waning moon is associated with release. As already mentioned, when we are working to *remove* a poor-health condition, it is the waning moon's powers that we work with. When working with drawing something to us, such as health or vitality, it is the waxing (increasing) to full moon that is worked with.

Most people have a certain level of trepidation at the thought of casting a ritual Circle and are fearful of making a mistake or of causing some kind of occult offence. It is very important to state that there is no such thing as 'wrong' when it comes to the ideal of working for the highest good in activities like spiritual healing. In Wicca, it is the intention of the heart that is important, not whether every word and action is perfect. Wicca is a faith that appreciates feelings rather than mental precision and flawless memory. If you feel you have made a mistake, either correct it confidently or proceed with the ritual as if nothing had happened. It is best not to worry about any mistakes you make, as this can block the free flow of energy being raised or stop it altogether.

Preparation

Preparation for this ritual is deliberately shorter than for a Wiccan coven healing ritual.

Ingredients

- cleansing herbs to burn prior to commencement, such as sage or frankincense
- a heatproof container for the burning herbs
- 4 individual candles of yellow, red, blue and green
- a staff or athame or wand
- a bowl
- a smaller bowl
- spring water
- 3 light blue floating candles or nightlights
- 1 bay leaf per individual to be healed
- a pen containing silver ink
- matches
- salt

Cleanse the area you intend to work in by wafting your burning herbs around the room/habitat, making sure you get into all the corners, windows and openings (like fireplaces).

Place an altar at the central point of the Circle you intend to cast.

Fill your larger bowl with spring water, put the three unlit floating candles in it and place it upon the altar. Put your bay leaf and silver pen nearby, along with your matches.

Place some salt into your smaller bowl and add a little spring water.

Place your four candles in a circle around you, positioned in their appropriate quarters: Air, East, yellow; Fire, South, red; Water, West, blue; and Earth, North, green. The Circle should be large enough to accommodate you and your altar comfortably.

A Simple Wiccan Healing Ritual

Beginning in the East and moving in a clockwise direction, light your four Circle candles one by one.

Once they are all lit and you are back at the East, take up your staff (or other item) (with your right hand if right-handed) and, facing towards the East, standing before the candle there, hold the staff up to the heavens and say: *'Here do I summon Air in at the East to bring the breath of life to this sacred Circle.'*

Bring your staff down towards the candle and, holding the staff about 1 inch (2.5-cm) above the ground, begin to define the Circle with it until you reach the South candle. Hold your staff up and, pointing towards the direction you are facing, say: *'Here do I summon fire in at the South to bring brightness and warmth to this sacred Circle.'*

Lower the staff towards the candle on the ground again and then continue to define the Circle with your staff until you reach the West candle. Hold up your staff as before and say: *'Here do I summon Water in at the West to bring love and clarity to this sacred Circle.'* Complete the Circle back to the East.

Lower your staff towards the candle and then continue to define your Circle with your staff until you face the North. Hold up your staff once more and say: *'Here do I summon Earth in at the North to bring strength and stability to this sacred Circle.'*

Hold your arms out with your staff in one hand and say aloud: *'Guardians of the four quarters, may you stand in protection over this Circle which is now duly cast. In the name of the Goddess and the Great Horned God, so mote it be!'*

You can now make a circuit of the Circle, sprinkling consecrated water from the saltwater bowl to 'seal' the Circle.

Your Circle is now cast and the four quarter-candles are lit around you.

Go to your altar and light the three nightlights one by one, saying the following as you do so:

Nightlight one: *'For the maiden.'*

Nightlight two: *'For the blessed mother.'*

Nightlight three: *'For the crone.'*

Complete your invocation by saying: *'Goddess of Earth, Moon and Stars, I call your gracious presence to this healing Circle.'*

Pick up your pen that contains silver ink and gently write the name of the person or animal you are seeking healing for on the bay leaf and then drop it onto the surface of the water. (You can include other people/animals too, as long as you use one bay leaf per individual, dropping each leaf singly into the healing bowl.)

Stand or sit before your altar with your hands palm outwards towards the healing bowl. Remain silently focused upon the individual for up to 15 minutes. When this time has elapsed, place your hands palms together upon your heart and say:

'Great Goddess and mother of all that is, I give you my thanks for hearing this plea and if it be for the highest good of [the name of your individual/s] by your grace and goodness, may they receive your healing.'

Wait a few more moments and then rise and blow out your healing candles, saying as you do so: *'To maiden, mother and crone I give my thanks. This healing ritual is now complete. I bid you hail and farewell. Hail and farewell.'*

You now close the Circle. It is important in all magical working to complete what we start – this is why a Circle once opened must always be closed upon the completion of any ritual or magical working, in order to keep command within our Circle and to notify any energies present that the ritual is finished.

Move to the North and, holding your right hand palm outwards with your fingers upright towards the direction, say: *'Hail and farewell, Guardians of the North. I say thank you for your presence. This ritual is now done. I bid you hail and farewell.'* Snuff out the candle. *'Hail and farewell.'*

Turn West, South and finally East, repeating the above closure at each one.

Dispose of any organic ingredients you have used during this ritual with care and respect.

A Wiccan Coven Ritual

This second ritual is the kind of ritual that would be performed by a Wiccan coven, which would include coven members, as well as the High Priestess and the High Priest. It can be performed with a minimum of two people – a man and a woman – but would be a little complicated to undertake on your own. The focus in this ritual is upon honouring and invoking the Sky Father and Earth Mother to hear the words of their assembled children and to help them to bring about healing where it is right for them to do so.

Once you have decided to perform a group healing ritual within a healing Circle, there is a certain amount of preparation to be done before the Circle is cast. This includes cleansing the area where you will be working, performing your own ritual cleansing and blessing and laying out your altar tools. All of this information is shared with you in the book wherever it is relevant.

Preparing for the Full Ritual

First of all, you will need to obtain the ingredients for your ritual, which will include altar items such as candles, incense, salt and spring water, and your four Wiccan Elemental tools. This does not have to cost a lot of money. You can use a kitchen knife for an athame, a twig or branch for a wand, a stemmed wine glass for a chalice and a flat circular breadboard for a pentacle.

The preparation of your equipment is normally done in the one or two days leading up to your chosen event. You will also need to consider what type of healing ritual you are going to perform before you begin. By this I mean the kind of healing event you are going to undertake, such as making a healing charm or perhaps casting a spell (if you are intending to create a *doppelgänger* or a cone of power, you will not need any extra equipment). Gather the necessary things and place them around or beneath the altar.

A full healing ritual can be performed at any time, although most Wiccan rituals are performed after sunset and tend to commence just prior to what is known as the 'witching hour' of midnight to one o'clock. Busy schedules might preclude this, and the important thing to remember is that it is better to carry out a healing ritual as best you can than to allow something to put you off doing it at all.

The Wiccan Coven Healing Ritual

All covens will have their own way of doing things, and many different varieties of Circle opening will be used, so there is no standard ceremony. This one is fairly representative, however, and if you are in a group who wishes to use it, it can be adapted freely to suit your own needs. The 'Maiden' mentioned here is a coven member holding the honorary position of handmaiden to the High Priestess. The invocation beginning 'Eko, Eko, Azarak' is extremely ancient. Nobody knows exactly what it means, or even what language it is in. There is evidence that it has been used in witchcraft for centuries and has therefore been hallowed by time and long usage.

When all has been made ready, the High Priest lights the candles and the incense and the High Priestess signals to have the Circle opened by sounding the bell three times.

At this signal, the High Priest takes a position at the altar and calls:

Eko, Eko, Azarak,

Eko, Eko, Zomelak,

Eko, Eko, Cernunnos,

Eko, Eko, Aradia!

The High Priestess and High Priest kneel in front of the altar, with him to her right. The High Priestess raises the chalice of water and puts it on the pentacle. Lowering the point of her athame into it, she then says:

I hereby cast out
all impurities and uncleanliness from this water.
Be now cleansed and blessed
in the names of the Goddess and Horned God.

She then lays down her athame and raises the chalice of water in both hands. The High Priest places the cup of salt on the pentacle, lowers the point of his athame into it and says:

Blessings be upon this salt
relinquished of all malignity and harm.
Let it be exalted to its highest good
in the names of the Goddess and Horned God.

Now the High Priestess stands facing North. Some covens suggest that she adopts the 'Osiris Slain' position, which is with arms stretched out wide to her sides at shoulder height. (Two Osiris positions remain in witchcraft as part of the Ancient Egyptian influence in its deep past. Both of these positions can actually be seen in temple paintings and statues of pharaohs and priests.) In this ritual the High Priestess opens hers arms in a gentle upward curve with the palms pointing skywards like an upturned crescent moon.

The High Priest invokes the Goddess into her, saying:

Queen of Moon and Stars, descend.
Mother of Earth and Stone, arise.
Spirit of the Goddess, abide herein.

The Maiden/group member/or other party then says:

Lady, we honour you.

The High Priestess says:

Gracious Goddess, we honour you.

The High Priestess makes a 'finger blade' by pointing the first and middle fingers forwards with the thumb resting on the fourth and little fingers and defines the outline of the Circle deosil (clockwise), saying as she does so:

Here do I build our temple for the Mighty Ones,
a sacred Circle forged of love and honour
for you, our gracious Lady, and you, our mighty Lord.
Be with us now, your children here assembled.
So mote it be.

The High Priest takes up the cup of salted water and sprinkles the Circle behind her.

The High Priestess then takes up her athame from the altar (or uses her fingers as before) and goes to the North, drawing in the air the Invoking Pentagram of Earth. Then she goes to the East and draws the invoking pentagram, then the South and then the West, returning to the North.

As the High Priestess does this, the High Priest, invokes the Guardians by calling out as the appropriate pentagram is drawn:

The Invoking Pentagram – starting at the top, the figure is
drawn in the air until the starting-point is reached again

I call the Guardians of the North,
summoned to watch over the Gateway to Earth.

I call the Guardians of the East,
summoned to watch over the Gateway to Air.

I call the Guardians of the South,
summoned to watch over the Gateway to Fire.

I call the Guardians of the West,
summoned to watch over the Gateway to Water.

When this has been done, the High Priestess replaces her athame on the altar and the High Priest stands up.

She then goes to the North-East of the Circle, makes a cutting motion with her finger blade and says:

Open may this doorway be.

They both now welcome any other members of the coven into the Circle one by one in the traditional manner, with a hug and a kiss and saying 'Blessed be!' to each. Entry is by stepping over the area of the Circle that has been 'cut'. Coven members enter the Circle and move clockwise to their places.

When all have been admitted, the High Priest brings over the salted water and sprinkles the line of the imaginary doorway, saying, 'Sealed may this doorway be.' He then returns to the altar.

When this has been done, the High Priestess and High Priest stand and invoke the Goddess and the God.

The High Priestess raises her left hand and points the index and little fingers outwards, drawing the middle and third finger into the palm of the hand. She calls out:

O Goddess, Mother of all that is,
be with us this night (day).
Grace us with thy loving presence.
So mote it be.

The High Priest makes the same gesture as the High Priestess, using his right hand.

He calls out:

O Great Horned God,
Lord of Nature and Protector of the Sacred Way,
be with us this night (day).
Shield us with thy awesome presence.
So mote it be.

Now the Charge can be read. This is a prose poem that states the principles, values, beliefs or philosophy of Wicca in some way. There are various 'charges' used in Wicca, such as the traditional 'Charge of the Goddess' by Doreen Valiente, which you can find in Chapter Nine. There is also the 'Charge of the God', and in line with this tradition, I have included below a 'Charge of the Great Horned God' for this healing ritual.

Charge of the Great Horned God

I am the summer winds that rustle through your spirit
and stir the whispering leaves of your soul.
I am the wild and darksome stag
that raises horn and hoof within your wildest places.
I am the oaken-mossed caress that softens you
with velvet fronds of green.
I am the guardian at the gates to the underworld –
open your heart to me.

I am the great and Horned One
with whom your earth and stream do dance their days
I am the wise one, carved with timeless gems of radiance inspired.

I am the one that strikes the lightening tree
And paints the sky with storm and sun.
I am the woodland warrior cloaked in frankincense –
open your heart to me.

I am the ripening light that warms your fruits and seeds
Lush colours sweetened deep upon the bough.
I quench my thirst on Urth's morning dew
I dance upon my Lady's mantle green
whose snaking paths I find and tread so free.
I am the dragon's treasure in your breast –
open your heart to me.

The Circle has now been cast and is ready for the healing element of the ritual to begin. You can call upon a healing deity or helper, or you can build a cone of power, make an amulet or healing charm, summon an Elemental healing spirit or simply focus your minds upon the individual or situation, with a central focus upon your altar that depicts the healing required.

After the appropriate amount of time has elapsed, end your healing focus, thank the archetype/s if you summoned any and bid them farewell.

Closing the Circle

Closing the Circle is always the last thing to be done before coming back to the everyday world.

The High Priestess and High Priest return to the altar, if they are not already there.

The High Priestess sounds the bell three times.

At this signal, the High Priest goes in turn widdershins (anticlockwise, the opposite direction to deosil) to the North, West, South and East and at each point draws a banishing Earth pentagram in the air with his athame.

The Banishing Pentagram – beginning at the bottom left, the figure is drawn in one continuous movement until the starting-point is reached again

As he draws each one, he calls:

Guardians of the North (West/South/East),
this ritual is now complete.
With thanks we bid you
hail and farewell.

After the final pentagram has been completed in the East, the High Priest rings the bell three more times and then states:

This sacred Circle is now closed.

All present say: 'Blessed be.'

This completes the ritual.

These two rituals can be arranged to fit any healing event, because each of them has a middle part between opening the Circle and closing the Circle where your own magic can be performed.

Chapter Eight
The Ways of the Wiccan Healer

Because Wiccans have no centralized doctrine, no written scripture and as a general rule no structured organization beyond an immediate circle of acquaintances, they remain free to define themselves, within the bounds of harming none, entirely as they wish. This can mean that two witch's viewpoints can be very different. If this occurs, the witches simply agree to disagree and respect each other's individual opinions and beliefs, because to be a witch means to live with tolerance. Therefore, in general terms a witch could be defined as someone who loves the Earth, lives with sensitivity and courage, touches people with honesty, compassion and understanding where invited to and relates honourably to life and all of its creations. Wiccan healers will always work to heal themselves first, before moving into helping others, because it is only when we have freed ourselves of our own limitations that we can hope to help others to do the same. This chapter takes us through some exercises and ideas that can help us to orient our spirit towards understanding the ways of a Wiccan healer and to absorb its principles into our own lives.

Wicca – a Religion of Freedom

Wicca represents a way of life. This means that a walk in the woods easily becomes communing with nature, looking up at the skies becomes cloud-gazing, buttoning up against a strong wind becomes listening to the voices of the Sylphs riding upon the air and a look from an animal or the sounds of birdsong become the possibility of a message. Wiccans perceive a more universal language – the language of the heart – which speaks beyond words and lives within silence. It is a language never heard by the cynic or the disbeliever.

Because of this, Wiccans see the world through different eyes. They do not see themselves as superior to or separate from the natural world, but are intimately aware of their relationship to it. So it would be true to say that the Wiccan healer is a natural (nature-all!) healer, who by their close relationship to the natural world can call upon and interpret the powers of nature when required. Anyone with sincerity in their hearts can open themselves to this – no qualifications are needed to get you there, except an open heart and the desire to know yourself and the nature of Creation.

The Threefold Nature of Wiccan Healing

Witches have always used magic as part of their healing. From a theological point of view, Wicca recognizes that the Earth is our mother, and that she holds great magic. The ability to make use of her magic is one of the gifts the Earth Goddess gives to those who sincerely venerate her. Consequently, working magic should be understood as a sacred act and never used for any evil or wicked purpose.

An extremely important aspect of Wiccan healing is its threefold nature: psycho/spiritual, emotional and physical. Wiccans believe in reincarnation and in the Law of Karma. We believe that we return many times to the earthly plane until we have experienced everything that is necessary for our Higher Self to evolve into a perfected being.

What this means with regards to the ethics of healing is that someone who is suffering in this life may actually need to be experiencing it. In these instances, it would be morally wrong to interfere with their karma by denying them the experience, even though the person concerned may be unaware of these needs dictated by their Higher Self. So we should never assume that anyone who is ill automatically benefits from recovery through pro-active healing. We should take care that we do not commit the error of helping someone whose Higher Self will subsequently be delayed in achieving a more perfected state because we assumed we should intervene in some way.

It is not easy to make this kind of assessment, because we cannot normally know whether we are interfering with a person's destiny or what they are destined to experience for the improvement of their future lives and spiritual progress. All that we can do is to ensure that we always act out of the very best of motives – to ease pain, to help infirmity or accident, to dispel anxiety and fear, and to ask the greater powers to restore a person to their normal state of health. We can only act according to what is presented to us, motivated by compassion, and leave the question of any personal suffering to a higher judgement than our mortal view allows.

Human Nature

It is human nature – our personality, our beliefs, our faith – that colours us as individuals. It is also human nature that can cause us most of our problems and difficulties, because when our barriers are challenged in any way we tend to react against this in order to remain comfortable and safe within what we know. Some people may say: 'This is me. This is who I am and so I *can't* do anything about it.' This is actually far from the truth. These people don't *want* to do anything about it.

Human nature is more often than not a conglomeration of habits, addictions, opinions, beliefs, prejudices and social conditionings that we cobble together in order to try and make sense of life and fit its demands. But it is not fixed. Just because someone has always had two sugars in their tea doesn't mean this has to continue. And just because someone has always responded to anger with anger does not mean that there is no other way.

Throughout time, human nature, especially when in a position of authority, has tended to be barbaric in its approach. We have conquered countries, cultures, commodities, creatures and kingdoms with aggression and abuse, or with the blade, the gun and the bomb. This is recorded in our history as a species. Of course there is goodness here too, and there have been great feats and accomplishments, but it is the unevolved aspects of human nature that require the temperate influence of love, wisdom, tolerance and compassion, if life on Earth is to change for the better.

The Wiccan healer understands that it is important to work first on themselves, looking at their own human nature and where that limits their life experience. If you don't like something about yourself, change it. For example, if you feel miserable when you have shouted at the children, stop shouting at the children. If you wish to be more confident, work at ways to be confident. If you have always wanted to sing, go out and sing. We should be honest with ourselves, though, so be realistic. Accept your talents and gifts and be who *you* would like to be, not what others expect you to be. Live your life as best you can. Live with passion!

Every small step we take towards our highest potential reveals the richness of a journey that is beyond the mundane and is very much a life-enhancing path. The rewards for the efforts made reveal the true wealth and richness lying in the human spirit.

Through the Eyes of a Child

As we remove the veils of ignorance by developing a deeper understanding of who we are, we can begin to see life as if through the eyes of a child. There is a state of innocence, a freshness and a joy that bubbles up from inside as we free ourselves of guilt, fear, suspicion and cynicism. The eyes of the adult often fail to notice the magical and the mystical. Nor do they very often see the obvious, for they are looking through conditioned eyes that censor understanding or experience. To see life through the eyes of a child, we need to return to our original state, before life made us weary or worn out, predictable or bored, and allow ourselves to experience the wonder of a sunrise, of moonlight on water, of laughter and sharing, or being in the moment.

Life is simple, it really is. It is we who tend to make things complicated. To see life through the eyes of a child is a way of describing innocence before it becomes blemished or tarnished. It is to see clearly. It does not mean being naïve or turning our backs upon our experience and understanding.

I remember a time when I was very poor and an old friend whom I had not seen for over a year turned up late at night from the USA. I had literally nothing to offer him except a glass of bottled spring water. So I decided to make it special. We got out the stemmed glasses, we lit candles, we made a fire from wood we gathered from the hedgerow and we sat together sipping water and talking into the early hours. I shall never forget that night, for I learned the value of 'sharing water with friends' and how little we needed in order to enjoy each other's company. I see it now through the eyes of a child.

We are all born with magic in our blood, and as with all things, we have the choice to explore it or ignore it. But the joy is always there, waiting to be found. It is simply a matter of opening to innocence and to the realization that we are just a small part of a vast Creation.

Self-importance, cynicism, arrogance, boredom and apathy are not part of the expression of joy and happiness experienced by a child, and so it is to these tired emotions that we should turn our attention in order to heal them and so return to a more original state of being.

Through the Eyes of an Eagle, Butterfly and Bee

When we expand our perceptions beyond our base human nature and return to the state of innocence, we can then begin to experience life through the eyes of other creatures and other life forms, such as a bug, tree or a flower, for example.

The origin of the shamanic journey was partially to experience life through the 'eyes' of another life form and so expand human perception as much as possible. Some life forms see through ultra-violet light, others 'see' with heat sensors or through vibrations, and yet others have no eyes at all. From our human perspective, we often define other life forms as pests and vermin, weeds and parasites. But in fact, all they are and ever will be are different expressions of Creation which we either approve or disapprove of and always for very human reasons.

Have you ever looked at life through the eyes of a fish or a bird or an ant? Have you ever explored life from a creature's viewpoint or tried to see any problems you encounter with other people from their point of view?

Many great legends contain such practices. For example, in the Arthurian legends outlined by Mallory in his *Morte d'Arthur* it is recorded that Merlin taught Arthur to expand his perceptions using these selfsame principles of becoming a fish or a bird – the purpose being to help Arthur to understand that life is far more than we are commonly aware of as human beings.

A Spirit Journey

This next exercise aims to expand your perceptions, as the mythical Merlin did with Arthur, and so increase your ability to 'see' what is really going on around you. By expanding your understanding in this way, you can experience the gifts that are present in each moment, such as joy, creativity, sharing, humour and compassion, without these being clouded by misconceptions, assumptions or limited belief systems.

Step One

The first stage to expanding your perception begins with questions that are phrased in such a way as to open the mind. Take the following questions and consider them carefully. There is only one right answer to each of them and no trickery is involved.

> Q1 If a tree falls in a deserted forest with absolutely no living thing present, does it make a sound?
>
> Q2 Is a green leaf still green in the complete absence of light?

The answers can be found on page 240, but please remember that these exercises have a purpose beyond the answer that can only be experienced if you go through the process yourself. Life is far more than an intellectual exercise in reading questions and answers. The realizations that arise through achieving results with this exercise change perceptions, improve intuitive skills and can clear fixed human opinions.

Once you have worked through Step One, move on to Step Two.

Step Two

Visualize a scene that would come easily to mind for you in as much detail as you can.

Now remove all traces of yourself and your consciousness from the picture, so that you are not there.

Step Three

Having expanded your perceptions beyond normal human conception and belief, you can now more easily take a spirit journey as a dragonfly, bear or fish for example. Choose a creature that you feel drawn to and comfortable with, then work through the following guidelines.

Remove your human ideas from the journey as much as possible before you begin.

Focus your consciousness upon the spirit of your chosen creature and, if you like, have icons of it around you, such as pictures, statues, feathers, etc. You may even like to consider taking the journey at or near a place where your chosen creature would live. Dedicate your journey to the spirit of your creature and ask for its guidance and protection as you travel with it.

When you feel fully prepared, focus your perception upon how the creature would experience life, with light, heat, sound or whatever, and how they would move, fly, hunt, play, and so on. Become as totally immersed in the activity as you can, and every time you start to think in a human way, such as 'How would a butterfly see?', know that you are in 'human perception' again and go back to simply experiencing the experience as totally as you can. The spirit of the creature will guide you as best it can, with the results depending very much upon your levels of openness and trust.

This third stage of the spirit journey can be taken with as many different life forms as you like. Each one will bring a new type of richness to your experience as a human being, because absolutely everything is connected. In other words, all life experiences are beneficial in some way.

Wiccan Morality

Wiccan morality is such that we only offer to help those who ask for it or have agreed to it openly, not manipulating free will or working magic for selfish or base personal gain or prestige. All Wiccans operate under the same guiding rules, and anyone moving beyond them must then take personal responsibility. If, for example, you come across an individual who offers curses or love-trapping potions, treat them with great caution. These people may call themselves witches, but are not to be considered wise, moral or ethical ones.

Wiccan morality also means that we do not treat anyone or anything we feel is beyond our powers or abilities, and there is always a right way to proceed, which will be obvious to anyone with sensitivity. For example, if someone turns up on your doorstep with chest pains, heart palpitations and profuse sweating, you would immediately call a doctor or ambulance. If on the other hand, someone came to you for support during a grieving process, perhaps you would feel qualified to relate to that and would feel confident in doing so. Please only operate in areas where you are experienced or comfortable.

Each and every one of us is born with particular gifts and potentials that can be developed into natural talents. Mine, for example, are transmogrification, bones, headaches, emotions and the soul.

I recall a time about 20 years ago, when one of my cats had a limp and was obviously in a certain amount of pain. I took him to the veterinary surgeon who considered the situation serious enough to take X-rays. The results showed that there was quite severe calcification around the joint and painkillers were prescribed with the commentary that very little could be done – it was arthritis due to some prior accident or trauma.

Dickon, my very dear cat friend for so many years, and I went home together. I felt very strongly that I should try healing on him, which I did, and to this day

I remember how powerful the forces were that came through my hands. After a few days had elapsed, I began to notice Dickon putting more weight on his leg, then jumping and cavorting as he used to do, until all seemed well and as it was before his injury. I was delighted.

A few years later, Dickon happened to need another X-ray of the same leg. This showed that all traces of the previous calcification had completely disappeared. He remained arthritis-free for the rest of his life – another 12 years. He died at the grand old age of 17½ as an old boy with absolutely no teeth, but a light and sprightly step to the end!

Understanding Wiccan Healing at a Personal Level

To understand Wiccan healing at a personal level, it is helpful to bear in mind that we are all ultimately the same. Our packaging may be different on the outside, but our inner needs remain constant. If we are balanced individuals, we thrive when in good health, flourish under the wings of love and harmony, and pale beneath subjugation and abuse. All humans have a need for food, shelter and warmth; all humans crave love and freedom of expression; and all humans have their hopes, fears and dreams.

The individual who understands himself will more easily understand the workings of another. The most powerful healers are those who have worked to build a deep relationship between their inner and outer spiritual worlds, the microcosm and macrocosm of Creation.

The journey to well-being can often begin with sickness or disease, and so it is important to remember that illness can be a very positive experience within someone's life. To the uninitiated, ailments are most often seen as irritations to be endured or cured as quickly as possible. To the wiser amongst us, illness can point the way to profound life-changing events.

The Wiccan healer does not judge a person because of any ailment they may have. In days of old, those who were different in some way were considered by tribal communities to have been 'touched' by the gods and were held in a certain amount of honour and respect. Examples of this include the epileptic, the hermaphrodite and the albino. To be different was to be favoured by the gods.

The Wiccan healer responds to whatever an individual actually is in any given moment without contempt or judgement, for we are all equal in the eyes of the Goddess who created us.

The Shaman's Death

Sometimes healers and wise ones experience what is called the Shaman's Death, where either ill health or a major life-changing event occurs that permanently affects one's life plan. These events can include loss of what is held dear, the near-death experience, serious accidents, chronic pain, fever, periods of intense illness and a long recovery, or perhaps a time of visions and powerful dreams. Most natural-born healers would probably say that they have had a particularly hard life and this often seems to be the case. Whether you have experienced these difficulties or not, it is important to remember that to understand suffering we need to know what it is, otherwise we have no way to relate to it.

To demonstrate that this is a truth, ask yourself how you would explain light to a person who has been blind since birth. As much as you would like to theorize about it, there is only one correct answer: you can't. Only what we can directly experience and place within our sphere of reality holds any kind of personal meaning. Therefore to be a healer, we must first have experienced what it is to be healed. To be able to walk beside another who is suffering, we must first know the nature of suffering. This is why, I believe, healers tend to have had a hard time throughout their lives!

The Home of a Demon

Mediaeval demonologists and sorcerers believed that a 'demon' could be summoned by the 'black arts' and sent out to do their bidding. This is actually a *thought form* and not a demon as such. A thought form is a deliberately created thought that embodies the feelings, attributes and characteristics that a magician requires in order to achieve a particular result. It is brought to an intensely sharp focus within the mind by trained concentration and magical discipline, and is then released to carry out its 'mission'. A proper thought form generated by an adept can be so powerful that it can sometimes actually be seen by other people as a shadowy moving shape. In effect, it is an extension of the magician's own mind. A demon, as described in old texts such as the Bible, was a *doubt*, a temptation to take the easy way out, to not do the difficult task that needed to be done, or a sudden impulse to question the validity of your own cherished spiritual beliefs. In this respect, the home of a demon is *within the human being* and nowhere else, certainly not in a land of 'hell'.

As I have mentioned previously, Wiccans do not believe in hell, the devil or Satan. Although witches are often accused of being Satanists and devil-worshippers, especially in the popular press, this is purely widespread ignorance of what witchcraft actually represents. It is not possible to worship something that one does not believe in!

In historical fact, the word *hell* does not originate in the Bible or anything connected with Judeo-Christian roots; it actually comes from the Vikings, Danes and other Scandinavian peoples who left their cultural impression upon England during the Anglo-Saxon period. Hel was the name of the Queen of the Dead in Viking myth, and the word came also to be associated with her kingdom, which was a place of great peace and tranquillity. Early translators of the Biblical texts used this name, often with an extra 'l' added, as a supposedly suitable English word to replace the Judaic *Gehenna* (Ge-Hinnom, 'the Valley of Hinnom'). This was history's first recorded 'city dump', based outside Jerusalem, which was expanded in religious belief to become a suitable dump for any human beings who were classed as 'spiritual refuse'.

In Wiccan belief, our devils are part of us and not a supernatural exterior entity. They are our own natural human weaknesses and our negative qualities. We all possess these, and it can therefore be rightly said that we are all 'possessed' by demons to some degree – it's just that some of us keep them more subdued and constrained than others.

It is normal to experience attacks from our demons from time to time. However, if a person is well-balanced, these attacks only last for a short time. It is when their influence begins to gain control that we become 'possessed', either by a particular demon or by several of them working together. A person may then go rapidly downhill, finding it ever harder to regain their proper state of health or well-being.

We now know that there can be literally hundreds of these demons. Self-discipline, mental resolve and willpower are vital ingredients in tackling them. We need to stop listening to them and start believing in our own ability to make appropriate and sensible decisions for ourselves, and so strengthen all aspects of our being.

Wiccan healing applies particularly successfully to the treatment of such demons by operating through the mind and spirit, enabling a person to find the inner strength to defeat their demons and free their body from these powerful subconscious pressures.

Naming the Demon

It was the mediaeval belief that in order to banish a demon you had first to discover its name. Naming the demon would imprison it in the physical world. It could no longer lurk in the shadows and cause its mischief. The same principle applies today.

To find and name your own particular demon/s or aspects of your shadow side, it is helpful to write a list of those personal characteristics that you either have problems overcoming or don't feel particularly comfortable with. These could include a weakness for sugary foods, or perhaps shyness, aggression or smoking, to name but a few. In each case you can give the demon a name and a personality in order to draw it out of your shadows.

If you decide you want to stop smoking, for example, consider what your smoking demon's name might be and give it a real character and lifestyle. You might call it 'Nico' (from nicotine). In this case, Nico is a smarmy individual who wants to take your money, regardless of your health. He is not your friend but someone who is greedy, devious and materialistic. Now every time that you want a cigarette you can see it as Nico sneaking his wily and selfish charms into your thoughts like a weasel. You can separate his temptations from your own self and therefore operate from a place that is not possessed by this demon but rather by your own integrity. From this place you can move through life making informed decisions on your own behalf and in your own best interests. The hold that the temptation or weakness had over you simply becomes an ignorant little demon you successfully managed to exorcise from your spirit.

This is a way of dealing with all personal weaknesses. By naming the drama, the pattern and the game we can begin to free ourselves from the habitual parts we have chosen to play in each of life's scenarios.

Healing Your Ancestral Past

It is a belief in magical terms that karma is carried within our blood and passed down from generation to generation through the mother to the child via the mitochondrial DNA (female DNA), as a kind of spiritual or soul genetics. When I am speaking of healing our ancestral past, it is this family bloodline that I am referring to.

Personally, I feel very strongly that a lot of the problems encountered by young people today are caused by a family bloodline that is literally heaving with unfinished business. This leaves the offspring totally unable to identify the problem, let alone with the tools to work on the solution, because the notion of family karma is anathema to them and indeed to everyone else in their family. I wish to make it perfectly clear that there is no 'blame' to be attached to any particular family member here; it is just a question of addressing the ignorance about the importance of family healing. In order to be able to step confidently into a happy and healthy future, in my opinion we must first look to healing our past.

What I mean by healing a bloodline is taking full responsibility for its patterns – the failings, the ignorance, the traumas, the injustices, the blames, the prejudices, the wars, the poverty, the wealth, the successes, and so on. I can remember that it was when I became a mother that I decided to take on any remaining family karma. Everything that life had brought to my family tree, I acknowledged. I did not know exactly what had transpired within my bloodline throughout its history, but what I could do was spend time focusing upon my ancestors, sending healing back through time to them, sending acknowledgement of any injustices, suffering and pain they may have endured, and also sending love back through time to each and every one of them. You see, it is our *intention* that is important. If you have the intention of healing your family bloodline, it will have an effect.

If you wish to heal your own bloodline, look at family patterns – those things that repeat themselves generation after generation, such as absent fathers, eating disorders, stress-related health problems, issues around wealth or poverty, success or failure, addictions such as alcohol, or perhaps violence and abuse. Identifying your family patterns will make you more aware of the resonances of your bloodline.

Be aware that the way you live your life can affect future generations of your family. To heal your bloodline is to undertake an act of total unconditional love for the generations of your family yet to be born!

Here is a ritual for healing a family bloodline.

A Family Bloodline Healing

Timing

On a Saturday during a waning moon.

Ingredients

> 1 indigo-blue pillar candle
> cypress aromatherapy oil
> an aromatherapy burner and tealight
> spring water

Find a time when you will not be disturbed for 30 minutes, and make the area that you have chosen both peaceful and comfortable. Pour four drops of cypress essential oil into your burner, fill it to its brim with spring water and light the tea light beneath it.

Make yourself comfortable, and when you are ready, light your indigo-blue candle. As you do this, say: *'I light the fire of transformation. May its flame be dedicated to cleansing and purifying my bloodline.'*

Sit with a straight back either in a chair or upon the floor in a meditation posture and begin to visualize a tunnel going back in time behind you. Visualize yourself turning around and facing the entrance to that tunnel. Stand in the opening and remain there throughout your ritual.

Without entering the tunnel or becoming emotionally involved, simply send healing vibrations back through time. Do this either silently or with the repetition of something like: *'Peace, love, comfort and ease to all beings. May all beings from my ancestral past be at peace.'* Whatever manifests in your imagination, hold to the intention that you are healing your family's past and remain focused upon that intent.

Continue this exercise for a minimum of 15 minutes and a maximum of 30 minutes, then extinguish your burner and candle, keeping the candle safe until you perform this ritual again in 28 days' time.

Maintain healing your bloodline in this way every 28 days until your tunnel feels unobstructed and bright and is simply a tunnel. When this occurs, bury your indigo candle with great respect and imagine that you are laying your ancestral past peacefully to rest.

If you wish you can move into another phase which involves a green candle and rose aromatherapy oil. This time you anoint the candle with rose oil and as you light it you make a positive affirmation for your family's future: *'I light the flame of love. May its enduring peace embrace my family name all the days of my life and all the days to come.'*

The green candle ritual is best performed on a Friday during a waxing moon. Again, this ritual can be repeated every 28 days on a Friday until you feel that your future is filled with love and brightness; you can use the same candle each time until it is fully spent.

Rightful Justice

Illness can often occur at those times when our security, stability, income, status or relationship is threatened. This can involve a whole gamut of justice issues, ranging from indignation at a minor false accusation, right through to a costly legal case about a whole manner of things to do with rightful justice.

Sometimes the line between what is appropriate and what is not is a fine one. Because of this, when working justice magic, we must remember that many factors should be taken into account. Sometimes life must take a particular course in order for the past to be healed or addressed (if you believe in past lives this would include them too). Sometimes we have contracted at some deep inner level to help someone by being crossed by them, so that they can learn from their mistakes. Sometimes we may have simply agreed energetically to be part of some divine process that evolves the human spirit and so we should not be too narrow in defining what real justice actually is.

With this in mind, the following ritual ensures that all of the above are included so that the most appropriate outcome is reached for all concerned.

A Justice Ritual

Timing

On a Thursday, during a new-to-full moon.

Ingredients

> a piece of clean paper
> a red ink pen
> a red candle
> Hecate Anointing Oil:
> > 7 fl. oz (200 ml) of sweet almond oil
> > 5 drops of lavender oil
> > 3 drops of myrrh oil
> > 2 drops of cypress oil

When working ritual magic with Hecate, you may like to anoint a candle with Hecate oil and burn it in honour of her. Her candle colours are red (full moon), black (waning/dark moon) or white (new moon). Hecate is a triple goddess of great power and she rules over justice, along with other deities.

At your chosen time, set up your magical table or altar. Anoint your red candle with the anointing oil you have mixed up yourself whilst holding the justice issue in your thoughts. Put down your candle and light it.

Take up your red-inked pen and write the same issue on a piece of paper in clear writing. Surround it with pictures, magazine cut-outs or statues of hounds, stags or lions (all sacred to Hecate), with the red candle in the middle of everything and the piece of paper in front of the candle base.

Anoint your forehead with the Hecate oil and then say:

My Lady Hecate, I seek rightful justice. Guide and guard what you deem is right and true about [state issue]. May your divine justice prevail over all concerned. May the outcome be for the highest good of all. My Lady, in you I place my trust and faith. So mote it be!

Take up the piece of paper to Hecate and burn it fully in the candle flame, visualizing the situation being taken to the spirit of Lady Hecate. Give your thanks for any assistance you may receive.

Try your very best to let go of the whole situation now and leave it in the hands of Spirit. By burning the piece of paper you are releasing it on *all* levels.

Taking Personal Responsibility

Part of the difficulty we seem to experience in life is with owning up to and celebrating who we really are. We are very good at blaming others, judging others, comparing ourselves with others, being jealous or envious of the gifts or lifestyle of others and feeling either less or more worthy than others. Where do we *actually* fit into the picture?

The only way that we can ever be successful is to live the life that has been given to us in the ways that it manifests through us. We must try to find out who we are, how we think and feel, what makes us happy or sad, what we need to work on and improve about ourselves. Above all else we must try to learn and grow through these experiences, so that we can stand up and say 'I am who I am' and know exactly what that means.

To take personal responsibility is to think for yourself, to work things out using your own life's experience and understanding, to accept that you are not always going to be right and not always going to be wrong! It is to believe in yourself and to have faith in your ability to be who you were born to be. Realize your potential and dare to be yourself, for that is ultimately all you can be.

No one – absolutely no one – has the keys that open your life doors for you. You really are the only person who holds the answers to your questions.

If we think about the word *question* for a minute, we can see that the word *quest* sits very neatly within it. To quest is to seek. So, in order to find an answer to a question that is beyond any superficially intellectual idea we may have of it, we must go on our own personal quest.

Myths, Legends and Quests

All great civilizations have had their myths and legends, and we could say that for the most part they seem incomprehensible to us today. The language that the spiritual chroniclers of old used was elusive, while the journey to mastery of the self has a particular landscape, flavour and colour to it that runs way beyond any mundane social language. It is an experiential journey that has its own language, poetry and imagery.

Mastery of the self is not easily won. The journey can be challenging. To complete our quest, we may well have to travel into strange lands where we feel vulnerable and alone. We may have to stand up to a weakness in ourselves and make it strong. We may have to face challenges that seem to have been almost deliberately manufactured to stop us from advancing, and so on. The various stages of the journey remain the same; it is the travellers who make each story unique. Your particular life's journey could be called your own myth or legend – the great story of who you are and how you live your life, told in the timeless prose of the ancients.

In order to get to know what you are, where you have come from and what your life's quest has been so far, it can be helpful to make a mythic life map. This can offer insights and understanding about yourself and your life's journey.

Making a Mythic Life Map

To make up your own mythic life map, consider first the myriad of creatures, landscapes, mythical beasts, saviours, opposers and allies you could use to illustrate parts of your life path – the boatman, the ogre, the unicorn, the dragon, the castle and the dungeon, to name but a few. To help you get started, you can refer to the chart below.

Chart 10: Characters and Meanings

Character	General meaning
Boatman	Moving from one place to another
	Emotions
Chalice	Love
Darkness	Ignorance or difficulty
Demon	Danger
Dragon	Protection
Fruit tree	Abundance
Giant	Overwhelming challenges
Guardian	Help and assistance
Hare	Fertility
Keys	Opportunities to change
Light	Realization or happiness
Lightning bolt	Sudden change
Ogre	Frightening obstacle
Rabbit	Fears
Songbird	Self-expression
Sorcerer	Magical assistance
Stag	Dignity or stature
Swan	Beauty
Unicorn	Travelling deeper into your soul
Veil	Mysteries, the unknown
Weasel	Unhelpful influences

Keep a notebook to jot down the thoughts and inspirations that come to you. Feel your way and take your time in deciding what best describes your life's experiences. It may be languishing in a dungeon for feeling trapped, or riding on a unicorn to represent the feelings of freedom you experience as you get to express your real self more easily. You could include a tower surrounded by thorn trees to depict a time when you felt locked away from the outside world. Another part of your life could have involved singing – on your mythic map, you could leave the tower and move along your life path towards a nightingale who is singing from an apple tree, the tree of love, because singing brings you love and joy, and so on.

Once you have decided how to detail your life within a mythic landscape, take a largish piece of paper and draw a path of some kind upon it, in any shape or pattern, with a beginning (your birth) and an ending (which would represent you in the present day). This path can be stony, sandy, under-ground, winding, a maze or a labyrinth, go up and down mountains, along watercourses, and so on.

Once you have drawn the path, divide it into your ages of childhood, teenage years, young adult, mature adult or whatever, so that you can fit your life onto the length of your path quite easily.

You can then begin to fill in the details. Find ways that express your life as it has been for you, both the good and difficult parts. Those of you who do not feel comfortable with drawing or painting could write your life as a mythical story in words rather than pictures.

This is a profound teaching and one that can move you deeply, so remember, too, to be gentle with yourself as you retell your life story in this way.

You can design as many mythic maps as you like until you are happy with the result.

The ways of the Wiccan healer involve healing the self and developing a deeper and wiser understanding of life. We have shared some of the ways that witches prepare themselves for healing, both through self-development exercises and by taking personal responsibility. We now move into healing with the natural world, which is another ingredient utilized by the Wiccan healer.

Chapter Nine
Healing and the Natural World

To a Wiccan the natural world is sacred. Nature is the canvas upon which the Goddess paints Creation, thus the Wiccan healer will always be close to nature, spending a great deal of time in relationship to it.

We can learn about the complexities of our own human nature by learning about Mother Nature because the two are inherently linked – we are, after all, part of life and depend upon the natural world for our sustenance and, even more so, our existence. By developing a relationship with nature, the Wiccan healer will automatically develop an understanding of human nature, which will be extremely helpful when it comes to healing both self and others. We must remember that medicine originated from nature and that we ourselves resonate with the natural world, not with the cacophony of sounds and energetics experienced in a busy city. To explore nature is to explore ourselves, and this is good food for any soul.

To the Wiccan soul, the natural world is a sanctuary, a haven, a sacred place where trees provide the temples, stars the ceiling and the grass the carpet. Most Wiccans prefer to hold their rituals outdoors, where weather and privacy permits, to honour and be part of the natural world. It is, after all, a gift from the Goddess and God to us, their children.

Connecting with Nature

As we spend time in nature, we make more and more connections that refine our understanding of the Elements and the natural world. This helps us greatly when we are considering what tools to use in a healing ritual or charm. A piece of flint, for example, carries not only the solidity of the Earth Element but also Fire, which is why we can raise sparks with it when we grind two pieces together. Flint is fiery, hard and sharp, and thus a good protection stone, for we seek these qualities when seeking protection.

Although each of the four physical Elements is individual, they can also mix with others quite easily. Their simplest physical expression would be the watercourses (Water), the atmosphere (Air), the land (Earth) and temperature/light (Fire). As we gain more familiarity with the natural world, however, we can see that absolutely everything has its own particular Elemental signature, with each having a predominant Element. Wood, for example, is primarily Earth, but also carries Fire (because it can be burned) with a little bit of Air (necessary for combustion) and a smattering of Water (sap).

By deepening our connection to the Elements as they present themselves in the natural world, we can build our own Doctrine of Signatures. This will allow us to gain a deeper understanding of why a particular plant is, say, under the governance of Fire and not Water, or why a mineral is associated with the Moon and not the planet Venus, and so on. Herbs, flowers, trees, grasses, nuts, fruits, vegetables, fungi and minerals all carry their own unique signatures that place them somewhere upon the table of correspondences *(see Chapter Four)*. To give an example, jasmine is a night-scented flower. Because it is associated with night, it corresponds to the Moon that governs all night-blooming plants. This means that jasmine is also a Water Element plant, because the Moon is associated with the Water Element. Plants that are hot, spicy and intense come under the governance of Mars or the Sun – the Fire-based heavenly bodies – for obvious reasons: they contain the heat associated with them.

It takes time to gain an understanding of Creation, but then again, anything worth knowing requires a certain level of research, effort and dedication. To begin with, as you travel the wilds of the natural world, start to make connections between the nature and character of particular things in order to build your own understanding. The art of being able to make connections is a vital part of all Wiccan practice.

Honouring the Natural World

We rely upon nature for our survival and, because she gives to us so freely, it behoves us to honour her and give thanks to her. It is also important that we act on her behalf and on behalf of all life by choosing green options; supporting organic initiatives; and campaigning for freedom, food, water and shelter for all people across the globe and for the protection of wildlife and the wild world in general. It is so easy to say 'I love the Earth'. It takes much more effort to put that love into practice by actively protecting nature and physically contributing our time and energy to a world where *all* life can live in harmony and peace.

I would like to share a ritual with you that can be performed anywhere within nature. It is a way to give thanks to the Earth and to send out healing intentions to her, to show the essence of Creation that we are appreciative of our world. We tend to take so much for granted. With this ritual, we can take time to honour Creation and return the love that is showered upon us so freely.

An Earth Healing and Blessing Ritual

This ritual's meaning and purpose are to thank our Mother the Earth for all of her gifts, and for each person present to pledge something that will heal and help the Earth in some way, such as rubbish clearance, tree planting, recycling, and so on. It has been adapted here for the solitary Wiccan or practitioner, but can easily be performed as a group activity too. Please feel free to 'spread your creative wings' when it comes to expressing your own love for the Earth during this ritual.

Ingredients

a veil (optional)

2 red candles

flowers and other offerings of your choice

a pledge offering such as a flower head, leaf or stone

a drum/rattle (optional)

For the beginning of this ritual you may choose to wear a gossamer veil. Depending upon the time of year, you can also garland an altar or shrine to the Earth Mother with flowers, grains and other offerings such as crystals, stones and shells. For this ritual we built a central shrine to the Goddess, with a clay statue adorned with flowers beneath swathes of red cloth that covered the shrine. It is not so necessary to cast a working Circle for this ritual, for its purpose is to bless and celebrate the Earth, which is everywhere beneath our feet at all times, and the ritual itself is performed in a circular spiral, but you can cast a sacred Circle if you like.

Cover your face with your veil if you are using one. If you have candles on an altar, light them now.

Walk a distance away from your altar/shrine (approximately 7 feet/ 2 metres from the centre). If you have a drum, begin to beat the rhythm of a human heartbeat, slow and steady.

Walk around your shrine in an ever-decreasing clockwise direction (the Wiccan term for clockwise is *deosil*) seven times. With each circuit consider one of the following:

1. Mother Earth
2. Father Sky
3. The four Elements and four seasons
4. The trees, plants and herbs
5. All the birds and beasts
6. The human kingdom
7. The great mystery of Creation

Lay down your drum. Stand facing your shrine and respectfully say: *'The veil is lifting from my eyes, Mother, from my eyes.'*

Lift your veil up and over your head very slowly, with the sacred understanding that you are symbolically parting the Veil of Isis as you perform this act. Say: *'I can see clearly now that you are a part of me and I am your child. I am your child.'*

Bow your head.

As a child of the Earth, you have spoken to the Goddess and she will now speak to you through 'The Charge of the Goddess'. As you speak the words, visualize that it is her speaking to you and to all those present. (This Charge was written by the late Doreen Valiente who for a time was Gerald Gardner's High Priestess. She also wrote several books on witchcraft.)

The Charge of the Goddess

Listen to the words of the Great Mother, she who of old has been called Artemis, Astarte, Dione, Melusine, Cerridwen, Diana, Arianrhod, Isis, Bride, and by many other names:

Whenever ye have need of anything, once in the month, and better it be when the moon is full, then shall ye assemble in some secret place and adore the spirit of Me, who am Queen of all witches. There shall ye assemble ye who are fain to learn all sorcery, yet have not won its deepest secrets; to these will I teach things that are yet unknown. And ye shall be free from slavery; and as a sign that ye be really free, ye shall be naked in your rites; and ye shall dance, sing, feast, make music and love all in my praise. For mine is the ecstasy of the spirit and mine also is joy on Earth; for my law is love unto all beings. Keep pure your highest ideal; strive ever towards it; let naught stop you or turn you aside. For mine is the secret door which opens upon the Land of Youth and mine is the cup of the wine of life and the Cauldron of Cerridwen, which is the Holy Grail of immortality. I am the gracious goddess who gives the gift of joy unto the heart of man. Upon Earth, I give the knowledge of the spirit eternal and beyond death I give peace and freedom, and reunion with those who have gone before. Nor do I demand sacrifice, for behold, I am the Mother of all living and my love is poured out upon the earth.

Hear now the words of the Star Goddess, the dust of whose feet are the hosts of Heaven, whose body encircles the Universe:

I who am the beauty of the green Earth, and the white Moon among the stars, and the mystery of the waters, and the desire of the heart of man call unto thy soul. Arise, and come unto Me, for I am the soul of nature who gives life to the Universe. From Me all things proceed, and unto Me they must return. And before my face beloved of Gods and men let thine innermost divine self be enfolded in the rapture of the infinite. Let my worship be within the heart that rejoiceth; for behold, all acts of love and pleasure are my rituals. And therefore let there be beauty and strength, power and compassion, honour and humility, mirth and reverence within you. And thou who thinkest to seek for me, know thy seeking and yearning shall avail thee not unless thou knowest the mystery; for if that which thou seekest thou findest not within thee, then thou wilt never find it without thee. For behold I have been with thee from the beginning and I am that which is attained at the end of desire.

Take up your flower head, shell or other votive offering and, holding it in the palms of your hands, consider what you could pledge to undertake that will serve the Earth, heal the Earth, love the Earth a little more.

Kneel before your altar/shrine and, holding your offering out, say the following words, or words of your choosing:

My Lady, Queen of Earth, Moon and stars, blessed be thy Name. It is I, [state your magical or chosen name here], come to pledge my heart to your ancient ways. I make this offering in the name of you, my Mother, and vow this day that I shall heed the whispers of your wisdom in my being. I pledge [state your promise/pledge here] for the benefit of all life. Erce, Erce, Erce, blessed be thy name.

(Erce is an Anglo-Saxon name for the Earth and is pronounced 'Air-keh'.)

Place your offering down before the Earth Goddess and sit in communion with her for as long as you wish.

If you cast a sacred Circle, close it in the usual way. If not, stand up and bow your head again towards the Earth, bending down and touching her if you feel you should with your hands. This completes the ceremony. Blow out your candles and say: 'Blessed be!' The fulfilment of your pledge should be undertaken as soon as you possibly can.

Healing with Plants

Witches work and commune with all aspects of the natural world. This is because, to them, nature is not separate from human existence, but a vibrant and active part of it, providing many remedies and medicines as well as being a welcome tonic for any soul that spends time in her environments and habitats.

In the past, the natural world was far closer to us than it is today, due to a total dependence upon local harvests. Because of this, natural things carried a much more tangible meaning than they tend to do today. In days of old, for example, flowers were given their own language and admirers would send bouquets to each other that contained secret messages. If an admirer sent you myrtle and red carnations, the message would read: 'I feel attracted to you and would like to meet you.' You might perhaps return a bunch of daffodils, which would mean: 'I don't feel the same about you.' This practice was very popular in Victorian times, when subtlety in affairs of the heart was often required.

In magical terminology each flower, plant and herb has its spirit, known as a deva, its own signature, its own particular power and a variety of chemical constituents. Many plants have been associated with healing for thousands of years, such as St John's wort and angelica, willow and myrrh.

Gathering and Harvesting Herbs

When a Wiccan works with flowers, plants or herbs, they ask the devic spirit of the plant for permission to pick it or use it in some way, as a matter of respect, for they are asking that plant to give up a part of itself for their use. There is no special wording that must be used. Simply speak as you would to a beloved member of your family – because in a way all life around us is like a family member, sharing Creation with us. Many people can get caught up in thinking that magic is made up of words and rituals that must be perfectly executed in order to work. It is not. It is so simple – magic is relating with aligned spirit, soul and body.

When gathering healing plants, the witch will use everything that is safe and which is to be found for the most part in their local environment, as long as this is away from pollution.

Plants should be picked on a dry day before midday and if herbal, before their flower heads have appeared, unless it is the flowers themselves you are harvesting. Specimens should always be unblemished and free from disease.

When gathering wild plants, the witch will never take more than necessary, to ensure continuance of the species in that place. They will also be aware of endangered species – many plants are now protected, and you would be wise to educate yourself about endangered species, so that you remain within the law.

After gathering a plant or herb, the witch will give thanks for what they have taken.

The witch's healing cupboard may contain several choices of herbs for every-day complaints, depending upon the time of year and the local habitats involved. Some witches may grow their own magical herbs to ensure a regular supply, but will also take advantage of modern techniques such as ordering from a herbal supplier where quality and correct identification can be assured. Unless the witch is qualified to treat medical conditions, the herbs gathered will only be for exter-nal use, or for inclusion in incenses, rituals or charms, and not for administering internally.

We have established that in days of old there was little separation between magic and medicine, and so Wiccan herbs of healing were also often used as cures for spirit possession or evil as well as for physical and emotional complaints. Herb bundles would have been created using magical incantations and protective formulae that are not mentioned here, because our focus is upon the healing aspects of plants rather than on their use against spirit possessions.

The following pages include details of a handful of herbs that can be used for healing some common complaints, but please be advised not to treat yourself without seeking proper medical guidance and also do not handle or take herbs or use oils if you are pregnant or on medication. All the herbs outlined, unless other-wise stated, are not for ongoing or long-term treatment, and I would strongly advise you to buy your herbs from a recognized supplier to ensure they are of medicinal quality and not polluted in any way.

If you do decide to collect herbs yourself, please make absolutely certain you do not endanger any local plant life, have harvested the correct species, have only gathered healthy specimens and, most important of all, can take a chosen herb safely. Remember that they are not to be taken from areas where there are any pesticides, insecticides and chemicals.

Always clean herbs thoroughly. And I remind you again, please do not handle or administer any herbs or oils if you are pregnant, on medication, suffer from allergies or have any kind of medical condition, without taking appropriate medical advice first.

Angelica

Angelica archangelica/Archangelica officinalis

Part used: *Root*

Angelica protects against disease, cleans the blood and is a wonderful tonic to the system. It is primarily used for stomach problems, and as a kidney flush, nerve tonic and skin cleanser. Do not take it if you have diabetes or diabetic tendencies. Due to its similarities to a poisonous plant called hemlock, you are strongly advised to purchase your seeds and roots from a herbal supplier and not to harvest them from the wild.

> Boil 1 pint (570-ml) of spring water with 1 tsp of dried root obtained from a herbal supplier. Leave to cool and then add to the bathwater as a skin tonic and purifier.

Birch

Betula alba

Parts used: *Leaves and bark*

Birch leaves have sometimes been prescribed for baldness and for skin complaints.

> **Leaves:** Take a handful of fresh undamaged leaves (about 1 tbsp) gathered on a dry day and drop them into half a pint (285 ml) of cold spring water. Bring to the boil and then simmer for five minutes. Leave the infusion to stand and cool. Rub into hair and scalp.

> **Bark:** Birch bark has been traditionally used like paper. For complaints of the skin or the hair, people would write their wish for healing upon birch bark and then return the bark to the area surrounding the tree. (Do not strip bark from trees – it can destroy them if not taken correctly.)

Centaury

Erythraea centaurium/Centaurium erythraea

Parts used: *Herb*

Also known as feverwort, centaury is an excellent treatment for intermittent fevers, constipation and for sluggish digestion. It is also said to alleviate rheumatism.

> Infuse 1 oz (30g) of the dried herb in 1 pint (570-ml) of freshly boiled spring water. Leave to cool and sip a small cupful shortly before each meal. Sweeten with honey if required.

Cleavers

Galium aparine

Part used: *Leaves and juice*

Cleavers is an excellent tonic for the lymphatic system, providing cleansing and clearing of any toxic build-up including abscesses and other skin eruptions. It is a favourite of geese, hence its other name of goose-grass. The seeds can be gathered, dried, roasted and made into a coffee substitute. Do not take cleavers if you have diabetic tendencies.

> **Leaves:** For a gentle lymphatic spring clean eat approximately five of the individual small green leaves from the rosette tops of a fresh young plant. Harvest these in areas away from towns, roads and workplaces to avoid toxins and pollution.
>
> **Juice:** Wash the affected area of skin clean first with a mixture of 1/2 tsp salt in 1/4 pint (150 ml) of warm spring water. Apply freshly extracted cleavers juice to the affected area and leave it to dry. Cleanse and reapply every three hours.

Clove

Eugenia caryophyllata

Parts used: *Oil*

Introduced into Europe between the fourth and sixth centuries, clove oil is truly excellent as a temporary reliever of toothache until you can get to a dentist.

> Drop a few drops onto a cotton wool pad and apply to the affected area as often as required. Keep away from the eyes.

Coltsfoot

Tussilago farfara

Parts used: *Flowers and leaves*

Coltsfoot is a good treatment for all upper respiratory complaints such as coughs, colds and asthma. The dried leaves can be smoked as a tonic for the lungs.

> Put 1 oz (30-g) of leaves and/or flowers in 2 pints (1.15 litres) of spring water. Boil it down to 1 pint (570-ml), cover and then leave to stand for 25 minutes. Sip in cupful doses as often as required. Can be sweetened to taste with honey.

Dandelion

Taraxacum officinale

Parts used: *Leaves and root*

Dandelion purges the system of impurities and is a good diuretic, balancing water retention safely without losing any essential fluids. Fresh young dandelion leaves can be used as a salad vegetable in the spring.

> Steep 2 tsp of fresh young leaves or dried root into half a pint (285 ml) of boiling spring water. Stand off the heat to cool; strain and take half the mixture in the morning and half the mixture in the evening, warm or cold. Sweeten to taste.

European Vervain

Verbena officinalis

Parts used: *Herb*

Vervain can be used as a skin tonic and to treat eczema and other skin complaints. It can also calm the nerves after a stressful day. It is a remedy for bladder problems and considered to be an aphrodisiac. A simple charm against headaches can be made by constructing a necklace from its leaves.

> Add 1 tbsp of the dried herb to half a pint (285 ml) of boiled spring water. Cover and leave to stand overnight. Strain and apply as a skin wash up to twice a week.
>
> To make a tea, steep 1 tsp of the dried herb in half a pint (285 ml) of boiled spring water. Strain and sip a cupful whilst still warm before going to bed. Sweeten with a little honey to taste. Not for regular use.

Garlic

Allium sativum

Parts used: *Juice; tablets*

Garlic is a highly effective blood cleanser and can lower high blood pressure. It was widely used during the First World War on open wounds to stop infection.

> Crush 2 cloves of garlic and keep the juice; dilute this with 1/4 pint (150 ml) of spring water and apply to open sores and suppurations of the skin with a sterilized swab.
>
> **Tablets:** To avoid losing friends, it is recommended that you purchase organic high-quality cold-pressed garlic tablets from a wholefood/health shop/ supplier. Take the dosage recommended on the bottle, especially in the spring.
> *Do not take garlic if you have low blood pressure.*

Lavender

Lavandula officinalis/Lavandula augustifolia

Parts used: *Leaves, flowers and oil*

Lavender has been used for centuries to clear the head, to calm the nerves and ease dizziness.

> **Leaves:** Take a handful of the fresh leaves and/or flowers and rub directly onto the temples when feeling light-headed or headachy.
>
> **Oil:** Purchase lavender oil and rub onto the temples, forehead and back of the neck when suffering from a tension headache. Add a few drops to a footbath after a long day to ease tired feet. Put the neat oil onto insect bites to relieve itching.

Lemon Balm

Melissa officinalis

Part used: *Leaves*

Lemon balm calms the nerves, eases insomnia, soothes the symptoms of a feverish cold and eases female reproductive complaints such as menstrual cramps and headaches. It can bring on menstruation, so please do not use this herb if you are pregnant.

> Add 1 oz (30-g) of the herb to 1 pint (570-ml) of boiled spring water. Leave to stand for 15 minutes, strain and sip whilst still warm. Can be sweetened to taste.

Onion

Allium cepa

Parts used: *Bulb*

Onion is an excellent remedy for all bronchial complaints, and the following recipe is completely safe to use with children. I was brought up on it. Whenever I had a cough or cold, out came the onions!

Peel and cut a fresh organic onion into rings and place them in a cereal bowl. Cover with approximately 2 heaped tbsp of organic dark brown sugar. Cover with another cereal bowl of the same size and leave to stand overnight. A syrup will appear in the morning. Strain this off from the onion rings and bottle it. Take 2 tsp every hour on the hour until symptoms are relieved. Make fresh every evening for the following day and administer for as long as required.

White Willow
Salix alba

Parts used: *Tablets*

White willow contains salicin, a painkilling ingredient that is now marketed synthetically as aspirin. Its natural form is known as white willow bark and can be used to alleviate headaches, inflammation and bodily pain. People sensitive to aspirin or to salicylic acid are best advised to avoid white willow bark.

Purchase white willow bark tablets from a good healthfood outlet or herbalist and follow the dosage suggested on the bottle. Do not take if you are on painkillers, or any other medication, without proper medical advice.

Tussie Mussies
Also known as a nosegay, the tussie mussie is a circular herbal bundle made up of flowers and herbs with disinfectant and fragrant qualities. They were very popular in the sixteenth century as a preventative against disease, and in fact are referred to in the children's nursery rhyme about the plague:

> *Ring a ring o' roses*
> *A pocketful of posies …*

These posies would have been tussie mussies containing roses, which in those days were not only used to mask any unpleasant smells but were also employed in medicines, especially the leaves of red roses. (Rosewater can be used to moisturize the skin and rose oil can reduce swelling and inflammation.)

A tussie mussie can have any focus – it can be made for a lover, a friend, a birth, a death or for healing, depending upon the flowers and herbs that are included in the bundle.

To Make a Healing Tussie Mussie

Ingredients

    1 open rose for the centre

rosebuds

sprigs of:

    rosemary

    parsley

    myrtle

    lemon balm

    lavender

Rue stems

Calendula/marigold flowers

Lady's mantle leaves or ivy leaves to edge the posy

floristry tape

ribbons (optional)

Working in a circle around your central rose, gradually build up a posy of assorted herbs and flowers (any varieties with healing qualities can be used). Keep your arrangement tight by binding them in place with floristry tape around the central stem of the rose.

When your flowers and herbs are in place, finish off your tussie mussie with decorative leaves from lady's mantle, ivy or any other large-leafed healing plant. You can if you wish add ribbons around the edge or within the arrangement before giving it to a loved one as a healing gift.

Trees

Witches have many individual skills and specialties. Some will work closely with the powers of the trees and when walking in the woods will be aware of the energy of the trees, which they may refer to as tree spirits or dryads. These Elementals are acknowledged in witchcraft and help to build the magical atmosphere of a wood or habitat. Witches closely aligned to trees will have a good working knowledge of the qualities of each species of tree. All parts of a tree can be used for one purpose or another, perhaps for making a wand or staff, for dyeing cloth, for medicines, for support and guidance, for magic and healing.

Because they are the lungs of our planet, we would be wise to protect trees, honour their valuable contribution to our world and realize that without them, we and many other life forms would cease to be.

Tree Spirits

Tree spirits or dryads are the energetic or astral aspect of a tree's physical form. Although, magically speaking, Gnomes have overall responsibility for the physicality of the natural world, it is the dryads who are seen to be the individual energy or spirit of each species, and it is to them that the witch will turn when seeking permission to use any of their materials.

Connecting with the Dryads

When approaching a tree spirit or dryad, we should move slowly with steady and controlled steps up to the tree, letting it know that we are friendly. I find that I can 'breathe' in unison with a tree if I place my hand upon its trunk (the best place being just before the trunk splits, because this is considered to be the heart of the tree) and then connect energetically to its slower rhythms by breathing deeply and slowing myself down. This sets up a kind of circular breathing where the tree and the 'toucher' become one.

Once you feel attuned to the tree (and you should actually physically begin to feel a tingling energy in your hands and even your whole body), you can speak with the tree spirit either mentally or out loud and ask its advice or

> guidance. The dryad will bring you its wisdom through your thoughts, perceptions and feelings, so take note of any mental pictures, ideas or teachings you may be given.
>
> When your communing is complete, say thank you to the dryad, remove your hands and quietly and slowly leave the area.

In days of old trees were highly venerated. The practice of touching wood comes from a time when tree spirits would be invoked by touching certain woods for luck or protection. Another practice of these tree-worshipping days is still enacted today in Clun, Shropshire, where on Arbour Day the oldest tree in the village is decorated with flags to celebrate its presence and its blessings upon the local community.

The Healing Powers of Trees

Throughout the past in many tribal cultures, and in some places to this day, it was common practice to plant a fruit tree when a child was born. Traditionally in Europe, pagans planted an apple tree for a boy and a pear tree for a girl. However, any fruit tree could be chosen to mark a birth. Once the tree was planted, it was tended with great love, because it became like an external part of the child's soul – the child and tree would go through life intimately linked together by their bonding at birth. It was a superstition that if the tree was felled or became diseased, that the bonded child would also suffer, and vice versa.

Trees have been intimately linked to us in many ways through history. It was a northern European custom to pass a child with rickets through a split in an ash tree nine times at sunrise and then to paste up the hole in the trunk. If the tree healed, the child's rickets healed as well. To relieve tired feet, travellers would place alder leaves in their shoes. Hawthorn berries were favoured as a tonic for the heart, and crab apples were prized for their antiseptic and detoxing qualities. Trees really have been our friends and allies for thousands of years, providing food, shelter, medicines and oxygen through their many and varied forms.

All trees can be approached for healing, through the dryads, and each will provide a different kind of strength or ability that you can attune yourself to.

Chart 11: The Healing Aspects of Trees

Species	Magical definition	Uses	Healing ability
Alder	The Elf Tree	Make an elf whistle by hollowing out a young branch	When requiring balance or harmony
Apple/ Crab Apple	The Tree of Love	Make apple honey by very gently boiling the fruit without sugar for a long time	When feeling negative or unloved, or having relationship problems
Ash	The World Tree	Make wishing helicopters with the seedpods on a windy day!	When sacrifices are or may be required Carry leaves or branches to undo hexes against you
Birch	The Cleansing Tree	Make your own birch broom with twigs bound with jute or twine to sweep the home	When detoxing or feeling blocked
Elder	The Witch Tree	Rub fresh leaves on your body to repel flies	When rehabilitating, starting again or recovering from broken bones
Hawthorn	The Hedgewitch Tree	Eat the flowers to see faeries	When feeling vulnerable or psychically challenged
Hazel	The Divination Tree	Make your own divining rod with a forked hazel branch	When confused about which direction to take or what to do
Oak	The King of the Forest	Crush acorns, roast until golden brown, grind and then roast again to make a coffee substitute	When seeking solace or protection and strength
Olive	The Tree of Peace	Eat the fruit for a healthy heart	When love and wisdom are lacking
Rowan/ Mountain Ash	The Lady of the Mountains	Make a protective charm by binding two small twigs at the centre in a cross shape with red thread	For endurance and protection
Willow	The Wishing Tree	Tie a white ribbon to a willow tree on a full moon and wish for healing	When emotional or seeking comfort
Yew	The Spirit Tree	All parts are poisonous	When grieving or missing someone

Chart 11 offers a unique way to work with the trees. All you need to put it into practice is a knowledge of trees. To begin with, you might carry a tree identification book when out walking. You can then visit whichever tree most fits your needs and simply 'be' with it for as long as you like. You can also let yourself be guided to a tree by following your intuition and trusting that the tree you are led to is the one that has something to share with you, regardless of what any books may say about its particular qualities.

If you would like to connect more closely to trees, adopt one in your local area, take care of it and build a relationship with it. Then in return you can ask for its guidance or support, healing or whatever you need, marking the event with perhaps a ribbon tied to one of its branches or a wish wrapped in one of its leaves.

We can also sit with our backs to a tree trunk and journey with its dryad to find healing solutions.

Journeying with a Dryad

Ask for the protection and guidance of the Goddess and Horned God before you touch the tree. Centre and calm yourself with some deep breathing.

Having made your connection to the tree and its dryad as already described (see *page 136*), sit with your back against the trunk and close your eyes.

Now visualize in your mind that there is a door in the trunk of the tree. Knock three times upon the door. It opens. You are greeted by a tree spirit whom you ask to grant you entrance. You are invited inside the tree and into the domain of the dryad.

You look around this new environment and take in the scenery. You can now ask the dryad to take you on a journey to find a healing solution, personal guidance or even some support and friendship, if the spirit is prepared to co-operate!

Journey wherever the dryad takes you — perhaps into a room, or down a tunnel, or through a maze of roots and rocks. Whatever happens, trust the dryad and go with it. If you remain by the entrance, this is also fine.

Spend as much time as you need in order to find solutions and then return to the entrance and the doorway, bid your farewells, give your thanks and step back through the door to your everyday world. Open your eyes.

You can leave a strand of your hair or any natural/organic gift for the dryad, although any act of care for the tree's well-being is best.

Oak, Ash and Thorn

Wherever oak, ash and thorn grow together is said to be a magically charged area where the Elemental presence is strong and powerful. If you find these three trees growing together, it could become your place of power, your place of healing and renewal, and also your place to make wishes or connect to deeper aspects of yourself by journeying with the dryads or by simply connecting to the trees there as already described.

Solitary thorn trees are known as faery trees. Hawthorn is one of the trees connected to the Faery Queen and so highly magical and protective. It is a wonderful tree to build a relationship with, especially when you feel you have lost your magic, your beauty or your potential.

All trees with thorns can be utilized when seeking protection from harm. Working at a sympathetic level, the thorns can act to provide a psychic barrier. When working with thorn trees, be aware, though, that a blackthorn cut should immediately be treated medically, as it can easily go septic.

Nuts and Cones

Nuts and cones have long been associated with conception and fertility. It was a traditional practice to give a couple a bag of hazelnuts on their wedding day in order to bless their marriage with children.

Walnuts, pinecones and acorns are also fertility charms. Carry an acorn or make an acorn necklace to help you conceive a child or to prevent illnesses. You can also make a healing or conception wish and place it in an acorn cup, between the cup and the nut, and then bury it beneath an oak tree on the eve of the dark moon.

Rocks and Stones

From the smallest pebbles to the grandest megaliths, the stones and rocks of our world are mighty presences that are aeons old. Their sheer time on the planet reminds us that we humans are very young beings upon the Earth.

Anyone who has worked closely with stones knows that they are extremely wise and able to hold, receive, store or transmit energetic information. Crystals and gems are part of this stone kingdom, as are salt, talc and sand. It is of interest to note that the human body also has crystalline structures within it, such as the teeth, meaning that we too have aspects of the mineral kingdom within us.

Stones can offer us great support and strength at those times when we feel weakened or vulnerable and perhaps out of touch with the natural world. To spend time in conscious communion with a rock, pebble, crystal or gem, simply by holding them in our hands or touching them, offers us the opportunity to experience their healing tones in profound ways. Stone magic is simple: we allow their teachings into our world through 'listening' as we touch one.

The art of listening well is to be in a state of receptivity, rather than a state of seeking. Accept impressions and feelings into your being and then, with the aid of conscious awareness and scrutiny, you can utilize these impressions in self-development and divination.

Connecting with Stones

Make a physical connection with your stone of choice by either holding it or touching it in some way with part of your body. Slow down your breathing and find a place of deep calm within yourself.

Once this has occurred, state slowly and clearly that you set your intent to connect with the stone if it harms none and is appropriate for you to do so.

If you perceive that all is appropriate, mentally communicate with the stone that you come in peace, seeking its support, wisdom or guidance. Remain open to the stream of consciousness that will pour into you if you allow it to, bringing images, symbols, senses and understandings that will lead you to those places inside yourself where truth can be found.

For those who have a little difficulty getting out of the mental chattering of the mind, after calming yourself, visualize an open window in the stone. Imagine yourself becoming small enough to enter this window. You can then mentally open it and step inside.

What have you stepped into? Take in the scene, the feelings, the flavours and the messages. Remember what has been shown to you before giving your thanks and saying farewell.

You then mentally step out of the imaginary window, return to normal size and come back to everyday consciousness, closing the window behind you and bringing any messages or insights with you to integrate into your spirit.

Crystal Pyramids

Some witches work with crystals as part of their healing practices, and one effective way to keep your home or workspace clear of negative or stale vibrations is to create a pyramid shape with obsidian pieces. Obsidian is made of volcanic lava and because it is a dark stone is an effective absorber of unwanted vibrations. All black stones are able to perform the same function, although obsidian is excellent because it does not require cleansing.

Creating a Crystal Pyramid

To create your own crystal pyramid, place a piece of obsidian in each corner of the building and another in the loft or attic, as near to the centre of the building as possible, so that if lines were drawn between each crystal, a pyramidical structure would be evident.

Do not attempt this if your attic is not easily accessible or safe. Place the piece in, or as near to, the centre of the upper floor or ceiling instead.

Not only do obsidians keep the environment clean but, as with all pyramid shapes, they can recharge the atmosphere within them, bringing more stability and balance.

The Witch's Necklace

Stones that carry special significance to the Wiccan are hag stones, or holey stones. These are stones (primarily flints) with a hole through them and represent the Goddess and Her protection. Hag stones are often carried or worn by witches as good luck charms, because they have the ability to avert any negativity.

To make up your own hag-stone necklace, loop both ends of a thread through the hole in your stone and then pass the ends back through the loop to secure the stone. Add beads according to preference and then knot the ends. Your hag necklace can now be magically consecrated in a Circle to activate and bless its potential.

Apart from a hag-stone necklace that is worn for more personal reasons, some witches will wear a special witch's necklace during rituals. The traditional witch's necklace is made up of alternately strung jet and amber beads. Together they symbolically bond the masculine and feminine aspects of Creation, with equal representation and importance being placed upon both. Some witch's necklaces are made of acorns, or berries, or silver; in fact any type of necklace, appropriately dedicated, can be worn during sacred rituals.

You may like to make your own special necklace to wear during your rituals by stringing beads, berries, nuts, charms and/or crystals together so that you feel closely connected to nature's blessings as you perform your magic.

Healing Sites

All of the Earth is sacred to a witch. Historically, however, some places have been considered more sacred than others, such as the White Horse at Uffington in Oxfordshire, and we can still feel the power of such sacred places and the sheer majesty of their presence. They seem to enhance the landscapes that contain them, as if our ancestors were building some kind of sacred stage that incorporated the local scenery as well.

Any sensitive person can feel the powers inherent in certain areas, whereas in other places they may feel little or no energetic pulse. Our ancestors lived so closely aligned to the land that these vibrant energy forces would have easily been felt by them.

Many sacred places can be used for healing. The Water Element has the strongest associations with healing, and so all watery places will provide an ideal environment for healing rituals, especially those involving the emotions, relationships and family. It really does depend what kind of healing is required. If someone is very mentally stressed, for example, the excess energy would benefit best from grounding and releasing, and so the Earth as well as the Air Element would come into play.

Crossing Water

To our ancestors water was a vital commodity, a sacred Element. Rivers were named after goddesses, or dedicated to them, thus automatically sanctifying them and raising their importance. Witches and other pagan practitioners have for aeons defined their working Circles with consecrated water, and watercourses were often used in the old days to delineate land boundaries.

The superstition that witches cannot cross water more than likely arises from subverting the original pagan belief that no negativity can travel across sancti-fied water. When the Church was attempting to abolish witchcraft, it adopted this belief but with a far narrower definition – namely, that water just stopped the evil intentions of witches and sorcerers. Witches have no problems crossing water, although, because traditionally rivers and streams were used as boundary demarcations, witches of old were reported to have reaffirmed themselves or their recent magic as they crossed water in order to acknowledge movement from one place (boundary) to another and so maintain a true course and intention as they journeyed into what could well be another parish, land or dominion with perhaps different physical and magical rules and regulations.

'Crossing the waters' was also a term for travelling from a lower to a higher state of consciousness, a vital ingredient in any self-development and healing. This practice became closely associated with riddles. Our forebears loved riddles. The art of conversation through the battle of wits was considered a worthy pastime, for it was language that gave us the ability to 'name' things, and with that naming to know their nature and either communicate with or to gain knowledge of them in order to understand or to control them. With Isis, Queen of Witches, for example, we know that she plotted to obtain the secret name of Ra in order to name and claim his powers.

In days of old, the humble riddle graced many a spiritual tale as a way of ascertaining the stage the traveller was at on their spiritual journey of consciousness, or of providing the means to exercise and stretch their perceptual skills.

In order to expand our consciousness, and thus become more closely aligned to our healing gifts, we must first know the right questions to ask, and we can only ask these questions when we are in the right place within ourselves to find them – hence the riddle. We must find the answer to the riddle in order to 'cross the water'.

The Irish had tales (called *imrama*) about wayfarers crossing the waters to the farthest isles (magical dimensions) in order to gain wisdom and inspiration. At certain significant crossing-places on rivers or lakes, votive offerings were made (and still can be today). At key places on watercourses, you can, if you wish, make a votive offering to ask the river spirits to be with you on your journey, to guide you to greater wisdom, to seek their healing assistance, or even just to give them a gift in acknowledgement of the water they provide.

It is no coincidence that there is a magical alphabet called 'Passing the River'. Consider using it to make a river-blessing charm, or conversely to seek the river's blessing upon whatever journey has brought you there by casting your request or blessing into the waters as you pass by.

Making a River-Blessing Charm

To make a river-blessing charm or request to the water spirits, whilst still at home think of the words you will use and then translate them into their corresponding letters from the 'Passing the River' alphabet (overleaf).

Write the charm or request on a stone using water-soluble non-toxic ink.

Take the stone to the water's edge and announce your presence to the water spirits by simply introducing yourself and stating your reason for being there.

Hold out your stone and after a few moments of contemplation and communion with the water, drop it into the water with thankful and respectful grace.

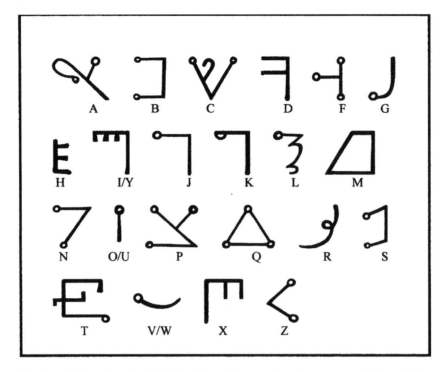

'Passing the River' magical alphabet. You will notice that there is no symbol equivalent
to the letter 'E'. This is because, like many magical alphabets, it is based on Hebrew.
The conventional solution to this is to use 'I' or 'Y' instead.

Wells and Springs

Hilltops, mountains, springs and wells were all formerly considered very sacred,
most often for very logical and sensible reasons. Breathtaking vistas, unusually
shaped trees, time-moulded caves or perhaps grassy mounds towering above the
surrounding flatlands would all have been considered special places, because
they would evoke particular feelings or reactions, either because of their unusual
placement in relation to their surroundings or because they offered something
of the magic of the times. Ayers Rock in Australia would be a prime example
– the burnt red rock rises majestically out of the flat earth as if from a different
location, outside space and time.

To our ancestors, the hilltop provided a good vantage-point, the mountain offered protection, the springs provided much-venerated water, while wells were considered gateways to the underworld and the latent potentials that existed there. Women seeking fertility, for example, would drop votive offerings into a well or spring dedicated to the Goddess to seek her favour with the conception of a child, because Water is the Element that has long been associated with birth as well as with healing.

Our foremothers traditionally cleansed and blessed wells and springs on May Day or conversely 40 days after Eostre (Easter). This is a custom that can easily be continued today by performing a well blessing or dressing at this time of year.

Blessing a Local Well

It is often only when we are sick that we think to make a connection with the instruments of healing, such as medicines, healing wells, deities and herbs. Then we may wish to appeal to the gods or to the healing waters (of, say, Lourdes for example), but for the most part we remain blinkered to these healing gifts all around us and don't consider giving thanks or showing appreciation for what we have been given before we need help. The purpose of a well blessing is to give unconditional acknowledgement — in other words, with no personal appeal or wishes attached — for the qualities of a particular healing well and to show our appreciation for what the Earth Mother has raised from her depths in order to help us to heal ourselves.

A well blessing can be a simple or more complex affair. At its simplest, we can clear the water, lay a flower head upon it and honourably bless the well's existence, seeking nothing in return. At a more complex level we can dress the well with flower garlands, leave precious offerings such as a statuette, crystal or hand-crafted gift we have made especially for the purpose, or perform a community well dressing.

A well dressing is achieved by mounting a layer of clay onto a wooden backing board, upon which a design or pattern is etched out. This is then filled out and decorated with flower petals, grasses, twigs, leaves, grains and seeds pushed into the wet clay and built up into an image such as that of a dove and a rainbow, for example. The board is then displayed at the well as a way of honouring it.

Making a Healing Wish

There are several variations on the tradition of seeking the granting of a wish at a well. Women seeking help with conception would take a deliberately bent silver pin to a well and, after making a votive offering, cast it into the waters whilst repeating their wish to conceive. The reason for bending or breaking the object was to symbolically 'kill' it to allow its spirit to enter the spirit world, thus bearing the wish with it. It is more responsible to nature if we do not emulate this practice but use a flower head or other organic product instead.

Once at the well, state your intent and that you come with respect for the local spirit or guardian of the well. Ask for their attention as you make your request or wish and then gently cast your offering into the water.

If you can reach the water, you have the option of filling your cupped hands with it. Take it into your hands and then, with your eyes closed, turn clockwise three times, ending with your back to the well. Then tip the water back over your left shoulder towards the well, making your healing wish as you do so. If you do this, it is wise to remember to wash your hands afterwards.

Another option is to cast your gift into the water first. Then close your eyes, turn three times clockwise and make your healing wish. You can then look into the well and see if your reflection can be seen clearly in the water. If it is, you know that your wish has been acknowledged by the water spirits there.

You may also leave a piece of coloured 'clouty' rag at a well and ask for a health condition to be removed. Healing wells were often decorated with these rags and became known as clouty wells. The word *clouty* makes references to the old custom of removing pieces of clothing (or, in days of old, bandages), i.e., casting a clout, and leaving them at the healing wells in order to try to remove the cause of the illness or ailment. Bandages are no longer discarded, but leaving coloured rags at healing wells is still a popular activity today.

Safeguarding Sacred Sites

In the past, many of the holy springs that were once sacred to pagan goddesses were claimed by the Church and renamed after saints instead. Churches, cathedrals, monasteries and abbeys were all built upon ancient sacred sites and the pagan element erased. St Boniface, for example, felled a yew tree in Germany that was dedicated to the thunder god Thor and used the wood from it to build his chapel to St Peter, thus taking the site's inherent powers away. This was common practice – to override the original uses of pagan sacred sites and re-establish them under the rulership of the Church. However, the pagan heritage of many places remained intact, such as the Temple of Mithras in Carrawburgh, Northumberland, or the Madron Healing Well in Cornwall, which is still adorned with token offerings and tats of coloured rags today. The ancient pagan beliefs in the sanctity of nature and her shrines have survived their suppression because no matter how much indoctrination the Church attempted, somewhere within the human spirit there remained a deep and profound belief in the gods and goddesses of old.

Today, however, across the world, the gifts offered to us through the sacred sites of our mother the Earth are slowly disappearing, along with the knowledge of their meaning and purpose. Thus we are gradually losing the richness not only of our local cultures but of our ancestral history as well. In the USA, many of the Native American sacred sites are under threat, including the Medicine Lake Highlands in northern California, whose healing waters have been used by the native people for thousands of years, and Puvungna Island, in southern California, which nearly became a shopping mall. Bear Butte, which means Bear's Lodge, referred to inappropriately by white people as the Devil's Tower and made famous by the film *Close Encounters of the Third Kind*, is seeing a conflict between the spiritual practices of the tribal people and the financial rewards of tourism. The

Zuni Salt Lake in New Mexico and Manataka, now called Hot Springs National Park, in Arkansas are both sacred healing sites that have nearly vanished beneath bricks and business. It is not a question of denying the need for progress, but it is vital that we maintain a balance between the 'civilized' and the sacred within our lives, our culture and our lands. We must respect the Earth and defend her, for once these sites are gone, they are gone forever.

The Wiccan healer is prepared to voice their concerns for life, to engage in ecological issues in order to safeguard the planet's existence for those generations yet to come and to ensure that the spirit of our Earth does not die because of human ignorance or abuse.

Taking care of all the habitats in our environment also means that at those times when we are seeking solace, healing or guidance, we have already built a relationship to the place we are visiting and so perhaps will be more favoured than a stranger might be. To give you an example, if I came up to you and started telling you some of my fears, you might well back off and consider me strange because you don't know me at all. However, if I were a close friend and spoke along the same lines, you would be happy to listen. The same applies to the sacred. If we get to know it, honour it and live by its standards, when we need its embrace, we will know where to find it.

Chapter Ten
Magical Witchcraft Cures

In this chapter we touch upon some of the healing practices at the heart of Wicca, utilizing the powers inherent in the natural world and the human mind and working with trees, herbs, flowers and minerals in order to create ribbon charms, perform cord magic and make knotting spells. We will also be finding out about the cone of power and the *doppelgänger*, exploring some helpful healing amulets and potions and dipping into the folk medicine of the old wyfes.

It goes without saying that we have a medical profession today, which in past times was not readily available to the ordinary people, and so I advise you that no treatments in this section should take the place of appropriate medical care. Our medical knowledge today precludes the use of a lot of what appears in medical folklore, and we should remember, too, that in olden times ailments included syphilis, consumption, leprosy, diphtheria, scurvy, smallpox and typhoid, to name but a few, while in our modern world general practice is much more likely to treat lifestyle conditions like diabetes, high blood pressure and cholesterol. Medicine must move with the times, but some ways of healing are as relevant today as they were to our ancestors.

The Cone of Power

Probably the most widespread method of Wiccan healing is through the raising of the cone of power. The cone of power can be thought of as a focus of energy that an individual practitioner or member of a coven can pour a share of their own power into, thus building a magical charge. This charge is then released to accomplish its designated task. It is believed that during World War II some New Forest witches raised just such a cone of power to prevent Hitler from succeeding in carrying out Operation Sea Lion, his planned invasion of Britain.

The cone of power requires strong visualization skills and the ability to project the image into the real world so that we 'see' it there. A bell is rung

Chart 12: Colour Correspondences to Use When Raising a Cone of Power
Red: For strength, courage and dynamic energy to deal with heavy conflicts
Orange: For reproductive problems and good health
Yellow: For mental conditions, mental stress and the need for positive change
Green: For balancing body, mind and spirit and for support in all psychic and material problems
Electric blue: The most popular healing colour, blue can be used for all healing rituals, but is most commonly called upon for calming, releasing and healing those with emotional strains, physical needs and a general inability to cope well
Indigo: For those needing to connect to their deeper side, for sleep problems and karmic issues
Ultra-violet: The colour to visualize whenever you are sending a cone of power to someone in pain or during surgery, operations or recovery from open wounds, as it has antiseptic as well as cooling properties
Magenta: For those feeling unloved, unwanted and spiritually wasted; helps to lift the spirits towards a greater peace
Gold: For raising the masculine to its highest potential (solar powers)
Silver: For raising the feminine to its highest potential (lunar powers)
Rainbow: For depression or lacklustre feelings

to signal the start of the visualization. Then a cone-shaped column of psychic energy is visualized rising from the surface of the altar. It should taper to a point just below the ceiling of the room, or if in the open air, it should be approximately 7 feet (2 metres) high. There are various colours that the cone can be, depending upon its purpose. As a general rule blue is most commonly used for healing, but you can refer to Chart 12 in case another colour appears more appropriate.

As the cone of power is raised, the High Priestess of the coven or the solitary individual should ask respectfully out loud for healing energy to be granted in the names of the Goddess and Horned God, or whatever personal names you may know them by (for example Cerridwen and Cernunnos), stating 'if it be for the highest good' to ensure acknowledgement of the best outcome for all concerned.

At the point when the cone reaches its optimum power, a bell is sounded a second time. If everyone in the group knows the person the healing is intended for, the apex of the cone is visualized as extending through space and curving down to enter the top of that person's head, even if they are many miles away and their exact location is unknown. If, however, only one person present in the Circle knows the recipient, they alone visualize this while all the others visualize the apex of the cone as curving down and entering the top of the head of the person who knows the recipient. This person then acts as a kind of 'transmitter' for the raised energy.

In cases where a cone of power is raised by a solitary practitioner, they must either know the recipient or have something of theirs (such as a handwritten letter) in their hand, to act as a link for the transmission of the cone energy.

The *Doppelgänger*

Doppelgänger is a German word meaning 'double'. The principal use of the *doppelgänger* technique is to enable a person to overcome fears, doubts, phobias and inner weaknesses. It is a magical method of strengthening our inner self through resolve, bravery, dignity and calmness in the face of terror, doubt, misgivings, uncertainty or panic. It can also produce very real improvements in certain health problems, both of the mind and body, especially when practised over a period of time.

The method works by creating an exact double of yourself so that you can allow all the things you wish to free yourself from to happen to your *doppelgänger* instead. By using visualization, supported by willpower, you can vividly create, in as much detail as possible, an exact duplicate of yourself standing beside you. Children often have imaginary friends that they see with as much clarity as they see living people. The *doppelgänger* technique is an intensely magnified adult version of this, except that we do not see an imaginary friend but an imaginary self.

A *doppelgänger* does not have 'human' feelings, and so we should not feel guilty about loading our shadows onto them. They have been created by us to fulfil this role and can only work when we use them as an astral double who is willing and able to take on our problems for us.

Creating a Doppelgänger

A *doppelgänger* can be created in any environment or situation, but with your first attempt it is probably best to build your astral double in a quiet and supportive environment.

After ensuring that you will not be disturbed in any way, settle and centre yourself in a comfortable position. Gradually begin to extend your perceptions to visualize an exact double of yourself, clothed and positioned exactly as you are, appearing beside you as an exact mirror image of yourself. Build as strong an image as you can through your willpower and concentration until the double appears as real to you as possible.

Once your *doppelgänger* has been created, pass onto them any negativity you are experiencing.

You can then call upon your *doppelgänger* to appear at any time in the future when you feel the need for them to take on any of your problems, remembering that they will manifest as an exact astral carbon-copy of you as you appear at any given moment.

Simple Candle Healing Rituals

The Fire Element is transformative; which is why candles are so regularly alight during any kind of healing and ritual work. At times when perhaps you can't cast a magical Circle or perform a full ritual, you can light a candle instead. In urgent cases you can use a white candle when other colours are not available.

In candle magic, people sometimes engrave symbols into the wax, such as Runes, symbols or sigils, and dedicate them to the particular type of healing before the candle is lit. If you do this, refer to the charts in this book for appropriate symbols. However, the simplest way to perform candle healing rituals is to anoint an appropriately coloured candle with a fragrant oil or herb that is associated with the result required, and then light it with the healing intention clearly in your mind. Sit in quiet contemplation for about five to ten minutes, focusing upon the person or people receiving the healing thoughts you are transmitting through the transformative qualities of the candle flame.

Candle Anointing

The act of anointing a candle imparts a certain magical flavour to it, and although the burning of candles is a regular feature on Wiccan altars, witches also dress certain candles in oils in order to activate a deeper connection to a single candle's focus. Anointing a candle, therefore, creates a bond between the witch and the candle, which in turn increases the potency of the magic and raises its significance in the cauldron of the subconscious mind.

To begin, decide which is the most appropriate colour to work with and refer to Chart 13 below to find the complementary oils or herbs of that colour. These should embody something representing your hoped-for result.

Pour a few drops of your oil into a bowl. Hold the candle in your left hand if you are right-handed and the right if you are left-handed. Moisten your fingertips and then smooth the oil from the centre towards both ends until the whole candle is oiled.

The anointing process can be enhanced by softly chanting as you dress the candle. This chanting lulls the anointer into a trance-like state. You could repeat words like:

Here I bring the powers of Air
to heal what pains Amanda's ear.

Or:

Candle dressed with oils that soothe
the grief that ails Katrina Booth.

This is a typical use of the rhyming couplet employed in so many Wiccan rituals. Once anointed, you can place the candle on an altar or prepared area and reaffirm its purpose each time you light it. Burn it for as long as you feel necessary. Always observe safety measures when working with flames. Never leave a naked flame unattended.

Magical Spells

Spells and witchcraft are inextricably linked. Although today many people dismiss spells as fantasies, they have been an integral part of a witch's magic for centuries and for very good reason: they work!

The word for a magical spell originates from the same root word we use for 'spelling' with our modern-day alphabets. This is because the symbols or inscriptions used in the spells of old would effectively 'spell' out what was required without there being any need for literacy, which was extremely significant, as many people in the past could not read or write. Travellers and traders would have found these magical inscriptions mysteriously charged with something they could not understand and so spells and other magical inscriptions would have greatly impressed the merchant or peasant passing by.

When the Vikings invaded Britain, they brought their own magical alphabet with them, known as the Runes, which are still used today for protection, prophecy and divination. Consequently, when anyone wished to record a piece of magical instruction, they used writing in letters of an alphabet, thus they *spelled*

Chart 13: Candle Correspondences

Candle colour	Magical uses	Ailment	Anointing oil	Herb
Red	Energy Willpower Protection	Conflict Laziness Lack of self-confidence	Coriander	Bay leaves
Orange	Creativity Success Health	Low energy levels, lethargy	Cinnamon	Marigold
Yellow	Intellect Travel Change Study	Mental stress Fear of change	Lavender	Dill
Green	Harmony Friendship Relationships	Relationship problems Feeling out of balance	Thyme	Vervain
Blue	Healing Family issues	Emotional stress All ailments	Jasmine	Sandalwood
Indigo	Sleep Deep fears Spiritual integration	Insomnia Obstacles, frustrations	Cypress	Parsley
Violet	Spiritual inspiration	Surgery, open wounds Emotional and physical pain	Lavender	Valerian
Pink	Love	Sadness, grief	Rose	Myrtle
Purple	Luck Spiritual empowerment	Change of fortune/fate	Lilac	Oak
Gold	Compassion Success Fathering issues	Male-to-male problems such as those between father, brother and son	Frankincense	Cloves
Silver	Healing Intuition Mothering issues	Female-to-female problems, such as those between sister, mother and daughter	Sandalwood	Coconut
White	Purity, grace	Can be used in place of any coloured candle	Lotus	White roses

the magic, a witch made a *magical spelling* and so a spell was cast! This is why the word *spell* is used to define this type of magic.

Magical spells do work, but until the workings of the mind were explored by Carl Jung, one of the fathers of modern psychology, little was known about its more hidden powers and therefore about how the process might work. Jung named the unharnessed part of our mind, which is unfocused and flitting from one random thought to another, 'the unconscious mind' and the awake or more reasoned part of our thinking 'the conscious mind'. The raw power of magic, to my view, lies in this un/subconscious mind. The occult practitioner aligns their energy, intent and conscious focus using this raw unconscious power source to 'drive' the spell and help it to remain strongly focused upon its set goal. If there is some level of misalignment within the practitioner, emotionally, mentally or energetically, it is highly likely that the spell itself will go slightly awry or be subtly altered and thus has the potential to alter the end result. This is why all magical requests must be treated with the utmost respect and only undertaken with care and awareness. We will get exactly what we have put out for!

For example, when Sandy had some financial problems, she decided to make a money spell and duly referred to a magical book in her home. However, not only was she missing some ingredients, which she randomly replaced with others that she did have, but she was also unaware of the importance of focusing positive energy upon the result and of not allowing any subconscious financial worries to cloud her mind during the ritual. So she spoke of her 'need' for money and this is precisely what she got – the *need* for finances to repair all the electrical equipment that almost immediately started to go wrong! She contacted me and we neutralized the spell, after which everything returned to normal. So, be aware at all times during spell casting!

Journeying to the Underworld

There is a barrier between the subconscious and conscious mind, which is referred to in magic and psychology as the 'endocyclic' barrier. This barrier disappears during sleep, but is present under normal circumstances when we are awake.

There are various ways in which a 'door' can be opened in this barrier. One way, for example, is through hypnosis, in which a sleep-like state is induced. A skilled hypnotist can temporarily suspend the endocyclic barrier, allowing both sleep and wakefulness at the same time. Another way to suspend the barrier is by inducing a trance-like state. The whirling dervishes of North Africa, for example, perform a ritual spinning dance to produce such a state. Fasting is another way of altering the mind's perceptions and opening the door to the subconscious.

To connect symbolically with your subconscious, you can also link your activities to the underworld. The *underworld* is a term used to describe a mythical place that can lead us into our subconscious. Journeying to the underworld, through rituals and offerings, can develop your connection to your subconscious realms.

The underworld is also a place of shadows, fears and unformed realities waiting to be claimed, and as such is a rich and pregnant cauldron of potential. This is the same cauldron where our spells' powers are simmered, formed and powered.

Gateways to the subconscious in the natural world include hawthorn trees, wells, bogs, lakes, monoliths and stone circles, and faery mounds. All these are places where appeals to the underworld can be physically and symbolically made.

Here are few ways in which you can journey to the underworld to experience the power and potential of your own subconscious mind:

Make nature spirit doorways out of leaves and twigs and lean them against magical trees you find or put them in other places you feel drawn to.

Consider which underworld archetype/s you feel drawn to and find out all about their associations (herbs, trees, flowers, etc).

Create an altar to an underworld archetype and develop a close bond with them. If you like, write your own shamanic journey to take yourself to meet them. Accompany your journey with a slow rhythmical drumbeat if you wish, or ask a friend to drum for you.

> Find your own hawthorn tree locally and connect to the Queen of Elphame
> (Faery Queen of the underworld). Dress the tree with ribbons for magical
> wishes and appeals.
> Research local wells and bond with the lady of the waters there.
> Research underworld myths such as the story of Persephone and Demeter and
> seek their real meaning.
> Make a percussion instrument such as a rattle, drum or cistrum that is used only
> to summon underworld attention'

Twilight is a powerful doorway to the underworld in our daily spectrum, the direction being towards the setting sun, so spells and appeals made at this time of day will also link to the underworld.

Another way of accessing the underworld is through chanting. Many of the world's tribal societies produce trance state or a semi-trance state through repetitive chanting, often for days and days. This is done by Australian, African, Asian, American and European tribespeople, so is probably the most common method.

When we consider chanting, we are approaching a magical spell. Chanting focuses the mind and wears down the endocyclic barrier by continual repetition. It focuses *part* of the mind, the part that contains the message or thought of the chant. A spell is not a chant, but it works along very similar lines. If the message is repeated often enough and with sufficient depth of meaning, it produces echoes deep within the unconscious mind. These echoes are magnified by our natural psychic energy, which is released in a burst as a result. But now it is not a random burst that might produce any kind of unexpected and unwanted effect; now it is a *shaped* and *moulded* burst of power that fits the wording of the spell like a piece of a jigsaw puzzle.

A spell needs to be worded in a short, simple and easy-to-understand way so that it will be 'sharp' enough to bore down through the endocyclic barrier deep into the subconscious mind. It is useless to devise a spell like: 'May great-uncle Frederick Smith's extrasystole condition develop in such a manner that it gives him less concern and physical discomfort.' This is not an effective spell.

Reworded and simplified, it could say: 'May Fred's heart palpitations calm.' But even this is really too long and the even simpler phrase: 'Heart's ease for Fred!' is better still. This is a good spell, and if repeated for a time during a magical ritual, or even without a ritual but merely within a mystical atmosphere, it will produce a corresponding release of psychic energy shaped to the same desire, and so a result is likely to occur.

Casting a Healing Spell

The best kind of short spell is a rhyming couplet, which is a simple and straightforward two-line summing-up of the requirement, with rhyming words at the end of each line. The reason why this is better than a single line is because a short poem is 'absorbed' more readily and more deeply by the subconscious mind. One line is a statement; two short rhyming lines act like a symbol and the subconscious mind reacts to symbols, not to logic.

A good example would be:

> The ruby ring I lost today,
> Returns to me without delay.

A rhyme that states your desired wish in the present tense, as this one does, is again more easily absorbed by the subconscious mind.

Another example would be:

> My toe is free of all its pain.
> A sprightly step is mine again.

All it takes in order to come up with a rhyming couplet for your own spells is a little thought and imagination. Anyone can do it, and you do not have to be in any sense a skilful poet.

When performing any kind of spell work, remember that whatever you ask for will be answered in some way, shape or form. If you call for health, there may well be a healing journey to undertake. If you are seeking prosperity, then all areas of your life where abundance is an issue will become highlighted, for in all spell work we must energetically rise to meet our request if we are to change the fabric of our reality to any great degree. Weaving any kind of magic will demand that we come into closer alignment with whatever we seek. This is why experienced spell weavers are always very careful what they ask for – they know what any request may entail!

Cord Magic

There are two principal uses for cords in Wicca. First, they may be worn around the waist to indicate the individual's particular degree of attainment within the Craft, and second, they are used for working cord magic.

Cord magic is one of the simplest forms of spell casting and yet it is extremely powerful. Like most of the magical techniques described in this book, it can be applied to just about any purpose, but here the focus is upon healing. For actual cord spells, each witch works as an individual and this is therefore a useful method for solitary Wiccans.

Casting Cord Spells

To cast a cord spell, a coloured cord is required. For healing, pale blue is the most usual, although if healing is required for mental stress, worry or psychological problems, yellow is most appropriate. The most usual length for this kind of cord magic is 6 feet (1.8 m), although some witches prefer to work with 9-feet (2.7-m) lengths.

A spell chant is composed that briefly and succinctly states the purpose of the spell, remembering always that in all works of magic, whatever the method used, the phrasing should be in the present tense as though the desired result had already happened, not in the future tense as for normal requests. So, for example, it should be 'John *is* healed', not 'John *will be* healed.'

As the chant is spoken, the cord is knotted one knot at a time along its length. This serves to magically 'tie' the words of the spell into the cord. It is most usually done six times, producing six knots, with a seventh knot binding the two ends together.

There are different variations on this basic technique. For example, each repetition of the spell might have its own specific knot, or else the cord may simply be knotted with no direct relationship to the number of repeats of the chant. This is a matter of individual preference.

After the knotted cord has been fashioned, it should be kept in a special and secure place, usually the place where magical equipment is stored when not in use. It is a nice idea to have a special cord bag or pouch, perhaps with an embroidered magical design on it, for keeping the cord safe.

One almost universally recognized custom is to untie the cord again when the desired result has been achieved. It can then be reconsecrated (magically cleansed) to be used again whenever needed.

Consecrating Tools and Equipment

To consecrate your cord (or any other magical equipment), lay it out upon your altar and once your Circle is cast pass the four Elemental tools three times over it, beginning with the athame.

Pick the athame up and face the East, saying as you do so, *'Witness, ye Guardians of the East, the cleansing and consecration of this cord with the powers of Air.'*

Put the athame down and take up the wand, turning South. Pass it over three times and say, *'Witness, ye Guardians of the South, the cleansing and consecration of this cord with the powers of Fire.'*

Continue in this way with the chalice and finally with the pentagram.

Hold out the item to the altar and say in a commanding voice: *'Mighty Ones, bear witness that this is now duly cleansed and blessed by your sacred powers. So mote it be!'*

A variation on cord magic is to tie the cord around a tree while chanting a healing spell and leave it in place until the result has occurred. The table of trees and their magical properties *(see page 138)* can be used to select the most appropriate one for the purpose, but if you are limited by your environment at all, willow or oak can be used for general health and healing purposes.

Another variation of the basic method that is more generally used within covens rather than when the healing is for those not initiated into the Craft is to gently and loosely tie the cord about the person who needs the healing, either around the affected part of the body or simply around their waist. They keep the cord in place until they go to bed, when they should carefully remove it and keep it safe until the magic has worked. This variation can obviously only be done when the person requiring the healing is present at the ceremony and consequently is generally confined to fellow witches or friends who have associations with the Craft.

Binding Spells

Cord magic can also be utilized for what are called binding spells. A binding spell is not a physical restraint, nor does it mean that witches interfere by stopping the free will of another. In Wicca, witches are not allowed to send or intend harm to any life form, but they do have every right to protect themselves from harm sent to them by others. When this happens, it is often a binding spell that is put in place to bar the effects of the negative thoughts, words or deeds. Again, these spells are very simple to perform.

The most important factor in any binding spell is to keep your own magic pure. No matter how dark or nasty the energy being directed at you, you do not send back anything negative to the perpetrator at all, be it anger, malice, revenge, jealousy or any other unpleasant emotion. Whilst performing a binding spell, your thoughts are simply upon blocking the harm directed at you, and that is all. In effect, it implies a 'rising above' the negativity. To my view, binding spells should only really be used when other courses of action such as communication, mediation and reconciliation have failed.

How to Work Binding Spells

I have included two different types of binding spell here, one that works with cord magic and one that works with the powers of the natural world.

A Cord Binding Spell

For the cord binding spell you will need to obtain a length of red cord either 6 feet (1.8-m) or 9 feet (2.7-m) in length and consecrate it in a magical Circle to dedicate it to the highest good of all. Once this has been performed, you can use the cord for a binding.

Anytime between the new and the full moon and preferably during the witching hour (midnight to 1 a.m.), cast a Circle. Light a red candle and dedicate your activities to a protective deity of the Fire Element. You can burn a protective incense associated with Fire if you like as well, such as frankincense.

If you know who the instigator of the harm towards you is, focus your mind until you have a very clear image of them. If you are uncertain who is sending you harm, focus upon something that can represent the harm, such as a spear, arrow or sword rising before you. Hold your cord and dedicate it to healing the present situation by saying a few words such as: *'Behold this cord before you now, to bind this harm and heal the row.'*

Begin from the right and move along the cord to the left, tying knots into it at intervals, either thinking of the perpetrator or the symbolic image as you do so. You can repeat a chant such as: *'Duly bind this harm from me, for highest good, so mote it be!'*

Continue along the cord making as many knots as you wish. Thirteen is a good number, because it is associated with endings and transformation, which is what you seek — the ending of one situation and the birth of another, more positive one.

When you are done, give thanks to the protective forces you have invoked, blow out the candle and declare your ritual closed.

Once the knots are in place, take your cord to an out-of-the-way place to store it and then completely forget about it.

When the desired result has been achieved, undo the knots in reverse order and cleanse your cord, reconsecrate it and put it back in your store cupboard ready for use when another spell of cord magic is required.

Binding with Nature

As well as using cord magic for bindings, it is possible to work directly with the powers of nature, especially as you become more confident in magical correspondences and in making wise connections. One such connection I made personally was with bluebells. Many years ago bluebell roots used to be an ingredient in glue, because they contain a sticky glue-like substance. Knowing this, if we wanted to do a nature-based binding spell on someone we believed was trying to harm us in some way, we could work with the bluebell devas to bury our spell in a bluebell wood, on the empathic understanding that the glue in the roots would sympathetically help to 'hold' the binding in place and cement the negativity in the roots rather than around us.

Agreement should first be reached with the spirits in the bluebell wood and with the devas of the flowers themselves. They will not agree unless they are happy to do so. Agreement may come as rustling leaves, the arrival of a bird, a birdcall, seeds or berries dropping out of the trees, or even the appearance of a misty shape around you. It can also come in the form of 'feeling right to proceed' or 'not feeling right to proceed'. At all times listen to your inner voice, your 'feeling', and then everything will fall into its rightful place.

A Bluebell Binding Spell

Ingredients

> 1 bluebell leaf
>
> twine made from the stalk of a bramble
>
> a gardening glove

At the time of the waning moon, go to a bluebell wood and make yourself known to the flower devas there simply by saying hello and letting them know you have come for their assistance. Leave them a little organic gift of some kind.

Wearing a gardening glove, gather a length of bramble (carefully, to avoid the prickles). Bramble has thorns and all thorny plants are protective.

Pluck a bluebell leaf respectfully and write the name of the perpetrator of the harm very lightly upon it with your right forefinger (or left, if you are left-handed).

Fold up the leaf and bind it all over with the bramble, saying as you do so, *'I bind the harm that comes to me. No harm pass this, so mote it be!'*

Carefully bury your bundle *at the edge of* the bluebell carpet, being careful not to disturb root systems or flowering plants.

Thank the devas for their assistance.

Walk away and do not look back.

Runic Charms

Runes are part of the northern European magical tradition said to have been brought to our world, Middle Earth, by Odin's sacrificial 'hanging' from Yggdrasil, the World Tree, for nine nights before receiving the Runes and their meanings. They have been used in magic for thousands of years and, like the Ogham alphabet of the Druids, have been carved into wands and staffs and used in charms, amulets and magical spells of all kinds. Having such a strong historical lineage, they too carry a strength and clarity that can be invoked for protection or healing.

Runes have intimate connections to the Norns, the northern European weavers of fate and destiny, and so make excellent guides when we are feeling off course or hindered by circumstances in some way. Carrying an appropriate Rune at those times can help the subconscious mind to clarify or identify what needs to be considered or acknowledged. A reading with the Runes can throw light upon any situation where shadows are falling and causing pain or confusion.

Chart 14: The Runes

Letter	Rune	Sign	Meaning
A	Ansuz	ᛪ	Messages
B	Berkana	ᛒ	New beginnings
C	Kenaz	<	Illumination
D	Dagaz	ᛞ	Transformation
E	Ehwaz	M	Progress
F	Fehu	ᛕ	Spiritual richness
G	Gebo	X	Partnerships
H	Hagalaz	H	A challenge
I	Isa	I	Inaction
J	Jera	ᛟ	Gradual success
K	Kenaz	<	Illumination
L	Laguz	ᚱ	Emotional harmony
M	Mannaz	ᛗ	Destiny
N	Naupiz	ᛏ	Delay
O	Opila	ᛜ	Separation
P	Perth	ᛁ	Choice
Q	Kenaz	<	Illumination
R	Raido	R	Reunion
S	Sowelu	ᛋ	Good fortune
T	Teiwaz	↑	Conquest
U	Uruz	ᚾ	Strength
V	Uruz/Wunjo	ᚾ or ᛕ	Strength or alignment
W	Wunjo	ᛈ	Alignment
X	Kenaz/Sowelu	< ᛋ	Illumination and good fortune
Y	Jera	ᛋ	Gradual success
Z	Algiz	ᛉ	Protection

Making a Runic Charm

To make up your symbolic charm using the Runes, you will need to consider the meanings behind each Rune and choose the one/s that bring you most closely to what you seek.

Having made your choice, you can put your Runic letters together to form a pictorial shape such as the example shown below, using the Algiz Rune, which is used for protection. By creating a shield-like pattern with this Rune, you will also psychically be calling in a radiating protective force around you.

The Algiz Rune

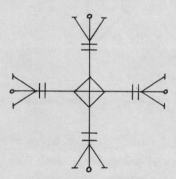

A Runic shield using the Algiz Rune

To take another example, a Runic charm for, say, emotional harmony in your relationships can be formed by combining the Laguz (emotional harmony) and the Gebo (relationships) Runes together. You can embellish your design with curves, lines and other artwork as long as it clearly maintains the original shapes of the Rune/s you are using within it.

Alternatively, you can display or carry a chosen Rune for the duration of your need in order to draw upon its qualities.

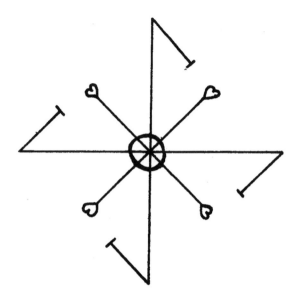

A Runic charm for harmony in relationships using the Laguz and Gebo Runes

Another regular use for the Runes is as a magical alphabet. Here the magical practitioner translates letters of our modern alphabet into their Runic equivalents, thus concealing letters and words that could be recognized by the conscious mind and by other people. This adds to the magical qualities of any spell or charm by providing a little mystery, as well as appealing to the symbolic nature of the subconscious mind.

Healing Amulets

An amulet is something that contains certain powers which we can call upon when we are seeking those particular attributes within our lives. The word *amulet* originates from the Latin word *amuletum*, which broadly speaking means an object that is believed by its owner to protect them from harm.

There are two types of amulet: man-made and natural. A natural amulet can be anything from the natural world that is associated with certain qualities, for example, rowan wood, ammonites, shark's teeth and garlic. Garlic is a well-known protector and cleanser which has been used for thousands of years to ward off 'evil'. Its pungency and potency are already present within it, and so in making an amulet of a clove of garlic, we are in effect 'expecting' that piece of garlic to protect us or cleanse us with its inbuilt powers. Sharks are fearsome and dominant predators, ammonites were believed in ancient days to be fossilized serpents and the rowan tree has long been associated with psychic protection.

All natural amulets have some association with inbuilt powers or abilities that are not just protective. An amulet can in effect be charged with any requirement such as healing, success, luck and virility, but it works because of our belief in its ability to protect us from difficulty in particular areas of our lives.

A man-made amulet is something that has been charged with supernatural powers of some kind to bring protection or particular qualities into being. Throughout the ages, man-made amulets were crafted in Sumeria, Egypt, Greece and Rome, where beliefs in deity, magic and the supernatural were part of daily life and religious practice. Some of the most famous amulets from these times are known as Devil Traps – inscriptions made up of magical alphabets designed to draw demons into them and thus protect a home or person from harm. Other man-made amulets include the six-pointed star, the eye of Horus and the infamous 'abracadabra'. Although adopted today by children's entertainers, in Roman times this was a charm used against fevers.

Some magical experts say that amulets are nothing more than comforters, with no powers apart from the beliefs placed upon them by the human mind. Others believe that certain objects do possess magical powers and that humans have managed over the years to tap into this resource very effectively. Whatever the truth may be, amulets are still very popular.

Chart 15 lists natural healing amulets that can be carried in a pocket or pouch, or worn and displayed as symbolic charms. There are literally hundreds of natural healing amulets and so if you are interested in this form of magic, it would be advisable to obtain books that concentrate specifically upon the subject for a more comprehensive list. Outlined below are simply a handful of amulets that you can use in your daily life to bring health, happiness and good fortune.

Chart 15: The Attributes of Amulets		
Amulet	*Healing ability*	*Use*
Acorn	Fertility	Make an acorn necklace by stringing them together on green thread
Amber	Chest infections	Wear close to the chest
Dragon	Longevity, happiness and love	Wear as a charm
Eucalpytus	Bronchial complaints	5 drops of oil in ½ pt (285ml) boiled water. Inhale the steam
Garlic	Protection and cleansing	Pocket or pouch
Horseshoe	Strength and protection	Display in home
Jet	Nightmares	Place under the pillow
Lavender	Headaches	Rub fresh leaves/flowers on the forehead. Inhale the fragrant oil.
Owl	Psychic protection	Display in home
Rosemary	To improve memory	Sprigs in pocket
Rue	For grief	Sprigs in pocket
Carnelian	Weariness	Wear as a piece of jewellery, or carry a piece in pocket or pouch
Haematite	Grounding	As above
Jade	Harmony and calm	As above
Moonstone	Emotional balance	As above
Peridot	Fearfulness	As above
Rose quartz	Wounds of the heart	As above
Ruby	Happy relationships	As above
Seashells	Safe travel over water, sea sickness	Carry when travelling
Sodalite	Insomnia	Place under pillow
Scarab	Protection	Carry or wear as a charm
Ankh	Long life and fertility	Wear as a necklace
Pentagram	Protection and knowledge	Wear as a necklace or as signs over doors
Eye of Horus	To see the truth	Display or wear as a charm

Charms

A charm is one of the terms used to describe a man-made amulet. It can be made of clay, metal, paper, ribbon or any other material. In times past, it would have been most likely a piece of clothing or part of a bandage that was tied onto a tree or beside a well. I have expanded upon this original concept and created a ribbon charm.

A Ribbon Charm

A ribbon charm is a simple and easy way to make a healing amulet for a specific purpose, which can then be hung from a tree, a window frame or in fact anywhere where it can blow in the breeze. The movement carries the wish.

Charms of all kinds are usually written in magical alphabets in order to keep them hidden from worldly view and to preserve the magic that has been placed into them. The reason for using magical alphabets is because all magic works at a subconscious or hidden level within the mind and the subconscious mind does not work in a linear way, but through a language of pictures, feelings and symbols. This can be demonstrated in how we experience dreams. Dreams rise from the subconscious and are often highly symbolic in the way they are presented to us. The most potent force within a dream is not the imagery but the way it makes us feel. It is clear from this that our subconscious understands symbols and not words from everyday alphabets, and so to create an effect at this primal level we must work with those things that can touch our inner world.

The simplest magical alphabet to use is the Theban or witches' alphabet *(see overleaf)*, because it most closely resembles the letters found in our own alphabet.

A Lunar Ribbon Charm

The following healing charm has been created utilizing the powers of the Moon, so can be made when you or someone that you know has need of emotional support, emotional healing or help with sleeping, or is dealing with problems within the family. The best time for activating this charm is at the full moon, especially if that moon is travelling through one of the Zodiac's Water signs.

Ingredients

3 feet (1 m) of pale blue decorative paper ribbon

1 pen with silver ink

paper

scissors

First of all, you need to work out what it is that you wish to write upon your charm and to make it as concise and clear as possible. For example, if you are seeking help with a family problem where two people are arguing most of the time and thus causing stress levels to be high in the home, you could write words that emulate the environment you would like to invoke, such as: 'Peace in my home, peace in my family.' In cases of sleep problems, you could write: 'I sleep with ease, both calm and deep.' These are just two examples of working with words that invoke the healing powers of the Moon.

Once you have decided upon the wording, you need to transcribe each letter into the Theban alphabet. It is recommended that you work it out first on a piece of plain paper before you transfer it to the ribbon.

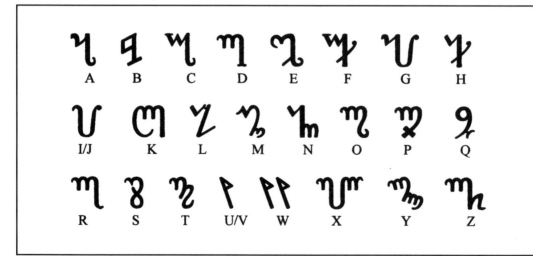

The Theban Alphabet, also known as the Witches' Alphabet

Having completed this, you then either write your Theban letters in silver ink upon the whole length of the ribbon, repeating the phrase from one end to the other, or write it along part of the ribbon, adding any patterns or symbols that will enhance your intent if you so wish. Some things that come to mind for emotional harmony are otters, dolphins, crescent moons, rainbows, lilies and pansies, because all of these are either related to the Water Element (emotions) or to soothing the heart. (Here is another example as to why learning about correspondences is so helpful!)

Hang your charm from a tree near your home where the Moon can shine upon it.

Once your charm is no longer required, bury the ribbon with thanks.

A Confidence Charm

Confidence comes with belief in the self, and so the Fire Element can be called upon in the making of a confidence charm because of its links with courage and energy. To make a confidence charm, therefore, we need first to find out about all the herbs, flora, fauna and minerals that reflect and complement this Element. This is the time to refer to books of correspondences such as Scott Cunningham's *Magical Herbalism* or *The Magician's Companion* by Bill Whitcomb.

To make the following charm for confidence, we shall be working with the lioness-headed goddess Sekhmet, the colour orange (the colour of the Sun, a Fire Element star) and the colour blue, for two reasons: to soothe and calm emotions and unhelpful emotional responses, and because blue is the complementary colour to orange (its flashing colour). I have also decided to use some herbs of Fire that can work together to build selfhood, confidence and courage. The herbs I have chosen are bergamot for strength, bay leaves for protection and healing, and frankincense for harmony, spiritual evolution and wisdom.

Ingredients

1 orange and 1 blue candle

orange thread

blue thread

a lioness charm or Sun charm

silver beads (with reflective surfaces to represent mirrors)

5 drops of bergamot essential oil

3 drops of frankincense essential oil

3 bay leaves

On the night of a full moon, preferably when the Moon is in a Fire sign, take your chosen ingredients to your altar space and lay them out. Light your two candles and dedicate your ingredients to the powers of confidence, courage and stability by holding them in your hands and stating your intention simply with a few words such as:

Here do I bring herbs and oils to build confidence and courage in [state name]. May all I perform be for the highest good of [state name] and by divine will may confidence and courage be woven here this night.

Take your threads and plait them together, adding silver beads and your charm wherever you feel is the right place, all the time thinking about bringing confidence and courage to the intended recipient.

Once this is completed, knot the ends together and anoint the whole amulet with the oils.

To complete the amulet, bind threads around the bay stalks and attach them to the amulet as well, going round and saying as you do so:

Thrice round is bound the bay
To chase self-doubt away.

Then say:

Lady Sekhmet, you of flame and light, fill this charm with your courage and strength. This I ask for the highest good of all and harming none. Thrice round I bind the bay to manifest your confidence and courage within this charm.

Lady of Brightness, fill this charm with your guiding light. This I ask for the highest good of all and harming none.

So mote it be.

Hold the charm in your hands quietly for a few moments and then lay it on your altar.

To close the activation and blessing, simply state:

This ritual is now completed. I give thanks to my Lady Sekhmet and bid you hail and farewell.

I give thanks to the Elements and to the spirit of the lioness for assisting me and say hail and farewell.

I give thanks to the Goddess and to the Horned God for their blessings and say hail and farewell.

Blow out your candles and say for the last time, 'Hail and farewell.'
Your confidence charm is now ready to be used.

You should now begin to see how a witch weaves their magic. The possibilities are literally endless when it comes to ways of bringing the magic to life. The important points are belief in the power of what you are doing, appropriate focus and concentration, and the use of correct and helpful correspondences for the type of magic or healing required in order to help you focus your intent correctly. Lists of herbs and other correspondences were originally compiled very much from people's own perspective and experience and in time you will be able to do this yourself when making up your own magical formulae. One way of using these correspondences is in potions.

Potions

In days of old, potions would have been concocted from herbs, aromatics, tree bark, resins and anything else from local surroundings that supported a particular cultural belief. But today species are declining rapidly and what was commonly available 500 years ago will for the most part have given way to other things as cultures have changed their farming methods and land management techniques. These changes have altered our countryside quite dramatically, and so potion recipes also have to adapt and evolve.

Fortunately, flower and crystal essences are now readily available for us to add to our recipes, which means we do not have to collect plants from the wild and thus inadvertently perhaps add further to the decline of species, because essence producers work specifically to conserve the planet. We can therefore work with essences, confident that we are still working in harmony with the Earth.

Essences work on the subtle anatomy very much like homeopathic medicine, which means that when investigated scientifically it appears that nothing is present in the medicine. Again like homeopathic medicine, essences can be very effective in treating all kinds of physical, emotional, mental or spiritual problems, gently easing symptoms, because overall they are subtler on every level than more conventional treatments.

Flower essences were first established by Dr Edward Bach in the 1930s, and today a myriad of essences are produced world-wide from a wide variety of sources. The flower essences in the potion recipes in Chart 16 can be sourced from International Flower Essence Repertoire (IFER), a flower essence supplier: *flower@atlas.co.uk*. Flower essences can be used quite safely on children, animals and adults. Essence potions for animals can be found in Chapter Thirteen.

Making your Own Potions

Chart 16 gives some modern-day potions utilizing flower essences that can be made up quickly and easily whenever the need arises. All you will need is a glass, spring water and the essences themselves.

Taking mental stress as an example, you would fill a glass three-quarters full with fresh spring water and to that add 7 drops of white chestnut, 7 drops of sweet pea and 7 drops of yarrow. Stir your potion gently and sip consciously. By 'consciously' I mean contemplating the effects you wish the potion to achieve, which in this instance would be mental peace.

You will notice that each potion comes with a suggested gemstone, which can help to balance particular symptoms. You can either adorn yourself with the gemstone by wearing items of jewellery containing it or you can carry a piece of it in a pouch or pocket.

You can also make up a gemstone potion by simply placing a clean stone of your choice in a glass and adding spring water. Cover and leave the mix to stand for three hours, remove the crystal and sip the energized water. Cleanse any crystal that you have used to make a potion by rinsing it in spring water or burying it in some fresh clean earth for a few hours.

You can utilize all three options together if you like, but remove the crystals from your energy field once the desired result has been achieved.

Do not substitute oils or herbs for essences, as they are not the same. And to avoid possible contra-indications, do not take these potions if you are pregnant, on homeopathic or other medication.

Chart 16: Healing Potions		
Healing ability	*Gemstone*	*Flower essence*
Children's Calming Mix	Carnelian	Lavender (Harebell), Chamomile (Deva), Daisy (Findhorn)
Emotional Harmony	Rose Quartz	Crab Apple (Bach), Zinnia (FES), Lotus (Himalayan Aditi)
Fertility Potion	Pearl	She Oak (Bush Flower), Fig (Masters), Lady's Mantle (Harebell)
Immune Booster	Green Tourmaline	Echinacea (Petite Fleur), Königin van Dänemark (FES), Celery (Perelandra)
Menstrual Cramps	Moon Dew, Moonstone	Evening Primrose (FES), Commelina (Indian Tree), Sandalwood essential oil rubbed into the area.
Mental Stress	Amethyst	White Chestnut (Bach), Sweet Pea (Harebell), Yarrow (Harebell)
Peaceful Sleep	Jade	Lettuce (Masters), Valerian (Korte), Ylang Ylang (FES)

The Witch's Healing Garden

Apart from gathering plants from the hedgerows, a witch would have gathered culinary herbs, herbs for health and healing, plants for magical rituals, flowers, vegetables, bushes and shrubs, all to be eaten or for their magical qualities. In earlier times the land was a very practical place, with everything used in some way, not quite like today. To a witch, the 'garden' provided an oasis of crops for medicinal, remedial and culinary use.

Traditionally, plants and trees were strategically placed. Holly or bay laurel by the front door would deflect both emotional and environmental storms and lightning. Red geraniums around entrances would absorb negativity. Honeysuckle around the gate would bind any harm that might try to enter, and rowan trees would act as protectors. Roses were planted around the front door to bring love to the occupants, and peony root was dried and made ready to break enchantments. Pots of herbs and spices for both culinary and medicinal use were always close by, even if all that was available was a window box. And so the witch's garden would have grown, with plants and herbs that had meaning and relevance to each witch's particular skills and abilities.

There are so many species to choose from that no witch would have known everything there is to know about healing plants. Witches would have simply worked with what felt familiar, comfortable and in harmony with their work. The same applies to you if you wish to grow a Wiccan healing garden: choose the plants that you feel drawn to or that apply to your personality or talents. Take time, too, to get to know the flora and fauna around you. Keep a journal and take walks with identification manuals – it is truly amazing what you may find.

A witch's garden will always have a place for animals, birds and insects, and will try to work with rather than against natural laws. The garden, too, will relate to its owner by bringing vegetation and herbs into the area via the birds and the Elementals. Since moving to my cottage four years ago, I have been gifted with a flowering currant, mullein, herb Robert, teasels, raspberries, love-in-a-mist, spotted medic, cleavers, poppies and speedwell. Every year, I check to see what might have been brought to me to find and work with, which provides me with a very symbiotic relationship with my garden. It is a great joy to discover another healing herb that life has brought to my door and which I may well have otherwise overlooked in the fields and meadows around me.

Another important factor in the witch's healing garden involves 'listening'. The witch will commune with nature, with the Elementals in the garden, and will try to heed the garden's wishes as to which plant will thrive where or which plants to bring into a particular area, and so on.

Communicating at this intimate level also makes sense of the tradition to plant four seeds for every one you wish to grow. The saying goes: 'One for the rook, one for the crow, one to die and one to grow.' If we follow this tradition, it becomes clear that we should not expect to take everything from nature, we should also give back to her by feeding the birds and animals and insect life that pollinate the vegetation and thus bring in a healthy harvest.

The witch is wise enough to share the garden with nature and finds natural solutions wherever possible to any problems that may be encountered. In serious cases of slugs, for example, witches are more likely to adopt a pair of slug-loving hedgehogs from a local wild animal rescue centre than to put down slug pellets which carry poisons.

Healing Plants

Each witch will have their favourite herbs and plants, although there are some that seem to appeal universally. These include vervain, yarrow, mugwort, ivy, mullein and myrtle, to name but a few. It is with this in mind that I have included here a posy of plants that I work with for healing and related issues.

It is as well to bear in mind, however, that some folk medicine is not so effective, or indeed advisable. One traditional treatment for the ague (feverish sweating and shaking) was to swallow a spider wrapped in a raisin! Wounds were sometimes bound with spider's webs, which often caused tetanus and infection, and a soup made of nine frogs was a mediaeval cure for throat infections. We can see from any selection of folk cures that some are ethical and safe and some are definitely not.

Here I have chosen a selection of familiar ingredients that are either well-proven specifics for certain ailments or are still commonly available in most parts of the world. Besides, to me a true witch is the one who can work magic from common and simple things, from ingredients that may even be completely under-valued in modern society. Like the majority of those who practised witchcraft in the past, I do not have the money, time or inclination to search out rare or expensive items when something from the hedgerow will do just as well.

I repeat the caution not to handle herbs, oils or potions if you are pregnant or on medication, and do not take anything internally without first checking its safety for you with a relevant authority.

Anemone (Mars)

Anemones are flowers of the fiery planet Mars, work hard at averting the 'evil eye' and appear in the garden early in the cycle of the year, so are good little plants to cultivate. In the language of flowers their signature is 'Your charms no longer appeal to me', meaning that with their magical assistance we will not be taken in by fantasy or illusion, but will be able to stand in our own strength.

Anemones work well in all healing charms and amulets where protection, vitality and zest are required. You can harvest the flowers and bind them in a red pouch to carry with you as you build in strength and purpose during the spring and to keep weariness at bay.

Basil (Mars)

Basil, considered by most people as a culinary herb, is also a very magical one. It provides strength and protection and promotes honesty and high spirits.

When feeling nervous or intimidated, chew one or two leaves, or make an herbal tea from seven leaves to ease nervousness and regain confidence in yourself or a situation. Basil is also helpful in decision-making and so can be utilized in spells and rituals where a choice must be made.

Fern (Sun)

So magical, the humble fern, with many tried and tested uses throughout the ages, yet so little thought of today! In mythology, fern seeds gathered on Midsummer's Eve would bring prosperity and invisibility to the wearer, but beware, for the fern is a powerful purgative and was used by old wives to treat cases of intestinal worms. The spores are, therefore, to be treated as toxic and gathering them is not advised!

Traditionally, it was believed that one or two little fern leaves put into the left shoe of a wayward partner would ensure their fidelity and faithfulness. The leaves of the male fern are shielding and cast into a fire will swathe the area with protective smoke (that also keeps midges away, by the way).

In the past, maidenhair ferns were used as a hair tonic. Fresh young leaves and stalks would be steeped in boiled water for a few hours and the liquid was then poured through the hair to discourage hair loss.

Fresh young leaves from the adder's tongue fern were gathered by the ancients and made into a salve for wounds and sores, and handfuls of crisped fern balls were made into what is called a lye cake, which was dissolved in the washing water.

Please never take any fern concoction internally; specimens should only include *young* leaves picked responsibly just for external use. Beware of ticks when walking in ferny areas.

Honeysuckle (Mercury)

Just like the fast-witted planet that governs it, honeysuckle has many and varied uses, from prosperity to bindings, from divination to finding lost objects. The fragrance of the flowers improves the memory and flowers sprinkled into prosperity sachets or over divinatory tools before use will increase their efficacy.

Meadowsweet (Venus)

For love, gentleness, peaceful vibrations and as a strewing herb, meadowsweet is probably unsurpassed. It is rich in salicylates, which are constituents of aspirin, and acts as a digestive soother and balancer. It has been used for hundreds of years as a strewing herb at weddings due to its pleasant fragrance and can be utilized in the same way today by those who are prepared to walk the fields and harvest it.

Also known as 'Queen of the Meadows', meadowsweet can be included in all love rituals, as it stands for the giving and receiving of love.

Mugwort (Venus)

Also known as artemesia, mugwort is named after the Greek Moon goddess Artemis and is considered one of the oldest herbs. In his *English Herbal of Physical Plants* (1694), John Pechey stated that it was a wonderful remedy for all female-related complaints and was 'frequently used by women, inwardly and outwardly'. A traditional saying chides us to eat nettles in March and mugwort in May, then we ladies would not go so quick to the clay (decline in health)!

Mugwort is a specific against fatigue, and travellers who carry a sprig on their journeys are said not to tire or grow weary. It should ideally be picked during the full Moon under a clear sky. In magical terms it has been rubbed onto mirrors and crystal balls to increase perception and can be used in magical charms against theft. Overall, though, it is an herb of love and harmony, especially for women. Do not handle if pregnant.

Mullein (Jupiter)

Mullein is one of the herbs gifted to my garden by the birds three years ago. It is also called hag's tapers. This makes reference to the fact that the flowering stalks can be used unlit in place of candles when performing Wiccan rituals outdoors or in places where fire is not possible.

Good for the lungs and bronchial complaints, mullein is also known as grave-yard dust, and its dried and powdered leaves can be substituted in any recipe where graveyard dust is indicated. When used in this way, it will aid sleep and calm restlessness. It can be included in any charms intended to lay the past to rest.

Myrtle (Venus)

Myrtle, like meadowsweet, is a bridal flower and is often included in wedding bouquets or worn as a wreath at weddings to ensure happiness, harmony and fertility. To grow myrtle either side of the entranceway is to invite love, harmony and fertility into the home. It is a witch's favourite for inclusion in all magic concerning issues of the heart, including relationship sorrows and joys. An infusion of the leaves acts as a strong antiseptic.

Potato (Saturn)

The stalks, leaves and green berries of the potato plant contain the poisonous aspects of the nightshade family of which it is a part, although the tuberous roots that we eat are completely harmless. Because it is a member of the nightshade family, the potato is governed by Saturn, the planet that rules all narcotic and poisonous species, so the most effective day to begin any magical work with the potato would be a Saturday.

Potato is a specific against rheumatism and skin problems, and it was believed that to carry a potato in a pocket relieved rheumatism. As the potato shrivelled and hardened with age, it was thought to absorb the uric acid that caused the joint pains. There is some truth to its efficacy, because it contains atropine, a curative still thought to alleviate rheumatism today.

Cut slices from an organic raw potato and rub them topically onto warts, skin eruptions and lesions twice daily until the skin clears, or alternatively cut and carry a potato in your pocket to ease any aches and pains.

Rosemary (Sun)

Rosemary contains several minerals and vitamins A and C. Since antiquity it has been known as the memory herb, both for remembrance of departed loved ones and for times when mental clarity is required, such as during exams, tests and interviews.

Carry rosemary when grieving or when mentally tested to ensure clear thinking and positive memory recall. It was an ancient custom to give potted rosemary to people who had taken to their bed, to freshen the air in the sickroom. It is said that where rosemary flourishes, the woman is boss!

St John's Wort (Sun)

Wearing a necklet of St John's wort was said to drive out demons and to alleviate depression. In magical terms it was included as part of an incense to release negativity, and strengthen courage and willpower. A tincture of the herb is still prescribed to ease melancholic emotions, and it remains an active constituent in the homeopathic remedy Hypericum, a cream topically applied to bruises and sprains.

Vervain (Venus)

Another witch's favourite is vervain, which was regularly used in divination, spell-weaving, healing and cleansing; wild vervain being preferable to cultivated varieties. Sacred to the ancient Egyptians as 'the tears of Isis' and to the Romans as 'Juno's tears', this herb has much folklore associated with it and is reputed to lift the spirits, protect against and banish negativity, kindle love in the heart and calm the nerves. It is a herb of Venus, the planet of love, and so is often included in love spells. The Anglo-Saxons included it in their Holy Salve recipe against demons because of its ability to banish negativity.

Across Europe it was a pagan custom on Midsummer's Eve, when huge bonfires were lit across the land, for all present to wear crowns of myrtle and vervain and after the celebration to cast their crowns into the fire saying, 'May all my ill luck depart and be burnt up with these.'

You can strew vervain around the corners of any room to encourage positivity and happiness, but keep it away from young children who may be tempted to eat the leaves by putting it into sachets and placing them out of reach.

Violet (Venus)

Violets are soothing flowers that were regularly used for headaches and bronchial complaints by our foremothers, who would make violet syrups to ease those hacking coughs.

A Violet Syrup

Ingredients

3 x 5 oz (150 g) fresh sweet violet leaves and flowers (plants can be purchased from nurseries or florists)
1½ pints (1 litre) of spring water
organic honey

Boil your water and pour it over the herb. Leave to stand in a ceramic container for approximately 12 hours.

Strain and then place the liquid in a saucepan and heat gently.

Add another 5 oz (150 g) of the fresh flowers and leaves.

Leave to cool in the ceramic container for another 12 hours.

Repeat this procedure for a third time and then add honey to the liquid until a syrupy consistency is reached.

Bottle and use whenever those winter coughs are threatening to bite by taking 1 tsp three times a day between meals.

For headaches you can rub the leaves into your temples and also eat Parma violet sweets to freshen the breath or sweeten the heart. Violet leaves are heart-shaped, hence their associations with love, and in springtime violet flowers can be added quite safely to salads. Carrying a posy of violets in your pocket was said to change your fortunes for the better.

Witch Hazel (Venus)

The witch hazel tree was used in olden days for divining rods and also employed as a charm to mend a broken heart.

For swellings and bruises, stings, burns and scalds, apply witch hazel leaves topically to soothe the area, to draw out any foreign bodies and bruising, and to ease pain.

Witch hazel tincture is commonly available from chemists today and is one of the 'must haves' in my medicine chest at home. Perhaps my long-term affection for this tree lies simply in its name!

Yarrow (Venus)

Yarrow is one of the old favourites in the witch's herbal collection and is used in rituals associated with love, fidelity and magical protection at all levels. One of its folk names is 'nosebleed' because it was believed that tickling the nose lining with a yarrow leaf would induce bleeding. In East Anglia this was used as a form of divination. A magical poem would be repeated:

'Yarroway, yarroway, bear a white blow,
if my love loves me, my nose will bleed now.'

If the nose bled, then the love was true. If you want to try this then that is up to you, but I wouldn't recommend it personally!

Other divination uses for yarrow include placing leaves in a muslin sachet beneath your pillow and repeating a magical chant. If you do this, it is said that you will dream of your future partner. A traditional rhyme is:

Thou pretty herb of Venus's tree
Thy true name it is yarrow.
Now who my bosom friend must be
Pray tell thou me tomorrow.

Yarrow is a wonderful herb for menstrual disorders, stomach cramps and skin problems, and can be taken as a tea.

Yarrow Tea

Ingredients

1½ oz (40 g) of fresh leaves
1½ pints (1 litre) of cold spring water

Add the leaves to the spring water in a cooking pan. Bring to the boil and then turn off the heat and leave to cool. Strain the liquid and cover it. Sip one cupful three times a day for three days or until symptoms cease.
To cleanse the skin, instead of drinking the decoction, apply it to the skin three times a day.

Yarrow is also well known as a psychic protector, so carry some with you when you need to find mental courage or security.

We now leave this section on the witch's healing garden and move on to another Wiccan activity, the making of healing poppets.

Healing Poppets

Just about everyone will have heard of the age-old method of cursing by sticking pins into a doll. In magic, such a doll is usually called a poppet. The pin-sticking is the dark side of an ancient technique and has grossly overshadowed the more positive side to the poppet: its uses for healing.

The idea with poppets is that anything done to the doll will then happen to the human being that the doll represents. This kind of psychic activity is part of sympathetic magic, the word *sympathetic* meaning an object or a person that shares some quality with something else.

Many things other than poppets are used to achieve effects through the channel of sympathetic magic. Sarah, a student in one of my courses, came to be strongly haunted by a ghostly presence in her home after a magical object was unearthed in her neighbour's adjoining chimneybreast. In this case it was not a doll poppet but a lady's mediaeval shoe. Shoes were often placed in chimney-breasts to act as spirit traps. It's a strange coincidence that neither Sarah nor her neighbours knew at that time about spirit traps, nor the fact that to disturb them would release the energy allegedly ensnared there, and yet the timing of both happenings corresponded completely. This level of synchronicity supports the fact that sympathetic magic can be very powerful.

The occult theory behind such a spirit trap is that a shoe is both an item very personal to its owner and also a container. In mediaeval times, a shoe would be ritually consecrated by a witch and placed somewhere close by within their home, where it would remain undisturbed forever. A chimneybreast was an ideal spot. Any 'invading' or excess spiritual energy, especially any negative energy sent out against the witch by an enemy, would enter the house down the chimney and land in the shoe, where it would remain harmless if not disturbed. It used to be believed that a chimney was a weak point in a building's psychic defences and any spiritual energy seeking entry could make use of it as a door. Death, in the form of the Grim Reaper, was believed to enter this way, and crows or ravens perched on a chimney were a bad omen, as their presence indicated that Death had entered the property. Today, the main surviving memory of this belief is attached to Father Christmas and the folk tale about the Three Little Pigs, where the wolf tries to enter their property down a chimney.

It was believed that a shoe could trap spiritual energy because it was an item personal to its owner, which is also the basis behind the power of a poppet.

Making a Healing Poppet

To make a healing poppet, a small doll is made out of clay, wood, straw or cloth. It does not need to be very large or look like its human counterpart visually. Then an occult link should be made between the doll and the person it represents. This is usually done by dressing the doll in some item of clothing that is personal to the individual concerned. The item is tied around the poppet and in cases of healing is tied around the portion of the body where the healing is to be focused. Again, it is very important to add that this should never under any circumstances be done unless the person concerned has specifically asked for healing.

Once the poppet has been suitably prepared, it becomes the central feature of a simple ritual designed to strengthen the sympathetic link between the doll and the person whose personal item it wears and to send magical healing power through that link. This particular practice is very old and could be classified as a kind of 'cottage magic', because it was most commonly used by the followers of the old ways in remote country villages and hamlets. These country people could not afford special incense, swords, robes and other magical paraphernalia. In past centuries these items were not only expensive but also very difficult to obtain safely, due to the religious conditions of the time.

Making a Healing Poppet

You will need:

> plain coloured cotton material or muslin cut into a rough doll shape
> needle and thread
> an article of clothing or personal possession from the recipient of the healing
> unbleached cotton wool
> herbs (optional)

Cut and sew your doll pieces together. It does not have to be perfect. You can stuff the poppet with healing herbs associated with the person's particular condition if you feel confident with herbal meanings, otherwise use unbleached cotton wool.

Wrap the body part of the doll that corresponds to the ailment you are working on with the personal item or possession and take the poppet to a table or altar where you can sit comfortably.

Activating a Poppet

Activating a poppet is extremely simple. This does not mean that it is any less effective. By focusing upon a single phrase, the power raised and transmitted via the sympathetic link with the poppet is actually greater than by many more involved rituals.

An invocation through a poppet is actually more like a mantra than a full ritual. The mantra has its origins in the Orient and is a technique which repeats a single thought over and over again, sometimes for hours on end. Its great power has been explained by comparing it to a spinning wheel of thought. If any distractions occur, they are flung off by the spinning mantra. This leaves the mind free to absorb and digest the single idea expressed within the mantra. In the West we have the expression 'single-minded' to define someone who cannot be distracted. The ability to 'switch on' a state of single-mindedness is one of the skills of magic.

A suitable invocation to use with a poppet might be composed as follows:

> Say the intention is to perform healing for a man named John who has a back problem. A poppet will have been made and a personal item added to the afflicted part of its body, in this case the back. The knot can be positioned at the exact spot where the pain is greatest.
>
> The poppet is then carefully laid on a table (or an altar if preferred) and a candle is lit beside it. In this instance, because the trouble is with the back, the poppet would be laid on its front. (If it were laid on its back with a knot tied beneath it, the knot would dig into the back and, with sympathetic magic, might worsen the ache instead of helping to relieve it.)
>
> The healer would then gently stroke the poppet as if it were a sick child and repeat an invocation such as:
>
> This is John Smith whose back gives pain.
> It is now healed and well again!
>
> You can repeat a chant for up to 30 minutes per day, or longer if you wish. The sustained repetition increases the energy raised, cementing a firm bonding between the poppet and the sufferer.

To create a suitable invocation for any kind of ailment requires a little thought and imagination. The most important thing about this particular magical technique is to keep the verse as short and to the point as possible. Do not be tempted to compose lengthy verses or include elaborate descriptions of the ailment. The aim is to focus the mind. Two lines of verse (a rhyming couplet) are best, as more will tend to broaden the focus and weaken it.

We have seen throughout this chapter just how varied and diverse Wiccan healing techniques can be and that there are many choices available to us. Once you have chosen the method you would like to work with, don't allow confusion to come in by stepping too far outside the guidelines. What I mean by this is that if you choose, say, the cone of power; work with that without confusing the activity by introducing any other magical techniques during the same ritual.

Chapter Eleven
Magical Willpower and Visualization

The will and the ability to visualize things clearly in the mind are the two most important factors to develop and master for anyone who wishes to work real magic. Quite literally, everything else connected with magic – the charts, methods, techniques, equipment, rituals, in fact, everything – is there to back up these abilities and to channel them towards the desired result. All of these magical and occult methods are used to support the willpower and visualization of the person performing the magic, for it is the powers of the inner human spirit that make the magic. And it is the developed character that weaves the most powerful magic.

This chapter helps you to develop your inner character, sometimes called your true will or magical will, your visualization skills and concentration, and to expand your mental capacities so that the magic and healing you perform carries potent and well-balanced energy that is both effective and in harmony with requirements.

As a witch develops their powers, which usually runs parallel to their advancement in the three degrees of the Craft, it becomes possible to perform magic and ritual without the use of tools or equipment. This is achieved utilizing the aligned intent and focus that have been developed through perseverance, self-discipline and normally several years of training. To embody real power, one needs to be an effective container for it.

Meditation and the Power of Thought

Magical meditation differs from some more traditional understandings of meditation as found in Zen, Buddhism and Sati, for example, where the focus is upon stilling the mind and detaching from thought processes. To meditate in magical training means 'to think deeply about'. Why, then, it may be asked, is it necessary to employ a word such as *meditation* instead of using simpler words? The answer is that although magical meditation *is* thought, it is *controlled* thought, which is rather different from our normal rather random and undisciplined thought processes. We could also say that magical meditation is *trained* thought.

Human thought is very powerful energy. It has constructed the pyramids; the civilizations of Greece and Rome; the Constitution of the United States of America; the literary classics of Plato, Shakespeare and Dickens; and explored outer space. All of these, and every other human achievement, are the products of *controlled* thought processes.

Another way in which the power of controlled thought can be more fully appreciated is to compare it with light, particularly when considering a laser beam. Light from a normal torch will spread out as it travels forward, so that a lens 2 inches (5 cm) wide will produce a circle over a foot (about half a metre) across on a distant wall. If it were possible to shine a searchlight from the Earth to the Moon, a beam of light that was perhaps 4 feet (just over a metre) across at the start would be, on reaching its destination, larger than the Moon's diameter itself.

A laser, however, produces polarized light. That is a beam where the individual photons of light are all aligned to point in the same direction rather than being scattered. We could say that a laser emits 'disciplined' light. A powerful enough laser on Earth would produce a spot of light on the moon's surface. Over much shorter distances the polarized light of a laser can produce a beam so intense that it can cut through metal.

It would be true to say that the objective of applied meditation is to help create a form of polarized thought, which compares with normal thought as a laser compares with torchlight. The achievement of this focused state of mind and thought is a great step towards the attainment of magical willpower and visualization.

A Meditation Exercise

Clear a time and place where you will not be disturbed for at least half an hour. Sit in a comfortable chair and have a notebook and pen nearby so you can jot down any notes.

Sitting in an upright position, commence what is called the fourfold breath. *Warning: This is not a practice for anyone with heart or breathing problems.*

The fourfold breath is simply a calming technique involving breathing in to a count of four, holding the breath for a count of four, breathing out the same way and counting for four before taking in the next breath, and so on. In order to maintain regularity and correct pace, I always say in my mind, 'One *crystal,* two, *crystal,* three *crystal,*' and so on, in order to set a rhythmic pace throughout the four patterns of breath. You can choose any word that you like to pace your own breathing pattern.

This technique of controlled breathing is a valuable basic occult exercise that normally produces almost immediate results by generating a feeling of well-being, calm and relaxation. Gradually, over a period of a minute or two, you will find that this serves to calm the 'ruffled waters' of the surface of the mind. A period of controlled breathing can be employed on its own at any time in order to relax and calm the nerves, and in itself is a useful therapeutic method for coping with stress.

Once a relaxed state of well-being has been achieved, choose a simple subject as the centre for your meditation. This could be anything you like, such as a word, a name, a person, a book, a place or an event. It could also be an object such as a matchbox, a leaf, a flower, a plate, an ornament, and so on. Whatever the subject, let your thoughts wander upon it. To explore and experience the patterns of these thoughts is magical meditation.

To come out of the meditation, open your eyes on an out-breath, stretch and move slowly.

Do not give up if nothing much appears to happen on the first few occasions when you conduct a meditation exercise. It may, for some people, take three or four attempts before the even flow of focused thoughts can be satisfactorily accomplished. No two people are the same; we are all individuals. However, meditation grows easier with practice, and the controlled breathing exercise that starts off a session will be doing a lot of good both physically and mentally by greatly reducing potential stress.

Scientific studies of human brainwaves have shown that regular meditation has a tendency to unite the different activities and regions of the brain in a state of greater harmony. It is known that the left side of the brain controls the right side of the body and the right side controls the left. The left hemisphere of the brain deals with the more logical and material activities of our lives, while the more romantic and esoteric subjects such as imagination, creativity, art, love, feelings, poetry and religious tendencies are handled by the right hemisphere. Magical meditation helps us to achieve a much more harmonious relationship between these two different regions by enabling us to get beneath the surface of our daily experiences and agitation. This, in turn, will allow more inner abilities to influence any particular activity and help to balance the different aspects of the personality. We can become calmer and better people through the process of regularly applied meditation.

In effect, the practice of meditation enables us to establish deeper connections or circuits between the two hemispheres of the brain in addition to the ones that already exist on the surface of the mind.

The Flowers of Thought

To meditate the magical way is to think, and to think an undivided thought with great presence is to *will*. A thought rising from the will needs three things in order to survive and produce results: 1) direction; 2) a target; 3) nourishment. It is like a flower growing in the garden of our mind. If it can be viewed like this instead of as a distracting event, in time our lives will burst into flower.

For example, taking the saying 'We are what we eat', we can quite easily understand that whatever we eat and digest will be used to provide the bodily 'bricks' from which we are built. A healthy diet will produce strong bones and organs while, conversely, any unhealthy food or poison absorbed into the system will cause damage. The process of thought works in a similar way. If the mind believes sufficiently in something, with no reservations or doubts, then that thought will grow and become reality. All that is necessary is to form as clear an image as possible of the desired aim and to ensure that this image is 'kept flowering' – in other words, not allowing it to fade completely from the mind, even when attending to other matters. This is the nourishment of the thought.

For example, if someone wants to lose weight, they would form a clear picture of themselves *as they wish to look* and keep this mental image in their mind's eye no matter what else they may be doing. Gradually, their physical reality will begin to mould itself in a new direction, providing that the mental image is never allowed to fade and is never dismissed as 'nothing but wishful thinking'. This is the target and direction of the thought.

Visualization Exercises

Visualizing Objects

Arrange a table at which you can sit comfortably and place a small selection of ordinary household objects in front of you, for example, a knife, fork, spoon, a pencil, teacup, a few pieces of loose change or a book. There is no need to have many different things – two or three will suffice, with new items being selected every time the exercise is repeated.

Choose one of the objects and fix your attention upon it for a while. Try to fix its shape and colour firmly in your mind and, if you can manage this, also its surface texture – its particular physical 'feel'.

After concentrating on the item in this way for a couple of minutes, close your eyes and attempt to imagine the same object, its shape, its colour and texture, in your mind's eye.

If this level of detailed imagination seems difficult at first, do not worry and do not give up. Different people have different imagination skills. Regular practice is always better than a single attempt. If the object quickly vanishes from your 'mental screen' or is displaced by some other wandering thought, try to recall it again.

It is important to develop slowly but regularly. Someone who does only one press-up a day starting on a Monday will usually be able to do five or six by the following Monday, providing they stick with it and increase their total by just one per day. What applies to the physical body also applies to the mind – slow and steady progress achieves results.

As you develop this exercise over a period of time, remember that visualizing the 'feel' or texture of the object is also important.

You will have achieved the purpose of this exercise when you have reached the stage where you can hold onto the mental image and the textural feel of an object for several minutes without losing it to distractions or other intruding thoughts. At the same time, almost as a by-product, your willpower will also be developing.

Having achieved regular success, the next step is to aim for success in visualizing the object with open eyes. The image should be pictured as hanging suspended in the air before your gaze and it should appear solid and tangible.

Visualizing Emotions

A further great step in the process of developing creative visualization and willpower is something that forms a vital part of working magic at the higher degrees: doing the same kind of visualization, but with *emotions*, not solid objects. This is actually the technique used in what is called 'method acting'. If an actor in a film has to shed tears because the character they are portraying is sad, they are able to switch on the emotion of sadness in order to produce real tears and – equally importantly – to switch it off again afterwards so that they do not get emotionally disturbed in their own being. For a method actor, it is a tool of the trade, and for a magician or Wiccan it is much the same.

During a ritual, it can sometimes be important to switch on an emotion. This is especially useful when activating a thought form, which is what Wiccans are actually doing when, in the Circle, they send out energy for a specific purpose to a particular person. For Wiccan healing in particular, the emotion is likely to be a feeling of well-being, love or joy. Everyone taking part will, at a certain signal, switch on the visualization of the appropriate emotion and will it towards the sufferer, whether they are in the same room or many miles away.

It is very important when doing this that the emotional visualization is instantly switched off at the end of this part of the ritual, otherwise it will affect the people doing it. This would not only interfere with their own emotional stability but would also drain the energy from the healing thought-form that has been sent out on its magical mission.

It is not easy to learn how to visualize emotions properly, but it can be done and is regularly accomplished by advanced Wiccan practitioners. Once you have mastered the earlier visualization exercise, try to go on and develop this particular ability, but proceed with care and caution. It is very necessary to avoid any risk of retaining the visualized emotion in your own system afterwards and great attention needs to be paid to developing the art of 'switching it off' again. However, if emotional visualization can be fully mastered, the power of the will is also vastly increased, again almost as a by-product.

A quick and easy way to switch emotions on and off is to have a signal that marks the beginning and end, such a ringing a bell, snapping the fingers or clapping once at the start and finish. Any signal will do, as long as you use the same one each time, so that the mind becomes accustomed to this stimulus.

With a strongly developed ability to visualize and a powerful will, the effect of any magical work is greatly increased. All works of healing are particularly enhanced by the addition of visualized positive emotions. It is these skills that enable Wiccans to perform magic by the power of the mind alone.

Affirmations

To work with affirmations is, in effect, to programme the brain with repetitive sentences, similar to performing a spell chant. When we get into a mental rut or when we have negative beliefs, they can work powerfully against us and affect our progress through life. Therefore, to work with affirmations is to begin to clear old habit patterns and replace them with positive ones.

An affirmation is a positive sentence that contains the result you wish to establish as if it is already happening. For example, if you are feeling apprehensive about your job security, you could work out an affirmation that builds confidence, trust and belief in a positive future, such as 'I am confident that my life is unfolding exactly as it is meant to' or perhaps 'I trust that whatever happens is for my highest good.'

It is at a deep subconscious level that we carry the negative patterns, beliefs and fears that have often drummed into us by family, peers or society to such an extent that we can actually manifest them physically in our own lives. How many of us could say that what we fear is going to happen is often what happens? And yet to face these fears is not something we readily would choose to do, so they may often surface as a challenge in our lives before we acknowledge and heal them and so release them and grow from the experience.

A student of mine, Becky, had a very deep dread of authority and had buried within herself a fear that she was not a good mother. Just after taking part in a Wiccan workshop on the nature of power, her home life exploded right into the centre of one such primal fear – a new and zealous teacher at the school that all of her children had attended for many years alleged that some kind of abuse was occurring with her youngest child. All who knew Becky realized that this was absolutely untrue, and Becky herself knew exactly why this was happening – her fear of it had brought it out in order for it to be healed.

After a great deal of trauma, negotiation and intervention from professionals, her innocence was revealed, but Becky had to face many things during this time, including building confidence in herself as a mother and facing assumptions about her parenting skills with honesty and courage. She achieved most of this through her own brilliant efforts, by maintaining positive affirmations on her worth as a human being and by being supported a little by my guidance and her fellow students' encouragement. She is now much stronger, has a healthy belief in herself and her abilities and will no longer be pushed around by the unfounded opinions of others. She faced her fear! The positive affirmations she used have also increased her confidence, her creative abilities and her life direction, and continue to influence her sense of value within society.

By working with positive affirmations, we can support the evolutionary process of clearing our past in a positive and encouraging way. All you need to do is to create a sentence that supports your healing process and your needs and to repeat it as often as you wish throughout the waking hours. Every time a negative thought enters your mind, you quickly replace it with the positive affirmation that you keep repeating until you feel calm again. Gradually, the negative is replaced with the positive and you find yourself greatly healed of past conditioning or situations.

Postulates

Whereas affirmations involve the repetition of words, postulates involve images. To hold a postulate means to have a very clear picture in your mind as to a future that is yet to occur. For instance, if someone is seriously hurt in a car accident, you can hold the postulate that they fully recover by visualizing them in your mind functioning completely normally and going about their daily business having fully recovered from the experience. A postulate is a firm assumption that something is going to transpire and there is complete belief in it coming to pass.

One word of warning, though: do be careful when formulating affirmations and postulates – in fact with every aspect of magical work – that you remain on the right side of 'non-interference'. In other words, say just the following once before *all* potentially alterative work: 'If it be for the highest good of all and harming none' and then repeat your affirmation or visualize your postulate as many times as you wish. Saying this initial phrase ensures that you are prepared to accept whatever outcome is right for all concerned.

Vigils

The word *vigil* stems from the Latin word *vigilia*, meaning 'to be awake', and this is precisely what a vigil is – the act of remaining awake and aware. A healing vigil is the process of remaining awake and aware on someone else's behalf whilst focusing as much of your healing energy and strength on them as you can.

Perform healing vigils whenever it seems as if extra help is needed in order to achieve a desired objective. Vigils can be very effective during crises, helping to give another love and strength at a time when perhaps they are unable to have these for themselves. A good example of an appropriate time to perform a healing vigil would be after an accident or when someone's life is at a critical stage. Alongside the practical and medical support they may need, the healing vigil can provide that extra spark of healing energy that really can be experienced by the one you are performing the vigil for.

A close family member of mine, Louise, once suffered a major setback when she was suddenly completely paralysed from the neck down because of the acute rupture of a disc in her neck. She was rushed into the hospital for emergency surgery because she could not breathe properly and was in a serious condition. An operation was performed immediately to remove the ruptured disc and the calcified build-up. However, it wasn't successful, and a second one was performed 24 hours later. Anyone with any medical knowledge will be aware that there can be complications with this amount of anaesthetic being pumped into the bloodstream so quickly, and complications did develop. It was discovered that Louise was highly allergic to opiates and was not coming round from the operation. She was drifting in and out of consciousness and being monitored closely in the intensive care unit. Basically, she would not wake up and was close to death.

I had not been informed that a second operation was occurring, but picked up psychically that she was in some kind of serious trouble and knew a healing vigil was being called for. So at 9.30 p.m. I telephoned two trusted healers and asked them to join me in the vigil, which had to commence that evening. We prepared and synchronized ourselves from our respective homes. I personally continued the vigil until 1 a.m. the following morning, alert throughout the whole process and focusing upon Louise and her needs, and she survived the night. Today, she is alive and well and increasingly mobile once more. If she ever takes opiates again, however, it could kill her, and she now has to wear a medic-alert bracelet because of the seriousness of this allergy.

During the vigil, whilst Louise was drifting in and out of consciousness, she saw me standing in a shroud at the bottom of her bed keeping watch over her, and she thanked me afterwards for it, because it had made her feel safe and protected. Even though I had not spoken at all to her about what had been done on her behalf, she had been aware of the healing presence throughout that precarious part of her recovery and had drawn strength from it. I feel that the powers of a vigil, therefore, speak for themselves.

We can never know if what we have done for others on a healing level has worked, for we have no way of knowing what would have happened otherwise. I shall never know what would have transpired if the vigil for Louise had not taken place, but it is certainly worth noting the support that she drew from it.

Performing a Healing Vigil

The most important element of a healing vigil is the quality of time and energy that you contribute to it. What this means is that it is better to be completely concentrated upon your charge for five quality minutes than it is to sit for 15 minutes drifting in and out of concentration because you have other things on your mind. The level of mental focus really is a key ingredient in all healing vigils.

All you need to perform a vigil is a candle or a nightlight.

> Sit comfortably and light the candle in front of you.
>
> Focus upon the individual or situation you are performing the vigil for with as much concentration as you can manage without straining. If you notice yourself drifting, simply bring your concentration back to the vigil.
>
> You can remain 'vigilant' for as long as you feel is necessary or until you feel that your own energy is fading and you are in need of a rest. If you like, you can set up vigils with friends, so that as you end your session someone else takes over, and so on, until the vigil is complete.

Clear focus, clarity of intent and the power of your will are important factors in developing Wiccan healing skills. With the powers of concentration, it certainly seems that we can affect physical reality for good or ill, depending upon our state of being and what we believe. In this chapter I have shared how you can develop your mental energy so that your beliefs work for you, rather than against you, and this should help you to become an effective, wise and compassionate healer.

Do remember to preface any of your healing work with 'If it be for the highest good and harming none', for this determines that the outcome will be the best for all concerned.

Chapter Twelve
Animal Healing

As you know, the Wiccan heart moves out to all sentient life, and so animals are very much a part of any Wiccan healing picture. To this end, this chapter gives guidelines on the spiritual and physical attributes of animals and on treating your pets and other animals for simple everyday complaints. Please do be aware, however, that no one is currently allowed to diagnose or treat animal conditions unless they are trained as a veterinary surgeon. So remember to always consult your vet before commencing any of the treatments in this chapter.

To Wiccans, all animals have their place on Earth. Furthermore, animals have shown us that they have family ties, social structures and organized hierarchies. For example, the humble sparrow's pecking order is determined by the presence and size of the brown-coloured marking across the chest. The bigger the marking, the higher up the pecking order they are. Termites, ants and bees have very sophisticated societies and organized cultures. With regard to family ties, when a dairy cow is separated from her calf, she calls for her youngster for days. When an elephant is hurt, the herd stands round to physically support it and bring it comfort, and wild dogs take care of the injured members of their pack by leading them to the site of a kill so that they won't starve. And although they don't speak words, all animals have other ways of communicating through posture, facial expressions, colour flashing, other means of display and their own forms of verbal and psychic contact.

Let us not forget that if we wish to live the life of a Wiccan healer, we should behave kindly towards all animals.

Animal Healing Deities

When you wish to perform a magical ritual for the benefit of an animal, whether wild or domesticated, you can work with animal deities. *(For all animal correspondences, see Chart 17.)*

To give an example, let us say that a friend's horse is looking miserable because its companion has just died. Once a vet has established that there is no particular health problem, you could choose to work with the goddess Rhiannon because the feminine is most closely associated with family, friends and relationships, which is what the horse is pining for, rather than, for example, the masculine Wayland (another horse deity), whom I would probably choose to work with in cases needing strength, courage and vitality.

After looking up Rhiannon's correspondences, you could set up an altar in the appropriate colours on the appropriate day and with the suggested votive offerings. All you then need to do is to decide what type of ritual you wish to perform – perhaps a charm to hang over the horse's stable, perhaps an appeal to the lady Rhiannon for her intervention in finding companions for the horse, perhaps a spell slipped somewhere safe in its habitat or even a full Wiccan ritual of casting a Circle and dedicating it to Rhiannon. Spend some time in contemplation of the need and its most appropriate solution.

Once you have decided the best course of action, it is simply a matter of following the guidelines for your chosen event.

Chart 17: Animal Healing Deities and Correspondences

Deity	Animal	Votive offering	Colour and gem	Day of the week
Anubis	Dogs	Poppy, obsidian	Black Silver	Saturday
Bast	Cats	Cat icons, turquoise, catnip	Turquoise blue Turquoise crystal	Friday (hours of darkness)
Diana	Dogs	Mugwort (do not handle if pregnant), rue	Red Amazonite	Monday
Epona	Horses	Oats, vervain	White/black Azurite	Friday
Faunus	Cleft-footed beasts, bees, fish, wild animals	Honey, apples	Ochre Beryl	Friday
Freya	Cats	Primrose, catnip	Gold Amber	Friday
Rhiannon	Birds/ Horses	White feathers, braided horsehair and white horse icons	White Azurite, kyanite, rhonite	Monday
Thoth	Birds	Cinnamon	Yellow Amethyst	Wednesday
Wayland	Horses	Forged metal objects, fire	Orange Steel or iron	Tuesday

Flower Essences for Everyday Complaints in Animals

There are several ways of working with healing flowers, crystals and gems to treat everyday complaints in animals.

First you could try putting healing crystals into a pouch and placing this in the animal's bedding. In the case of birds and other animals, you can place the appropriate crystals into their water bowl and leave them to infuse in the water overnight before removing them and placing the water bowl into their enclosure. Alternatively, you can make up your own flower or crystal remedy mixes and add them to your animal's drinking water. All of these ways will be equally effective. It is just a matter of making the decision as to which one fits your lifestyle and animal the best.

One thing to bear in mind with all complementary treatments is that they are cumulative. They can often take longer to show a result than conventional treatments and so should ideally be maintained for as long as any symptoms continue.

All of the gems suggested in Chart 18 can be used in pouches or infused as an essence. Where more than one stone is indicated in the chart, you can either use just one of the varieties suggested or one or two of them. If, for example, your pet is suffering from depression and you would like to ease their process, you will see that lepidolite and rhodochrosite are indicated. You can, therefore, place a single lepidolite stone or a single rhodochrosite stone (or several smaller pieces in a pouch) in your pet's bedding, or you can mix samples of one or both crystals together to use either as they are or in a remedy mix.

Making your Own Crystal Remedy Mixes

Crystal remedies work best when made with spring water in glass or crystal bowls.

To make up your own crystal remedy mixes, place your chosen crystal/s into the animal's water bowl and cover them with spring water.

Leave to infuse overnight.

After removing them the next morning, give the crystal-charged water to the animal.

The water should ideally be renewed daily, following the same procedure each time.

When making essences in this way, it is important to keep your healing stones clean and to ensure they are of a good quality. Purchase them from a reputable dealer who knows that their stocks are gem quality and preferably have not been blasted from the ground with dynamite.

To Clean Crystals

The simplest way to cleanse healing crystals is to bury them in clean earth for anything between 24 hours to a few days. If you don't have a garden, you can fill some flowerpots with clean earth and use these to bury your crystals in. The length of time a crystal may take to cleanse depends upon the intensity of its use.

Afterwards, rinse your crystals off with spring water.

Once crystals have been cleansed in this way, you can hold them in your palms and make a simple affirmation that they are cleansed and blessed and ready to bring healing once more.

Chart 18: Crystal Remedies for Animals

Ailment	Crystal remedy	Timing
Depression	Lepidolite Rhodochrosite	Remove crystals when symptoms ease
Joint problems	Moss agate Azurite	Indefinite
Old age	Turquoise	Indefinite
Over-excitement	Jadeite Smoky quartz	Remove crystals when symptoms ease
Stress	Amethyst	Remove crystals once the animal is calm

Immune Booster

This remedy is best used when an animal seems to be a little off colour or is convalescing from any kind of veterinary treatment after medication has been completed. (Suppliers of flower remedies can be found in the back of the book.)

You will need:

> Olive Bach flower remedy
> Pansy, celery and echinacea flower remedies
> Spring water
> 10 ml glass bottle with dropper (available from pharmacists)
> 2 tsp vodka

Take your glass bottle and put the vodka into it. This will act as a preservative.

Add 7 drops of the flower essences in turn and then top up with spring water. Shake gently and label and date your bottle.

Add 7 drops of your remedy daily into freshly renewed water that your animal drinks from.

Your mix should remain useable for up to three months if stored in a cool dark place (not a fridge, as the electrical frequencies can affect the vibrational qualities of the essence). If at any point you notice it has gone cloudy or is spotted with flecks, discard it immediately and make up another mix. Clouds or bits in any remedy mix means that it has 'turned', i.e., has become polluted or tainted.

A Remedy Mix for a Timid or Intimidated Animal

If you have an animal that is becoming inward looking or withdrawn, it can be a sign of ill health, so do consult your vet in the first instance. However, if it appears that your animal's difficulty is behavioural, you could try the following essence mix. This will help it to integrate properly with other animals or people in the household, and improve its ability to relate positively and courageously with everything in its surroundings.

You will need:

> Larch Bach flower remedy
> Ruby gem essence
> Moss agate gem essence
> Spring water
> A glass or crystal bowl
> 2 tsp vodka

Take your glass bottle and add 2 tsp of vodka to it. Add 7 drops of each essence in the above order and top up with spring water.

Label and date the mix, which should keep for up to three months if stored in a cool dark place.

Household Remedies for Pets and Pests

In order to keep beasties under control in your living environment, you could try using some of the following natural remedies. When used regularly, they should deter fleas, ants, flies, mosquitoes and clothes moths.

It is also worth mentioning that if you have a word with the spirit of the creature concerned, asking them to leave or to move, they should comply within a few days. It has worked for me on most occasions, so is worth a try, and is a far kinder option than some more conventional treatments.

Ants

Many of us have experienced being inundated by ants that march around floors and cupboards in search of food. I had one instance where it became so difficult to use our kitchen table due to incessant marching lines of ants that I stood each table leg in a tin containing water, which stopped them being able to climb the legs any longer. Once they were out of the habit of using these particular trails, they left the building of their own accord. This definitely worked without causing any harm to any of them, whilst safeguarding the kitchen table and its contents at the same time.

It is well known that ants do not like tansy and so placing pots of tansy where they are entering should deter them from invading the house. Sprigs of tansy strategically placed should also discourage them from invading larders or store cupboards.

Moth Repellents

To protect precious items of clothing from moths, crumble dried and still fragrant artemesia leaves over tissue paper and put it over the clothes, or alternatively drop handfuls of cloves and chopped, dried orange peel into little muslin sachets and place them in clothes drawers.

Fly Repellents

Rub elder leaves directly onto your skin to repel flies when out walking in the woods or wilds. Alternatively, you can use yarrow leaves rubbed directly onto the skin in the same way. The best leaves to use are young undamaged leaves picked on a dry day, but please remember to make sure you have identified the correct plants first.

Mosquito Repellents

Mosquitoes can become a nightmare for those people who react to the bites and can spend days itching and scratching as a result. Being one of these people, I have experimented with various solutions, including taking vitamin B complex tablets and garlic capsules to try to 'sour' the taste of my blood. I have found that mixing my own insect repellent oils is more effective than using just one oil on its own, the most effective mixes being those made with pure essential oils.

In the recipe below, the wheatgerm oil provides the B vitamins that help to deter biting insects from being attracted to you in the first place, but should you suffer a bite, dab it regularly with lavender oil, which will relieve the itching.

To make up your own natural insect repellent you will need:

  7 fl. oz (200 ml) wheatgerm oil
  20 drops of pure citronella oil
  20 drops of pure lavender oil
  10 drops of pure eucalyptus oil

Add your essential oils to the base wheatgerm oil and stir. Cover and leave to stand for 24 hours to allow the mixture to blend. Bottle and store until required.

General Pest Repellent

Dried pyrethrum flowers are excellent deterrents for all household pests. Sprinkle them onto your pet's bedding and around any areas where pests are causing a problem, making sure you wear protective gloves to avoid possible allergic reactions. Although pyrethrum flowers are harmless to animals and humans, they can sometimes cause an allergic reaction and can also harm fish and helpful insects, so be sure to wash your hands before handling fish food or aquarium water, or any equipment associated with a pet insect.

Flea Repellents

There are two things that fleas do not like the taste of, and these are garlic and brewer's yeast. If you add either of these to your pet's diet, it is said to deter fleas from biting them because they do not like the taste that these substances leave in the blood. With a large dog, sprinkle one teaspoon of Brewer's yeast night and morning upon their food, or give one garlic tablet per day. With smaller animals and cats, halve the dose.

Jock was a small, white and particularly bald little dog when I first met him. His fur had been falling out due to his incessant scratching. He had what is now a very common complaint in pets – a flea allergy. Jock was given ½ tsp of brewer's yeast twice a day and within a very short space of time his fur was growing back and his scratching had stopped.

In these days of chemical cocktails, where products rely heavily upon compound mixtures to treat things like ticks and fleas, you may like to try the following natural blends. It would be wise, however, to check your animal regularly, as these mixes are repellents rather than treatments.

A Natural Flea Repellent

You will need the following ingredients:

> 7 fl. oz (200 ml) sesame oil
> 10 drops of lavender oil
> 10 drops of citronella oil
> 5 drops of rosemary oil

Add your lavender, citronella and rosemary drops to the base sesame oil. Mix and bottle. Leave to stand overnight to blend.

Pour approximately 2 tsp onto your palms and rub them together. Pass your hands over the dog or cat's body, gently rubbing the mixture into the hair and skin, concentrating on the areas behind the ears, under the chin (though not near the mouth), under the legs and around the tail.

There should not be an allergic reaction, but if the skin does appear to redden or react, discontinue use.

A Natural Flea Collar

You can make up your own natural flea collar by rubbing the following aromatherapy oils onto a material collar and renewing the mix once a week in normal circumstances and up to twice a week during flea epidemics. Check your animal regularly to ensure the collar is stopping fleas from attacking your pet.

> 5 drops of tea tree oil
> 5 drops of lavender oil
> 2 drops of eucalyptus oil

Mix the oils together and leave to stand for a few minutes. Take your collar and rub the mixture into the material. Fasten the collar to your pet in the usual way, making sure that it is not too tight.

Renew your oils once a week. If the skin becomes irritated or sore, stop using the mixture for two weeks and then just use one of the oils at a time to see if this stops the skin reacting.

Animal Familiars

An animal familiar is a well-known term for the witch's 'helper', although a familiar can be any wild or domestic animal that has a strong spiritual bond with a magical practitioner. The most common familiars are cats, dogs, ravens and crows, and they are usually actual physical presences. Some familiars, however, are energies such as a tree dryad, a wolf spirit or a dragon.

We do not exactly choose our familiars, or they us – it is more a mutual, symbiotic relationship. Whatever creature comes to you and remains over a period of time is one you could acknowledge and work with. It can make itself known through a dream, by coming to you physically or sometimes by appearing in a vision.

For me, for example, the spiritual essence of crow is my familiar. When I was a small child I would dream of these large black birds flying and swooping above me and then darting down to peck at my clothes. At first I was terrified by these dreams, but as my life matured, I came to realize that the birds were drawing my attention to them. Crows and ravens are almost always with me now and act as my protectors, guardians and guides. To the Celts the crow was a magical bird. He was revered in Ireland as a keeper of universal laws and truth. Crow is an important mythical creature, sometimes the trickster and sometimes the law-giver, but he is always oracular, with profound abilities to 'see' what is true.

To my view, familiars, like archetypes, are an aspect of our own potential. If we have dog as our familiar, we will carry the potential qualities of dog and we may be most at ease when fulfilling the qualities associated with dog, such as love, service, loyalty and guardianship. We may also receive challenges that call us to rise to our familiar's potential.

Familiars are spiritual allies, working co-operatively with us as we journey through life. When an animal ally appears to you, it is likely to do so on up to three different occasions, to give you the chance to recognize it as part of your life. If you realize that it has come to you during this time, the appearances or 'prods' will cease. But it is said in some circles that if you deny it three times the familiar will simply fade into the background and you may not be given another opportunity.

Once your familiar has been identified, you can obtain items that are associated with it such as a feather, a picture or statue, or even a charm, as long as gathering these items has not harmed nature in any way.

Visioning with Animals

If you would like to discover who your animal familiar is, you can record the following journey and play it back to yourself, or alternatively you can ask a friend to read it aloud to you. Remember that whatever appears is the creature for you, and do not be disappointed if you are visited by ant rather than eagle, or toad rather than serpent. We can sometimes have predetermined ideas as to what constitutes an 'acceptable' or desirable ally. To give you an example, one student of mine had a phobia about ants. They followed her everywhere, but she totally abhorred them. I suggested that perhaps they were trying to get her attention and she should journey to the spirit of ant to find out. She did just this, and yes, ant is one of her totems. Since this discovery, she has total respect for ants. She has claimed her ant power, which is very magical 'medicine' in her life today.

A Journey to Meet Your Animal Familiar

Switch off all daily distractions like clocks and phones so that you will not be disturbed for approximately 20 minutes, and then lie down in a comfortable position. Breathe slowly and calm yourself for a few moments before starting the journey.

Begin at the edge of an ancient wood. Looking around, you see a stile and sitting on the stile is a wood spirit. You greet each other and the spirit invites you to enter the wood.

You climb the stile and follow the wood spirit along a winding path. The spirit takes you to a glade where there is a stream and mossy stones to sit upon. The sunlight is filtering through the leaves of the trees. At the edge of the water the wood spirit shows you something wrapped up in leaves. It is a gift for you. You open it and the wood spirit explains that this is to be your power object as you travel to meet Lady Aradia, Queen of Witches. You stay for a while in the glade, feeling the magical atmosphere and listening to the sounds of the wood around you.

The wood spirit takes out a carved stone whistle and blows through it. After a short while, you hear something approaching the glade, and as you look around you see a creature coming towards you. This creature, the wood spirit explains, is your familiar, a friend who journeys with you as a helper and guide. You greet your familiar and get ready to leave the clearing.

Saying farewell to the wood spirit, you take your power object and go with your familiar deeper into the woods.

Following the path together, you travel through the wood. As you go deeper, everything falls silent. You notice that the path is leading to another clearing. There are curtains of ivy and honeysuckle cascading down across the entrance. Carpets of woodland flowers are beneath your feet. You feel the atmosphere is charged with a powerful presence.

Quietly you follow your familiar through the wild curtain and into the clearing. There upon a fallen tree branch is a beautiful woman, dressed in green, with golden hair and a raven on her shoulder. She is wearing a crown of stars and is singing a most beautiful song.

You approach with your familiar and sit down in front of her. She looks at you and you greet each other. She is Aradia, Queen of Witches.

Aradia bids you welcome. Her voice spans the ages and you feel yourself drifting away as you hear it. She says what you most need to hear, telling you three things about yourself that will help to free your spirit and bring you joy. You may speak if you wish and ask any questions that you may have. After sharing this time together, Aradia begins to sing her song again and you know it is time to leave and continue your journey.

You continue to follow the path. Deeper and deeper into the wood you go, with your familiar beside you and your power object in your hand. You can smell wood smoke, and further ahead you see a cottage surrounded by a hedge with a small gate. You are drawn to the cottage and go through the gate. The garden is filled with herbs and spices, with cottage flowers and gnarled old trees. The path winds through the garden, past a pond filled with waterlilies, towards the front door.

Approaching the front door, you see it is open and your familiar goes inside. You follow and find a room that has an old, old woman sitting in rocking chair by a large fireplace, with a cauldron bubbling over the fire. There is another chair by the fire and many different bottles and phials around the walls. You sit down before the old lady and wait. After a long pause, the witch reveals to you why your familiar has chosen you. Listen carefully and remember. Let memories come and go, let feelings rise and fall, and let yourself drift in this dreamy state for a while.

The witch rises from her chair and stirs her cauldron. Your familiar draws close and you know it is now time to leave. You go to the table and leave a gift for the woodland witch to thank her for your visit. You leave the cottage, going back along the path, walking with your familiar back towards the edge of the ancient woodland.

You pass by the clearing where you met Aradia, you follow the path to the glade where your power object was found, you travel back to the edge of the wood to the stile. Here you must say goodbye to your familiar, but you pledge to meet each other again. Turning with thanks in your heart for this magical experience, and taking your power object with you, you climb over the stile and bring your consciousness back to the present moment.

Power Animals

Animal familiars are not the only animals to work with us. A power animal may also do so. This is a creature that brings the energetic qualities that you perhaps aren't able to access at a certain time, or that you may particularly need. This does not mean that the creature is always big and powerful, however. An ant could be a power animal come to protect and serve us by bringing in exactly the right energy that we need to succeed as a team member. Physical strength is not always the requirement. Strong power animals do commonly appear if we are visioning or journeying in the spirit world, however.

A power animal can also be called upon during stressful or challenging times in this world to cloak you with their wisdom and protection and thus bring you a sense of security and the ability to cope.

The best way to work with power animals is to explore their particular abilities and meanings, so that when you do need to call upon a specific power you know where to turn. To give you an example, perhaps you are feeling in need of a change. The dragonfly is associated with change, as is the bat and all metamorphic creatures such as butterflies and frogs. With this knowledge already in place, when it comes to positive change, you already know which creatures you might work with.

Take note of creatures appearing around you, too – they can often material-ize just when we need them, to give their support and share a message.

Animal Clans

All of us, witches or otherwise, can, if we are invited to do so, belong to an animal clan. After a long questing journey on top of a hill with a Native American shaman, for example, I was invited by the spirit of the white buffalo to join the buffalo clan. That native part of me is now a member of that clan, the clan of the peacemaker and the provider and of sacred prayer. The buffalo clan is very close to the Earth and its people, something that is often reflected in my life and work as a witch. I see the buffalo clan as part of my extended family, and when I meet another buffalo member, there is always a sense of connection and comradeship, with very little need for words.

Entrance to a clan is usually by invitation from the 'energies' of that clan, which can come in dreams, visions or insights that increase awareness of a partic-ular creature and its associations. Make notes of significant dreams and experi-ences that have this flavour to them, and if you feel drawn to a particular clan, you should find that the path to follow simply starts to appear in your life.

Animal Messengers

You may or may not have noticed, but at certain times of your life certain creatures or birds will have featured strongly. Perhaps a buzzard soaring on the winds kept appearing when you felt you were going round in circles, reminding you that you can rise above anything, or magpies kept hopping around your home, chattering of good news to come, just when you felt you couldn't go on any longer, or cats were watching you with their cool, clear eyes, making sure you were psychically protected at times when you were vulnerable. I have many examples of this from my own life, so I know it to be true.

Once I got seriously lost in a large area of woodland and began to get really concerned that I would not find my way out. I called to my Mother and Father (Goddess and God) and asked them to send assistance. About two minutes later a group of about 20 song-piping wrens appeared, hopping from tree to tree along one particular pathway. I took the pathway and followed the wrens for about a mile as they wound a way ahead of me, singing from tree to tree, until I could see the edge of the wood. I will never forget the experience. I know that I was helped, and I say thank you again to the wrens that came!

I have also found that creatures will come and give us a message when we call, as long as we are sincere. Next time you need an answer to something, try turning to Mother Nature's animals by going into the wild and calling for guidance. (It goes without saying that you should always remain aware of local hazards and dangers when out in the wild and should act appropriately.) Wait and see which animal comes, but remember, it could be literally anything, so be aware. Once a creature has appeared, reflect on its qualities and what it means to you, for in this is the message you are being given.

As a starting-point, I have outlined in the pages that follow what certain creatures have meant to me on my spiritual journey, but do feel free to adapt anything to fit your own experience and belief system, for each creature will have a unique relationship with you.

Ant

Ant means that activity and business are going to be called for, as well as working closely and co-operatively with those around you. You are being asked to work as part of a team.

Badger

Badger is a guardian of the sacred knowledge and the Earth. He protects and guards with fierce determination. You may need to remain aware of possible challenges to your status, be tested on your divine purpose and therefore might also benefit from supportive bonds with family and friends.

Bat

Bat means change and transformation, but more in the sense of a birth, a change in consciousness. Your spiritual life is expanding, causing you to look at areas of your life in a new way. Expect a change – but a change for the better.

Bear

Bear means strength and courage. To dream of or to see bear means that you may be coming to a time of inner reflection or that you may need to be strong in a certain situation. Bear has come to say that you will not be alone and that you should seek bear when needing protection.

Butterfly

Butterfly to me represents the soul. You may well be entering a time of transformation. You are being reminded that all things change, and so some soul-searching or evolution may well arise for your attention.

Cat

Cat indicates psychic protection and psychic gifts. Cat will often appear at times when negativity seems to be blocking or stopping you in some way. Cat is asking you to make sure that you cleanse yourself and keep yourself in tune with the psychic realms, whilst reminding you about the importance of psychic protection and clear vision.

Cow/Buffalo

Sacred to many traditions around the world, cow/buffalo calls us to the power of prayer, to sacredness. This indicates a time when we may need to see a greater picture, to keep an open mind about events around us and not be too quick to judge. You are being asked to be compassionate to someone you know who is in need. This could be yourself.

Crow/Raven

Crow means change. He comes into your life at a time when you are wanting to change and are ready for the initiation necessary for your spiritual growth. Crow will help you to duck and dive through the transformational process. You can call on him at times when you feel isolated, lonely or out of tune with your universe. Being open and honest with yourself and others is best right now.

Deer

Deer comes to show that you are feeling edgy and anxious about something in your life. By all means take the swiftness of deer with you, but what if you must stand your ground like a stag and face the opposition? Deer indicates a time when you must decide whether to flee and ignore, or face and transform. Be gentle with yourself.

Dog

Dog can be a guardian and friend, and yet he can bite the hand that feeds him. Dog can sometimes be bringing you a warning about someone's intentions or something happening behind your back. Check out whether those around you have your best interests at heart. Make sure that you are not run into the ground or taken for granted. Alternatively, see whether you should consider being of service in some way.

Dolphin

To dream of or connect with dolphin is to unite with your ancestors. It indicates that you are either deeply involved with helping or healing others, or shortly will be. Dolphin is coming to share his healing gifts with you, bringing through all your ancestral memories to help you along the way.

Dove

Dove means love, peace, purity and innocence. If you dream of dove you are being shown the virtues of these gifts, which you must either learn to cultivate or put into practice in a situation around you. Spirit is hearing your prayers and sending you their messenger. A new relationship is likely. Love is highlighted.

Dragonfly

Dragonfly is transformation from emotionalism into creative joy. Dragonfly indicates that you are emerging as a new person, happy because you have found something or will shortly find something that fulfils you or takes you further.

Eagle

King of birds to the Native Americans, eagle can see great distances because he flies so high. If eagle appears, you are being shown how to 'see' something about your current situation. Fly as high as eagle and you will see it all with a clearer perspective. Open your mind to higher thoughts.

Elephant

Elephant is a regal animal, sacred in Hindu mythology and practice. When elephant comes into your life, perhaps there is something you must not forget to undertake or something important you have to remember. Elephant treads gently upon the Earth, guiding you to walk gently, too. Remember who you are and why you are here.

Fox

Fox is cunning and intelligent. He can live in cities and be completely invisible, should he wish. Fox is showing you his medicine so that you can learn how to be invisible in situations and so learn what it is that you want to know. Keep your wits about you and use them. You may be entering a spell of lesson learning and sudden opportunities.

Goat

One aspect of the Horned God is the goat-footed god, lord of nature and the Earth. If goat appears, you are being advised to treat life with respect, knowing that you are protected. You should also guard against making a scapegoat of someone or of becoming one yourself. Be sure-footed.

Goose

A sacred bird, the goose flies first in migration. She is the leader, the heralder of a new season. She is also a gatekeeper. Goose reminds us of the need to move forward, to welcome the new and to be prepared to lead the way by example rather than word. You may have to find the doorway that leads to this new season, which can feel frustrating at times, but with perseverance you will find it. Change is imminent.

Hawk/Buzzard

To dream of or experience a bird of prey can signify that something is preying on your mind or someone is bothering you. Birds of prey are usually a warning to keep yourself to yourself for a while and watch for things around you that may not be so good for you. Take time to talk with spirit, in case there is a message for you.

Horse

Horse traditionally carries the shaman to the spirit worlds. He is the trusted steed who carries us where we need to go. With horse, you are being asked to go with the flow, let yourself be led or taken to where you need to be. And when you get there, trust what you perceive or what is shown to you.

Jackal/Coyote

Coyote is a teacher and also a trickster. His presence would tend to indicate that you are feeling quite confused about something that is going on. Let yourself be teased by coyote, learn how to play the game of life and you will find out what the lesson is.

Lion

Lion signifies mastery and strength. With his presence, you may be asked to improve your physical strength or control over the lower passions – desire, greed and laziness, for example. Lion can also mean that you are being given the strength that you need to overcome things that are coming at you from others. Be strong and courageous – show that you can roar. Relate to solar powers for a while.

Monkey

Monkey is highly intelligent. He can outwit most opposition. To dream of or to meet monkey is to be shown that you may need to be agile in your dealings with something or someone. Do your research carefully and be prepared for things to run a slightly crooked path for a little while. Play, but try not to let your thoughts run away with you.

Mouse

Mouse is small and busy. She is a totem animal for the direction of South in some Native American tribes. South is summer, and mouse is a totem animal there because she is active, never still, just like a summer's day. To journey with mouse you must become small. Don't overstretch yourself or rush around too much. You have been in the shadows. Perhaps it is time to come out into the light. Avoid pettiness, but pay attention to detail.

Owl

Owl is traditionally a bird of wisdom and truth, and an omen of death. To me, owl is the 'soul' bird, the one that watches over us in both life and death. When owl appears, you may well experience closure around you – maybe the end of a project or relationship, not specifically death. If owl *has* come for this reason, he is showing you that the beings of light have sent their soul bird of the Earth to let you know that they are aware of the departed or departing spirit. Be wise yourself about life. Learn how to face up to your fears and trust the truth.

Pig

Pig is sociable, intelligent and bright and brings a sense of sociability and playfulness into your life. Make sure that you are taking enough time to balance work with play, though. Pig is also a protector, so be assured that you are being sent an ally for whatever may lie ahead.

Rabbit

If you experience rabbit, you are being asked to assess your activities. Perhaps you could withdraw a little and observe what's going on from a place where you feel safe, without necessarily taking any action at this time. Be gentle with yourself if a fear or challenge does arise. Fertile opportunities are coming, but you may well have to face your fears first.

Snake

Snake or serpent represents energy itself, the raw dynamic flow of life that pulses through our being. Snake is a powerful ally in the spiritual realms, one who is watching over you and guiding you through life. If you are shedding an old skin, be aware that snakes do this alone, so if you feel you have to withdraw and then begin to feel vulnerable, try to remember snake's way of developing a new skin. Snake is also a healer, and you may well be asked to heal yourself or someone else. Consider a detox of body or mind and check any desires to sink your fangs into others. *Wisdom* is also a key word with snake.

Swan

Swan is a regal bird. She is graceful and dignified. She is like a boatman carrying you to the spiritual realms. With swan, you are being taken into the realms of spirit in order to learn something, especially something of an intuitive nature. Swan is rebirth into greater understanding. To see a swan coming aggressively at you, however, is to be shown that you should be listening to your spirit!

Unicorn

Unicorn represents the soul. To perceive unicorn is to be shown that you are travelling deep within yourself to find the answer to something. Unicorn has come to show you the love and purity that live in the soul – and to help you to tap into them. Unicorn is magical. Let yourself become part of the magic that you may be longing to feel. Relate to lunar powers for a while.

Vulture

Vulture clears up the rubbish. He has the capacity to be very earthy or very heavenly, depending on whether he is feeding or flying. With vulture you are being shown that life has ups and downs, good and bad times. There will be times of limitation and times of free flight. Trust the process. Getting to the bare bones of a situation is indicated.

Whale

The largest mammal in the world, whale is gigantic and yet so gentle. To dream of whale is to dream of the wonder of life. What you are being shown is that you have wisdom and understanding that should be shared with others. Be sure you share your wisdom when you are asked for it, as you have much to give.

Wolf

Many people have dreams or visions involving this magnificent creature, whose powers of perception and guardianship are highly evolved. A beastie in folktales (perhaps because of its close associations with paganism), in fact the wolf is extremely loyal and intelligent and there is a highly evolved social structure within the pack. To experience wolf is to be asked to call upon the sacred in all your daily activities and to find your own wild spirit that is trying to speak to you from within. Be discriminating and learn to trust your feelings. A new direction is possible.

There are many other creatures not mentioned here. Please feel free to compile your own animal journal that you can refer to when the need arises and remember that what I have given here is only a guide.

The rich and varied aspects of our animal world provide a veritable cauldron of information that Wiccans can delve into when weaving magic. As well as visiting nature for communion with animals, you can also create little altars or charms to particular creatures at those times when you feel the need for their energies – bear for strength, badger for courage, eagle for clarity, and so on. This is simply done by carrying an image of the bird or animal, or displaying them in your home. If at any time I feel vulnerable, I open my wildlife photography book and display badger and then put owl statues in the four corners of my room. It works for me!

Finally, animals are well protected by law, and so I remind you not to treat anything but everyday ailments in your animals or pets. Always consult a veterinary surgeon, and on no account diagnose or treat animals unless you are qualified to do so.

Chapter Thirteen

Composing Your Own Rituals

Part of the joy of Wicca is when you are confident enough to begin writing your own rituals, bringing them alive with the richness and beauty of your own words and actions.

The essential idea behind a magical ritual is to align all the parts of our consciousness – those particular emotions, feelings and harmonic vibrations – that will produce the desired result. This is much simpler than it sounds. Witches focused upon their love of the Goddess and Horned God can raise a powerful energy within their working Circle by their loving attitudes towards these two deities. The energy that is triggered by such strong spiritual love can then be moulded by other aspects of the ritual into a specific form, for example, healing energy.

Embodying Magical Powers

Part of the purpose of working in a magical Circle is to charge the Circle with the divine energy of the Goddess and the God and to embody them through two human representatives, one female and one male. However, when working as a solitary witch, this is not possible. In this case, if you are female, you would speak the part of the Goddess as if you were the Goddess and would say 'The Charge to the Horned God' as if you were the Goddess speaking to Him, or vice versa.

To give you an idea of what I am saying, let us take the first two lines of the Charge:

You are the summer winds that rustle through my spirit
and stir the whispering leaves of my soul.

As the Horned God, the first line would read 'I am the summer winds...' and so on. If the Charge is to be spoken as if you were the Earth Goddess speaking to her consort, you would use the word *you* throughout instead.

We can see from this that any piece can be worded so that you are either speaking as if you were the Goddess or as if you were the God.

Rituals are made up of behaving as if we were the sacred powers ourselves, or making appeals to or celebrating them. When writing or composing your own rituals, it is important to have confidence in these forces of Creation.

Defining a Ritual

One of the first steps in composing your own rituals is to believe you have the right to do so.

Secondly, there needs to be a purpose behind any ritual, such as for healing, celebration, reverence or protection.

Once the focus of your ritual has been decided upon, you can research correspondences, work out the most suitable timing and collect the materials that support your choice, such as the appropriate herbs, oils, cloths, tools and equipment, prior to the date you have set for your ritual.

Structuring a Ritual

Thirdly, your ritual requires structure: a beginning, a middle and a completion.

The first step involves opening the Circle and invoking the sacred energies of your choice. The middle part involves undertaking your chosen focus, such as making a charm or creating a spell. The third part, which is as important as the other two, is thanking your spiritual helpers and the guardians of the four quarters and bidding them farewell before dismantling the Circle's energies by ensuring that all you have invoked is returned whence it came.

The two rituals outlined in Chapter Seven will help you to develop a sense of how rituals are put together and performed, and will provide a springboard for your own creative spirit.

Composing Rituals for Festivals

Wiccans celebrate specific dates on the Wheel of the Year *(see page 39)*, so the focus for these rituals is already determined. Imbolc, for example, is representative of the light returning to the world and of the Goddess rising in strength to nurture the seeds of the new year. Thus rituals at Imbolc will have associations with light, spring, new growth and promise.

Here is yet another example of the benefits we receive from understanding the powers of nature, the changing seasons and the Elements, for with this understanding comes the wisdom required to put a ritual event together.

Once the definition and structure of a ritual have been worked out, you are ready to perform it.

The space where the ritual is to occur can be made magical with candles, ivy fronds, incense smoke, flowers, faery lights, lanterns and anything else that you want to include. If you choose not to work naked, you can wear a simple or even an elaborate robe or outfit that perhaps you have bought specially or made yourself.

The more effort you put into your ritual event, the more beautiful and powerful it is likely to be. By 'effort' I am not implying that things have to get complicated, but simply referring to the fact that the investment of your own spiritual and physical energy into creating and performing your healing rituals will also contribute to their efficacy and strength.

In summary it is the worship of the Goddess and her consort, the belief in magical powers, the forces of will, having a clear purpose, creating a solid structure and building relevant magical content that generates a powerful healing ritual. Whether working alone or in a group, the ritual that is most effective is the one with heart and soul. Put your love and your spirit into your ritual words. Be thankful, be open and above all aspire to bring out your true magical self with style and confidence.

Chapter Fourteen
Stepping into Wicca

This book is now coming to a close. We have journeyed through many aspects of the Craft and shared some of its magic together. It is now timely for you to consider whether you wish to find out more about Wicca and to know which options are available to you should you wish to explore it further.

The Wiccan Coven

I have included details here of what you can normally expect to encounter if you explore joining a coven, so that you can make informed decisions about your options. There are, for example, at least three broad types of coven to consider. Gardnerian covens are the most popular and commonly encountered and most if not all of these work naked (skyclad). Gardnerian Wiccans are very nature-based.

Alexandrian covens are similar to Gardnerian in many ways, although generally speaking they also incorporate high ritual magic and Judeo-Christian terminology into their practices, so that that they tend to appeal to ritualists who are attracted to costumes, majestic tools and complex magical formulae. Alexandrian Wicca differs from Gardnerian and Traditional Wicca in that it includes what is known as high ritual magic, much of it being of Jewish origin, such as the Qabbalah. Where other types of Wicca make use of pagan names for energies and for the Goddess and God, the Alexandrians also use Judeo-Christian and other forms. Around the circumference of their circle, for example, are frequently written names such as 'Jehovah', 'Tetragrammaton' (a cryptic name for Jehovah), 'Messiah' and various other Judeo-Christian names such as those of archangels and sometimes sections of Catholic prayers. This is a generalization only. Different Alexandrian covens have different ways of doing things.

Traditional witches follow the old path as it evolved throughout its years of persecution, and they are generally more secretive and difficult to find. They tend to work robed and adhere strictly to the 'traditional', so would appeal to those who have traditionalist views about life as well.

There are also other kinds of covens, such as those of Dianic witchcraft, which generally do not admit men. Dianic witchcraft is popular in the USA and appeals mainly to feminists and women who worship the Goddess, but Gardnerian, Alexandrian and Traditional are the main divisions of Wicca. Of these, Gardnerian Wicca is the most popular throughout the world.

Joining a Wiccan Coven

When first researching joining a coven, you can look out for pagan 'moots' (meetings) that will be advertised in alternative magazines or shops or on the internet. At these moots you can meet others who have similar interests.

When taking your first steps towards joining a coven, it is you who must ask to join. No reputable coven will invite you or coerce you.

The coven best suited to you will be the one that feels like your family, bringing with it a sense of safety and trust. Each authentic coven will require that you get to know each other pretty thoroughly before granting your request to be initiated as a member. They will need to form an opinion of you and judge your sincerity in general terms and also judge whether you are compatible to work with their existing members. Some covens observe the traditional 'year and a day' waiting period, during which you would be expected to show enthusiasm in such things as regular attendance of 'open' meetings and overall commitment to the Craft, as well as a willingness to adapt to the individual character of the specific coven. Not all covens require you to wait a year and a day, but all have some period of 'getting to know you'.

All covens have two or three types of meeting. All have Sabbats and esbats, and most have open meetings as well. As already mentioned, a Sabbat is one of the eight ancient pagan festivals on the Wheel of the Year, and an esbat is a meeting for other purposes, such as Moon worship, spell work, teaching, healing and any other kind of magical activity. An open meeting is one where 'outsiders' can attend — that is, people who have asked to join but have not yet been accepted for initiation and are going through the period of assessment. (Some covens also perform certain public ceremonies which anyone can come along to watch.)

All Wiccan covens are presided over by a High Priestess, with a High Priest acting as a second-in-command and assistant. Most covens also have various other 'officers', such as the Maiden, who assists during rituals (i.e., a handmaiden), the Fetch (or Summoner) who contacts individual members if necessary, and so on.

Broadly speaking, first Wiccan degree represents knowledge and training, learning about herbs, psychic abilities, healing and so forth, and is in essence a practical degree. The second degree represents adopting fully the Wiccan way of life in thought and action, and is in essence about the personal application of the belief. The third degree represents the consummation of mystical union of the physical with the spiritual and the reaching of a stage of perfection according to the concepts of the Wiccan faith, and is in essence a mystical degree. It is the attainment of the 'mystical union' with the God (for a female) or the Goddess (for a male).

On reaching the second degree, a female witch is entitled, should she wish, to 'hive off' and start her own coven as its High Priestess (choosing a second-degree male to be her High Priest). To qualify for initiation into the second degree, a witch (whether male or female) must be deemed to be a 100 percent believer in the ancient sacred pagan precepts of Wicca and to act — particularly within the Circle — as a wholehearted Wiccan who can be a good example to other first degrees and trainees.

All covens have what is called 'Cakes and Ale', the celebratory part of joy, happiness, games, singing, dancing, bonding and unwinding after the end of the main ritual activity. Generally, the Circle is not closed until this is finished, and it is considered to be an essential part of the Sabbat and of most esbats. These days, any kind of food and drink can be used, not just cakes or ale, although 'Cakes and Ale' has become the title for this part of the ceremonies. According to Wiccan belief, physical enjoyment is a spiritual act honouring the way we were created by the Goddess, and the Cakes and Ale provides an opportunity to enjoy yourself, which is considered equally as important as the more formal ceremonial activities.

The Circle is considered to be a doorway between the worlds. All Wiccans believe that it represents a place within which a different and perfected universe exists, a universe operating according to the undiluted ideals of Wicca. This is a special magical place which is absolutely separate from the normal everyday world and its conventions, restrictions and inhibitions. Activity within the Circle is never mentioned to non-Wiccans and seldom even mentioned to Wiccans from other covens. Everything that goes on there is firmly considered to be a sacred act in honour of the Goddess and Horned God. The attainment of this level of belief is one of the ways in which an apprentice in the Craft is judged as being ready to receive the second degree, especially since a second-degree witch must possess the ability to cast such a Circle themselves.

A successful coven should feel like a family, a clan. Its members should be more closely bonded than is usually experienced. The Circle forms the mystic centre of this way of life, and some covens even consider themselves to be (within the Circle) a type of group marriage because their bonding is so close. Coven members often refer to each other as 'brother' or 'sister'. Obviously, new applicants who seek to join a coven are also judged on whether or not their personalities and vibrations are harmonious with the character of the particular coven. So if someone is rejected for initiation into a coven, it does not necessarily mean that the coven thinks they are not a good witch, merely that the personalities don't match. Someone who is rejected by one coven may well find they are fully accepted by another.

Joining a Wiccan coven represents a major step forward along the mystical pathway of self-development according to the ancient and sacred principles of the Wiccan faith, and it requires a willingness to allow the onset of the personal changes brought about by such self-development. This is one of the reasons why no legitimate coven will ever ask someone to join. The individual who seeks to join a coven must always ask freely and of themselves.

With legitimate covens, there is also no difficulty about leaving or resigning; nobody is ever forced to remain against their will. One just leaves, and that is that. In this, Wicca differs from many other religions, where it is often easy to get in but difficult to leave. In Wicca, the reverse applies — it is usually difficult to get in and easy to leave.

Take your time and remember that the right coven for you is the one where you feel totally comfortable and at ease.

The Solitary Wiccan

There are no rules that state you have to be a member of a coven in order to define yourself as a witch and there are those amongst us who prefer to practise alone.

Some covens provide the service of initiation into first-degree Wicca without the need to join a specific coven, which means you have been initiated as a witch by a witch but are not a member of any particular coven. If you decide upon this option, it is still up to you to approach the High Priestess or Priest and ask for initiation. You may find, however, that you don't wish to be initiated by anyone other than yourself, and if this is a strong feeling in you, then it is important that you honour your truth. There is such a thing as self-initiation, although I would personally say that initiation into the Craft by a High Priestess or Priest is more powerful. However, your choice is entirely up to you.

Having established yourself as a solitary, it is then up to you how you practise, because you can do as you wish within the areas of Wiccan belief. All solitary witches, however, will honour the Wiccan festivals and practise according to Wiccan customs, because they are still part of the broader Wiccan faith.

Being a solitary witch does not preclude you from joining a coven, nor does being a member of a coven preclude you from working as a solitary now and then. At any point you can change your mind and step into another aspect of

Wicca that turns out to suit you better, as I have done. I moved from coven work to solitary and finally to what I am today: a hedgewitch.

The Hedgewitch

A hedgewitch does not have to be initiated, living as they do on the edge of most things in this life. The word *hedgewitch* derives from German and means 'rider of the hedge'. In the old days, these people lived on the edges of the community. The isolation and the hedge provided a barrier between the community and their world and so provided a level of protection from prying eyes. Hedgewitches were practical in their service to society and lived by herbs, nature, prophecy and divination as well as magic and healing. They would have served their community through midwifery, healing, protection, house blessings and crop and livestock preservation, plus appeals to the spirits on behalf of others.

Holding certain powers because of their close relationship to nature and the magical world, hedgewitches would also have most likely used intoxicating herbs for visions and journeys in order to access information from the spirits that were so much a part of life in ancient days. This ability to stand in both this world and the spirit world was another reason why the hedgewitch lived 'on the edge' of society. They could be described as a kind of village shaman.

My understanding of a hedgewitch is that they have no loyalty to any particular magical practice, often being eclectic in how they practise their craft. Though they tend to have their own unique personal blend of magic, they do tend to honour the Wheel of the Year and perform certain rituals based upon life in the natural/supernatural world. They do things their way, as it feels right for them according to their highly developed intuitive nature. They are like the cunning folk or wise people of the past, often irreverent towards the set ways of others, shamanic, deep and different.

The main difference between a hedgewitch and other forms of Wicca is that hedgewitches are very practical in their dedication, rather than practising the more 'religious' tones of a coven. They offer services to their community, much like the shamans used to do. By 'community' they mean everything in their area — trees, plants, creatures, rivers, meadows — not just people. Covens also offer their services to the community, but it is not their primary focus as it is with the hedgewitch.

All Wiccan variations are different flavours of the same belief system, however, and so are very similar in parts. We can only ever generalize, because there are no doggedly fixed divisions within the Craft.

In Perfect Love and Perfect Trust

The Wiccan tradition advocates tolerance towards other religions and respects the ways of all authentic witches. Wiccans understand that any witch is a brother or sister in this ancient Craft and so, is a valued part of its rich fabric. They believe that there should be no divide when it comes to manifesting Spirit and its subsequent practices, and that all people, Wiccan or otherwise, should be free to celebrate their faith without prejudice, pressure or fear.

Belief systems are powerful structures that have caused a great deal of suffering across the world throughout the ages. Let us all remember that each of us has the basic human right to practise according to our beliefs, and that whether Witch, Sufi, Sikh or Jew, our faith is a very personal choice. May the 21st century be a century of co-operation, conservation and preservation of this beautiful Earth. May we all remember that the path to peace is best paved with hands of human kindness, and that finding peace within ourselves is vital if we wish to bring a lasting peace to the world around us.

And so may your heart beat to the rhythms of peace, love and joy. May the blessings of the Goddess and the Great Horned God guide you and protect you as you journey on.

BLESSED BE!

Answers

(to questions from page 106)

Q1: No, the tree does not make a sound when there is nothing present to hear it. Sound is made up of shockwaves spreading through the air or ground which only become 'noise' or 'sound' when they reach a living form that can register their arrival. If there is nothing there to hear them, they continue onward in total silence until they eventually fade away from loss of energy. This applies equally if you were to leave a tape recorder or microphone in the forest; these just convert shockwaves into electromagnetic waves, still in total silence, which only becomes noise if something listens to it.

Q2: No, a leaf is not green in the complete absence of light. Colour is only a reflection of non-absorbed light. If there is no light, there can be no colour.

Bibliography

Most of these titles will be readily available but in case of difficulty, the ISBNs have also been listed.

Yvonne Arburrow, *The Enchanted Forest*, Capall Bann Publishing, UK, 1993, ISBN 1-898307-08-3

Lesley Bremness, *Herbs*, Dorling Kindersley, UK, 1995, ISBN 0-86318-436-7

Jonathan Cainer and Carl Rider, *The Psychic Explorer*, Guild Publishing, UK, 1986, ISBN CN1369

D. J. Conway, *Magick of Gods and Goddesses*, Llewellyn Publications, USA, 1997, ISBN 1-56718-179-1

Scott Cunningham, *Magical Aromatherapy*, Llewellyn Publications, USA, 1996, ISBN 0-87542-129-6

Scott Cunningham, *Magical Herbalism*, Llewellyn Publications, USA, 1982, ISBN 0-87542-120-2

R. and A. Fitter, *Wild Flowers of Britain and Northern Europe*, William Collins, UK, 1974, ISBN 0-00-2190690-9

Sir James Frazer, *The Golden Bough*, Chancellor Press, UK, 1994, ISBN 1-85152-586-6

Mrs M. Grieve, *A Modern Herbal*, Penguin, 1982, UK, ISBN 0-01446-440-9

Glennie Kindred, *The Sacred Tree*, a self-published booklet, UK

John Lust, *The Herb Book*, Bantam Books, UK, 1990, ISBN 0-553-17273-5

Sally Morningstar, *The Wicca Pack*, Godsfield Press, UK, 2001, ISBN 1-84181-125-4

I. Opie and M. Tatem, *The Oxford Dictionary of Superstitions*, Oxford University Press, UK, 1989, ISBN 0-19-282916-5

Jean Palaiseul, *Grandmother's Secrets*, Penguin Books, UK, 1973, ISBN 0-14046-229-5

Mick Sharp, *Holy Places of Celtic Britain*, Blandford Press, UK, 1997, ISBN 0-7137-2642-3

Barbara G. Walker, *The Women's Dictionary of Symbols and Sacred Objects*, HarperCollins, USA, 1998, ISBN 0-06-250923-3

Barbara G. Walker, *The Women's Encyclopedia of Myths and Secrets*, Castle Books, USA, 1996, ISBN 0-7858-0720-9

Wylundt's Book of Incense, Samuel Weiser, USA, 1989, ISBN 0-87728-869-0

Index

About the Author

Sally Morningstar is a witch, teacher, and transformational healer with more than 30 years of practical experience. She's a warm and gentle person, with quiet strength and a joyful, slightly zany sense of humor. Having lived in many parts of England, she has settled in rural Somerset, where she's able to enjoy her love of nature and the countryside to the fullest. Throughout the seasons, she can be found (if she wants to be found, of course!) walking through woods and sitting by streams, deepening her understanding of the natural world and her relationship with Mother Earth. With Sally, her work and her life are virtually indistinguishable, so the concept of leisure time takes on a different color, but if asked to name her favorite leisure activity, it would probably be her passion for playing the Bodhran – the traditional Irish drum .

Sally runs training courses, a psychic and healing consultancy, as well as a remote-learning apprenticeship program. She has appeared on BBC, ITV and cable television in the United Kingdom; and writes for magazines, newspapers, and periodicals on witchcraft, healing, and natural magic. She's also the best-selling author of several books, including *Spells and Charms*, *Moon Wisdom*, *Love Magic*, and *The Wicca Pack*.

Sally Morningstar's contact info:

PO Box 2633
Radstock
Somerset
BA3 5XR
United Kingdom
 www.sallymorningstar.com

***

We hope you enjoyed this Hay House book.
If you'd like to receive a free catalog featuring additional Hay House
books and products, or if you'd like information about the
Hay Foundation, please contact:

Hay House, Inc.
P.O. Box 5100
Carlsbad, CA 92018-5100

(760) 431-7695 or **(800) 654-5126**
(760) 431-6948 (fax) or **(800) 650-5115 (fax)**
www.hayhouse.com

***

Published and distributed in Australia by: Hay House Australia Pty. Ltd. • 18/36 Ralph St.
• Alexandria NSW 2015 • *Phone:* 612-9669-4299 • *Fax:* 612-9669-4144 • www.hayhouse.com.au

Published and distributed in the United Kingdom by: Hay House UK, Ltd.
• Unit 62, Canalot Studios • 222 Kensal Rd., London W10 5BN
• *Phone:* 44-20-8962-1230 • *Fax:* 44-20-8962-1239 • www.hayhouse.co.uk

Published and distributed in the Republic of South Africa by: Hay House SA (Pty), Ltd.,
P.O. Box 990, Witkoppen 2068 • *Phone/Fax:* 27-11-706-6612 • orders@psdprom.co.za

Distributed in Canada by: Raincoast • 9050 Shaughnessy St., Vancouver, B.C. V6P 6E5
• *Phone:* (604) 323-7100 • *Fax:* (604) 323-2600

***

Tune in to **www.hayhouseradio.com** for the best in inspirational talk radio
featuring top Hay House authors! And, sign up via the Hay House USA Website
to receive the Hay House online newsletter and stay informed about what's going on
with your favorite authors. You'll receive bimonthly announcements about: Discounts and
Offers, Special Events, Product Highlights, Free Excerpts, Giveaways, and more!
www.hayhouse.com